Twayne's English Authors Series

Sylvia E. Bowman, *Editor*

INDIANA UNIVERSITY

A. E. Housman

(TEAS) 46

A. E. Housman

By TOM BURNS HABER

Editor of the Centennial Edition
of the Poetry of A. E. Housman

Ohio State University

TWAYNE PUBLISHERS
A DIVISION OF G. K. HALL & CO., BOSTON

PR
4809
.H15 H25

66690

For Willard Wood

About the Author

Often cited as a world authority in his field, Tom Burns Haber is an associate professor of Comparative Literature at Ohio State University, where he received his doctorate in 1929. He is the author of numerous published works on A. E. Housman, editor of a comprehensive centennial edition of the poetry, and has appeared in leading philological and literary journals in the United States and Europe. At present he is preparing a collection of Housman's letters.

Preface

Anyone who sets out to write a biography of A. E. Housman should be aware that his subject declared he needed none and took pains to discourage the writing of his life story. For extended periods biographical material is scanty. Housman made an art of incommunicability, and long after he left the scenes of his youth his former neighbors remembered him as "cold; never had much to do with anyone," and shortly after his death he was described by a university colleague as "alarming, remote, mysterious."

In the years of his maturity and fame as a poet and scholar, he had but few intimate friends; to the world he showed a side of icy repulsion. "Knowing my brother [Laurence] is no introduction to *me*" was his weapon for fending off would-be acquaintances. During his nearly thirty-year residence in London members of his family living there saw him only on his invitation, which he rarely offered.

Yet he wanted to be known, talked about. We touch here the center of the paradox of Housman's complex personality. Professing to scorn notoriety, he set himself in his early twenties to make his name known throughout the world of Classical scholarship, and a few years later he cut himself out of the royalties of *A Shropshire Lad* so that the price of his first book of poems would be within what the man of the street would pay.

Like Shelley, he carried the raw wounds of schoolboy persecutions throughout his life. Here is the source of the main themes of his poetry: the beauty and faithlessness of Nature, the swift passing of youth and its faith in things, the hopelessness of the undefended human creature beset by powers he cannot appease nor escape. To trace the outstanding events of Housman's seventy-seven years, the beginnings of his poetry, its literary sources and its development, and to assay his influence upon his time and the present—these are the main objectives of this volume.

[7]

The basic materials for a comprehensive study of the life of A. E. Housman and his writing are widely scattered, although the American researcher is most favorably situated, thanks to the drawing-power of the American dollar in auction rooms and other bibliophilic arenas, where the highest bidder is king. Most of Housman's scholarly prose is still interred in dusty rows of philological journals, whence by the terms of his will resurrection was forbidden; but a generous sampling of it and his lectures is offered in Mr. John Carter's *A. E. Housman: Selected Prose.*[1] Housman's numerous publications were faithfully cross-indexed by his friend and colleague at Trinity College, Cambridge, A. S. F. Gow, in his *A. E. Housman: A Sketch,*[2] pp. 64-129. It should be added that Gow's slender book, for its wisdom and firsthand knowledge of its subject, deserves a place on the smallest shelf of Housmaniana.

Beyond Housman's redoubtable papers on textual criticism and other classical subjects—Edmund Wilson was one of the first to come forward, in 1938,[3] with the suggestion that they be collected—other portions of his scholarly work still await the anthologist's net: his preface to Lucan; the prefaces to Manilius II, III, and IV, and other articles and reviews in English and Latin. Perhaps most needed on the shelf of essentials is a thick volume of Housman's letters. Although Housman was a lively correspondent, often willing to exchange letters with persons he would not meet face to face, the collecting of his epistles still remains to be done. This want has been somewhat relieved by Grant Richards (publisher of the second edition of *A Shropshire Lad,* 1898, and other later works of the poet-scholar), who scattered throughout his memoir of Housman[4] most of the more than four hundred letters he had addressed to his publisher during their association of thirty-nine years. One hundred and forty-one of the holographs of these letters are now in the Library of Congress; one hundred and twenty others belong to the University of Illinois Library.

Laurence Housman in his memoir of his brother[5] included numerous early letters written by Alfred to members of his family, the larger number to his stepmother and to his sister Katharine and Laurence himself. Many of these are not quoted in full, but some of the originals of those to the first two persons named have recently been given by Mr. Carter to the British

Museum. Laurence quotes also from letters to American correspondents, among them Houston Martin, who shortly after Housman's death published in the December, 1936, *Yale Review* eleven letters dating from November 25, 1932, to March 22, 1936. In the *Mark Twain Quarterly* (Summer-Fall, 1941), Cyril Clemens printed thirty-eight more from Housman to his publishers; and in the same magazine (Spring, 1943) William White brought forth fourteen others; he published fifteen more in the *Dalhousie Review* (January, 1950). Again, Cyril Clemens edited in *Poet Lore* (Autumn, 1947), seventeen brief letters dating from 1927 to 1933. I collected in 1957 thirty letters written by Housman to Witter Bynner,[6] a rising American poet-critic whose enthusiasm for *A Shropshire Lad* helped to found Housman's popularity in America. Lastly, a most illuminating series of forty-nine letters to Housman's artist-friend and his wife, the William Rothensteins—some running to the unusual length of three, four, and even seven pages—has lately been acquired by the Houghton Library of Harvard University, where are also to be found several other Housman miscellanea.[7]

The Lilly Library of Indiana University, six months after its dedication, exhibited in April, 1961, a wealth of Housmaniana—books and documents—collected by Mr. H. B. Collamore of West Hartford, Connecticut, and presented by him to the Library. This bequest contained seventeen more of the letters to Grant Richards, seven to various learned institutions declining the offer of honors, and twenty more to other correspondents dating over a period of thirty-five years. Also shown, and the pearl of the collection, was the choicest piece of autobiographical Housmaniana in existence: the two-page letter to a French correspondent, M. Maurice Pollet, answering his "gimlet questionnaire."[8] This rarity was accompanied by Housman's entries (1887-1914) in the jest-studded visitors' books of the Wise family, where Alfred was a frequent guest from 1877 to 1914.[9]

The guestbooks of the Wise family call up another, perhaps easier, enterprise: the assembly of Housman's juvenile poetry and the nonsense verse he wrote early and continued to write through the last decade of his life. Several specimens of both were printed by Laurence Housman in his memoir[10] and by his sister, Mrs. Katharine Symons, in the memorial volume *Alfred Edward Housman*,[11] published seven months after the poet's death by Bromsgrove School,* where Alfred was a scholar from his eleventh to his eighteenth year. Two long poems he entered in a school competition during this period were published in 1953 by Mr. William White: "Sir Walter Raleigh" (1873)[12] and "The Death of Socrates" (1874), the latter of which won the prize for that year. His humorous and satirical contributions, verse and prose, to *Ye Rounde Table* an undergraduate magazine he helped to found and edit during the latter half of his freshman year at Oxford (1878), have been recently described in the *Journal of English and Germanic Philology* (October, 1962),[13] shortly after a rare complete file of the *Table* was discovered by me in the Sterling Library of Yale University. The thirteen pieces written by Housman for this magazine form a landmark in his development as a writer and will be discussed in the biographical section of this book.

For the textual study of Housman's poetry the essential sources are in the remains of his four poetry notebooks, acquired about 1940 by the Library of Congress. These all-important manuscripts, our main—if not the sole—basis for practically all the texts of the posthumous poetry, though sadly decimated by Laurence Housman's cutting and erasure, still provide readable drafts, in whole or part, of all but twenty of the one hundred and seventy-seven pieces of the *Complete Poems*; and, for some of the lyrics, as many as three full drafts exist. Here, in brief, the researcher is granted an over-the-shoulder view of the poet at work. One needless and long-standing drawback hampers the systematic use of these precious documents: they still huddle in the Washington collection in the disordered, haphazard state in which Laurence left them in the autumn of 1939 after separating his brother's four poetry notebooks and readying them for sale. Thus the hopeful reader will find it practically impossible to identify in the collection earlier and later drafts, or to place with any certainty in its proper locus any undated sheet or fragment. At present the researcher's only road out of this maze is to have the entire collection—all the two hundred and twenty-four pieces of it—photocopied and then, with the aid of an analysis[14] Laurence made of the still-unbroken notebooks, to reconstitute the original four books in the order in which Alfred left them.

* Published the following year by Henry Holt & Co., this volume will hereinafter be referred to as the Holt memorial volume.

Not many Housman scholars have buckled down to this expensive and laborious business; it is a pity that the originals were not properly handled when their great value was recognized, over twenty years ago.

Just below the notebooks in textual value are Housman's copies of *A Shropshire Lad* and *Last Poems* that he prepared for the printers, later adding in both many last-minute changes. The former corpus is in the Library of Trinity College, Cambridge; the other, in the Fitzwilliam Museum of the same University. Both have been described by me in *The Manuscript Poems of A. E. Housman*.[15] To this list of indispensables for a thoroughgoing study of Housman's poetry, one more book should be added: Percy Withers' *A Buried Life: Personal Recollections of A. E. Housman* (1940),[16] which contains many Boswellian reports of conversations about the poet's writing and other reminiscences, unique in their kind and variety, carrying through the last nineteen years of Housman's life.

It is perhaps grossly superfluous to remark that A. E. Housman is not primarily a "scholar's poet." His desire was quite the opposite, and it has been fulfilled. The standard complete editions of his poetry are to be found practically everywhere English books are sold. The general status was recently summed up by a factotum of Scribner's New York bookstore: "Housman's complete poems? We could not be without them."

No book of any length about A. E. Housman would be worth the cost of its paper if it did not deal frankly with the vexed question of his liaison with his Oxford classmate, Moses J. Jackson. I believe that George L. Watson's interpretation of the known facts, courageously laid on the line by him in 1957, is correct. The evidence he so carefully marshaled in his biography[17] of the poet and the inferences he drew therefrom were supported the following year by Maude M. Hawkins,[18] who had in the course of a long exchange of letters with Laurence Housman and a series of visits in the home he occupied with his sister, obtained freely from them information out of family records hitherto inaccessible. It now seems necessary to accept the fact of young Housman's infatuation with Jackson and to recognize it as one of the two principal turning-points of his life, the other being the death of his adored mother on his twelfth birthday.

Housman's best poetry is love poetry, and the tone of it is

almost uniformly unhappy. Much of it seems to be addressed to a man, a revered friend passionately sought or surrendered as "too dear for my possessing." These symptoms of erotic malaise did not escape the observation of Housman's first readers; they were frequently alleged—and denied[19]—in reviews and articles about his poetry. And before his ashes were cold, the London *Times* obituary (May 2, 1936) significantly mentioned the "secret" of his life, hinting that in the near future the reason for his dark view of things might be revealed in documents he had "deposited in safe keeping for a number of years."[20] With the exception of his brother Laurence, A. E. Housman's family and near friends were stonily silent on the moot question or indignantly repelled the idea of any disastrous involvement with Jackson, who, for his part figures as an unresponsive idol, engaging—perhaps against his will or without his full knowledge—his classmate's affections during their final year at Oxford, 1880-1881. Something that went awry in this friendship caused Housman's academic failure and permanently embittered his introspective judgments and his outlook on the human scene.

It is, then, on this understanding of Housman's "cursed trouble," as he named his affliction, that the present study is partly based. But this understanding, once reached, has had no commanding part in the over-all view of the man or of the poet; nor should it weigh too heavily in the reader's inclination either to pity or to condemn. Understanding is all.

The word "homosexual," although not allowed a place in the great *Oxford English Dictionary* of 1928, no longer arouses the loathing and contempt it carried through the dying flurry of post-Victorian morality. For better or worse, we of the present era are a more tolerant breed and no longer shrink at the mention of the word and its human significances. Rather, we are shocked at the thought that children of sound middle-class parents only a hundred years ago were so heartlessly shackled in the bonds of a family discipline that drilled into their awakening minds the notion that those portions of their young bodies covered by their school garb were indecent, ignored by respectable people, and therefore never to be mentioned in the family group or elsewhere.

Repressions of this sort, in all but the most insensitive children, often result either in an explosion or a sublimation of some kind, proportionate usually to the mental energies of the individual. Housman's first reaction, when he called himself to judgment after he had failed his examinations and been sent down in disgrace from Oxford, was unbounded self-condemnation, followed by a passionate indictment of the "ways of God and man" that had betrayed him in his innocence to an existence he hated for its barrenness and isolation. The second poem[21] (dating in the mid-1880's) he entered in his earliest poetry notebook (A 61*) is an epitaph he wrote for himself: now, cured of the evils of life, he sleeps soundly, no longer grieving to think of God's mistakes in making him.

Knowing more of the nature of Housman's experiences than all but a very few of his contemporaries could certainly surmise or would admit to themselves, we can say that our total view of him as man and writer has come to a new focus by this identification of the main dynamic of his life and work. At the same time the breadth of view remains essentially unchanged; the difference is in depth. We may now, aided by the witness of his notebooks, observe that many portions of his poetry are more closely related to his biography than had been supposed—and that Housman was heavily diluting the truth when in 1933 he told M. Maurice Pollet that his *Shropshire Lad* reflected no more than "something of my temper and view of life."[22]

Perhaps the most radical new deduction our examination of the evidence will permit is that, when Housman insisted his poetry spanned sorrow "not mine but man's," he was stating precisely the opposite of the truth. Out of his own pain came his apperception of others'. Like King Lear on the storm-beaten heath, Housman saw in his own downfall, and saw for the first time, the defeats and tragedies of humanity. But he saw them, not with Lear's late-learned compassion—"O, I have ta 'en/Too little care of this!"—but with the passionate resentment of a proud and unyielding rebel against an ill-ordered universe that had injured *him*. As if his own misfortunes were too heavy or too unjust to be borne, he projected them into the lives of others: the shadowy Shropshire and London folk he never intimately knew and soldiers about to die, personifications of his brother George Herbert and other members of his family in the Queen's

---

* Housman's notebooks, A, B, C, D, will be thus referred to, by letter and page-number, throughout this book.

uniform. But the real field of action and the headquarters from which the bulletins of resistance and retreat were dispatched were in his own warring consciousness, where he himself may be observed in all the combatants. He is each in turn, and sometimes even his foes:

> Here the truceless armies yet
> Trample, rolled in blood and sweat;
> They kill and kill and never die;
> And I think that each is I.

In summary, it is a commonplace that the denial or displacement of normal human desire usually results in some kind of compensating activity. This process is to be seen in the two manifestations of Housman's genius: his scholarship and his poetry. So unlike, both had their source in the single imperious resolve to rebuke his evil destiny. As a classical scholar he rebuked it by an iron-willed ascetic devotion to the pursuit of knowledge that took him to the very summit of achievement; as a poet he rebuked it before the world in his poetry with a plangency and a violence that at times are hardly matched by the *saeva indignatio* of Swift. Considering the high peak of his scholarly attainment and the depths of despair revealed by his poetry, we may take some measure of the shock he sustained when his world collapsed under him in the unhappy spring of 1881 and of the herculean effort required to rebuild something in its place.

TOM BURNS HABER

The Talking Trees
Columbus, Ohio
August 3, 1966

Acknowledgments

Grateful acknowledgment of permission to quote is made to the following:

The Clarendon Press, Oxford, for the use of several passages of translation in Cyril Bailey's edition of Lucretius, Vol. 1.

The University of Minnesota Press for copyrighted material in *The Manuscript Poems of A. E. Housman.*

The London *Times* for excerpts from the obituary notice of A. E. Housman.

The Modern Language Association of America for quotations from Dr. William White's reprint of "The Death of Socrates."

F. E. Halliday, Esq., of Five Fields, St. Ives, Cornwall, for a quotation from his *Indifferent Honest.*

Among my numerous correspondents, to whom I am chiefly indebted, I particularly thank Mr. Willard S. Wood, of Del Mar, California, whose wide-ranging survey of the foreign press has brought up many things I might have missed, and who has crowned his many years of good offices by reading the manuscript with a Housmanian eye.

Contents

Chronology

1859 A. E. Housman born March 26 at the Valley House, Fockbury, Worcestershire.

1860 Removal of family to Perry Hall, Bromsgrove.

1867 (or earlier) Began writing verse.

1870 (September) Entered Bromsgrove School as a Foundation Scholar.

1871 Death of mother, on his twelfth birthday.

1872 "I became a deist."

1874 (August 8) Printing of his prize poem, "The Death of Socrates," in *The Bromsgrove Messenger*.

1877 (October) Entered St. John's College, Oxford, on an open scholarship, with stipend £100 per annum.

1878 (February 2 to June 22) Co-editor and contributor to *Ye Rounde Table: An Oxford and Cambridge Magazine*.

1880– Took rooms with classmates A. W. Pollard and Moses
1881 Jackson.

1880 "[I became] an atheist."

1881 Failed his final examinations and left Oxford without a degree.

1881 (May) to 1882 (December), at home, teaching at Bromsgrove School and preparing for Civil Service examinations.

1882– Clerk in the Government Patent Office; reading evenings
1892 in the British Museum.

1882– Shared London lodgings with Moses Jackson and a
1886 younger brother Adalbert.

1882 First published paper (on Horace), *Journal of Philology*.

1886– Lived alone at Byron Cottage, Highgate; wrote or revised
1905 all of *A Shropshire Lad*, two-thirds of *Last Poems*, and all but about twenty of the posthumous pieces.

1887 Moses Jackson to Karachi, India.

1889 M. J. returned to London to marry (see *Last Poems* 24).

1889 Death of Adalbert Jackson (see *More Poems* 42).

1892– Professor of Latin, University College, London.
1911

1896   (late February or early March) Publication of *A Shropshire Lad*.

1898   (September 14) Second edition of *A Shropshire Lad*.

1899   First paper on Manilius, *Journal of Philology*.

1901   (October 30) Death of youngest brother, George Herbert in Boer War (see *Last Poems* 17; *More Poems* 40).

1903–   Edition of *Astronomica* of Manilius, Books I-V.
1930

1905   Edition of Juvenal.

1911–   Professor of Latin, Trinity College, Cambridge.
1936

1921   (August 4) Lecture to the Classical Association: "The Application of Thought to Textual Criticism."

1922   (October 19) Publication of *Last Poems*.

1923   (January 14) Death of Moses Jackson.

1926   Edition of Lucan.

1933   (May 9) Leslie Stephen Lecture: "The Name and Nature of Poetry."

1935   Stay at Cambridge Nursing Home.

1936   (March 18) Last lecture to his classes.

1936   (April 30) Death.

1936   (October 26) Publication of *More Poems*, edited by Laurence Housman.

1937   (November 26) *A. E. H.: Some Poems, Some Letters and a Personal Memoir*, by Laurence Housman; with 18 *Additional Poems*.

1939   *Collected Poems*, edited by John Carter.

1959   (March 26) *Complete Poems*, the Centennial Edition, edited by Tom Burns Haber.

1961   *A. E. Housman: Selected Prose*, edited by John Carter.

A. E. Housman

CHAPTER 1

Home and School

ALFRED EDWARD HOUSMAN was born in the Valley House, about two miles from the village of Bromsgrove, in the County of Worcestershire, on March 26, 1859. His natal horoscope,[1] belatedly made for him a few years before his death by a professorial colleague at Trinity College, Cambridge, bore these forbidding interpretations of the astral influences that hovered about his birth-bed: ". . . you will have trouble and many bitter disappointments in connection with friendship and love. You will not have many real friends. . . . There is a strong inclination for a celibate life." It is easy to object that the reader of fate was merely being wise after the events; but, to offset this criticism, it must be added that the horologist also read, "You are somewhat lacking in mental concentration and perseverance. . . ." If Housman had *not* been endowed with more than the normal quantity of these two faculties, his name would have died with the man.

I   *"When I was young and proud"*

Happily unaware of his star-crossed future, Alfred grew up as his mother's favorite in a middle-class Victorian family increased in the next nine years by four brothers and two sisters. They were born in Bromsgrove, to which Edward Housman, a practicing lawyer, had removed his family in 1860.[2] Young Alfred, a quiet studious boy, took seriously his role of the eldest-born and was an apt learner, as his mother in the quieter intervals of her busy day guided his reading and sharpened his memory with long assignments, often chosen from the Bible. "Men are what their mothers made them," to use Emerson's phrase; and the terse, incisive language of the Scriptures, particularly the Old Testament, became the most influential literary element in the poetry that made Housman one of the outstanding lyricists of his generation.

The devoted pupil often has an inborn knack for teaching what he has learned, and Alfred served as tutor of the younger Housmans when the home schoolroom became the forum of their awakening intellects.[3] Reaching beyond the staid, prescribed subjects, the cadet instructor added astronomy to the family curriculum after absorbing a book he chanced upon in their library; and one of our first glimpses of Alfred's young flock in the pursuit of empirical knowledge shows him directing a fraternal orrery acting out the movements of the solar system with their front yard as the universe. Laurence, the youngest, who was given the leading role of the sun, was only to stand still; Basil was the earth and circled in kneebreeches about the sun, rotating as he ran. Alfred was the moon, skipping soberly about his brother, shouting admonitions to any part of the celestial scheme that threatened to stray from its appointed course.[4]

This was all good fun, but interest in astronomy did not end there. Robert, nearest Alfred in age, was inspired to build a working telescope from their father's cast-off camera gear; and thus, long before "progressive" education had a name, Alfred's willing pupils grew in firsthand knowledge of the world about and above them. Their tutor, meanwhile, was laying a durable basis for an interest in astronomy that grew to be one of the main concerns of his long scholarly career, culminating in his editing of the five books of the *Astronomica* by the Latin poet Marcus Manilius.

Coming down to earth and indoors, Alfred cleverly linked his students' will to learn with their instinct for play. He taxed his brain inventing labyrinthine games, often competitive to inspire the laggards and the youngest,[5] and assigned parts in the composition of dramas that were sometimes performed for the benefit or bewilderment of their elders. He gave out the subjects on which the young Housmans wrote their earliest poetry, tackling unperturbed their brother's first assignment: "Death." We are indebted to Laurence for preserving in his memoir of Alfred a generous sampling of these revealing juvenilia. Everyone, so he and his sister Katharine later testified, had to do his share in these coöperative projects; and their teacher came down hard on shoddy or unfinished work, except when one of the more callow contributors grew weary. Then Alfred would sometimes write the piece himself and magnanimously permit the delinquent to read or perform it as his own. A more ambitious collective project was the founding of a family magazine, a once-a-year production that attained a lively circulation among family and friends.

II *Bromsgrove School*

This work-and-play tutelage carried on into the formal schooldays of the Housman children, which began for Alfred when he was eleven and ready for Bromsgrove School, then called King Edward VI School, which he entered in September, 1870, as one of a group of twelve boys who had won the first Cookes' scholarships there, an honor which was successively earned in the years soon to follow by most of Alfred's home pupils. He held up a good example to his brothers and sisters by entering his own poems in the annual Bromsgrove School contests. His "Sir Walter Raleigh," submitted in 1873, did not win, but he took the prizes the two following years with his "The Death of Socrates" and "St. Paul on Mars Hill."

"Sir Walter Raleigh," edited by Dr. William White, appeared in *Études Anglaises* (November, 1953). This poem, Housman in his latter years thought superior to either of the two prize-winning pieces later submitted in the Bromsgrove School contests. Laurence, who reports his brother's statement, is not in agreement; but, because "St. Paul on Mars Hill" is out of comparison since no manuscript of it has survived, it may be said that "Sir Walter Raleigh," in spite of its inflated rhetoric and orotund patriotism, has sufficient worth to make its author's matured opinion not unreasonable. Compared with "The Death of Socrates," its praise of England's greatness perhaps sounds bombastic; but the two poems are entirely different in tone and subject and, again comparison is impossible. In Housman's autumnal preference for his earliest poem, he may have been swayed by four prophetic lines in the tenth stanza that carried him back to the schoolboy who sixty years before had so accurately forecast his own future:

> The lofty hopes of youth are fled,
> The buoyant fire of youth is dead,
> The golden dreams of youth are flown,
> And he must learn to be alone.

Some lines of the thirteen stanzas seem to prefigure what the poet in him would someday write: *the stormy breeze* (1.34)—*the rainy breeze* (*MP** 10:14); *earth and ocean* (1.25)—*Son of earth and son of Ocean* (*MP* 46:20); *And when the depth of ocean drinks/The light from heaven* (11.13,14)—*The sun is down and drinks away/From air and land the lees of day* (*LP* 1:3,4). Housman's boyhood absorption in astronomy and geography also appear in these glittering stanzas, numbers six and seven:

> He flies to other lands afar,[6]
> To lands beneath the evening star
> Where fairer constellations rise
> And shed their light from bluer skies,
> Where undiscovered treasure shines
> Locked in the dim and gloomy mines
> And red volcanoes howl and glare
> Like daemons on the midnight air.
>
> To lifeless plains where stillness broods
> Amidst eternal solitudes,
> To mountain chains whose peaks are lost
> And hide in heaven their endless frost,
> Torrents that shoot from steep to steep
> Inprisoned in their wildest leap
> And glaciers hanging over all
> Like seas suspended in their fall.

I quote a few additional stanzas, enough to allow a tentative balance to be struck between this poem and the one Alfred submitted the following year, 1874:

> Send forth thy gaze from zone to zone
> O'er pathless seas and lands unknown,
> O'er mountain crag and teeming plain
> To find the bounds of Britain's reign;
> But vainly where the sea expands
> And vainly through the endless lands
> Thou seek'st the habitable shore
> Where England's name is heard no more.—Stanza 1

* The symbols *ASL, LP, MP,* and *AP* have been used to refer to the four sections of Housman's collected poetry: *A Shropshire Lad, Last Poems, More Poems,* and *Additional Poems.*

[26]

What man was he whose genius gave
That speck upon the seething wave
Such power to stretch from clime to clime
The glory of her rule sublime?
The might to span the raging main
The strength to spurn the hurricane
To ride the seas with flags unfurled
And bid defiance to the world?—Stanza 3

When earth and ocean groaned amain
To bear the Spaniard's galling chain,
When every nation shrank dismayed
Beneath the yoke of Spanish trade,
When all creation formed the stool
To prop the pride of Spanish rule,
He rose to bid the world be free
And toll the knell of tyranny.—Stanza 4

And earth gives up to him her stores
And ocean strews his level shores.
Success around his forehead flits
And Victory beside him sits;
And thus while fortune on him smiles
And conquest leads him through the isles,
—The glory of his life is o'er
He falls, to rise again no more.—Stanza 8

Again he comes, again to dwell
Within the lonely prison cell,
Again the iron hinges grate
And close like heralds of his fate.
And now he leaves the prison gloom
And forth he goes to meet his doom,
Unterrified, and calm, and brave,
To change the prison for the grave.—Stanza 12

Alfred's success the following year with "The Death of Socrates" brought him not only the school prize but also the honor of reading a part of the poem at the annual Commemoration Speech Day. A few days later, August 8, 1874, he shared with his family the buzzing excitement of seeing his elegy in *The Bromsgrove Messenger*—the first of Alfred's poems to appear in print. Perhaps the main interest of the poem is the strong religious feeling that pervades it: proof of the active survival of the effects of the training he received from his mother, who had died

March 26, 1871. The description of the afterlife of Socrates certainly fits the Christian heaven as well as, if not better than, the Elysium of the Athenians. It would therefore seem that at fifteen, whatever settled convictions he may have kept or lost about the faith he had learned from his mother, Alfred had passed through the first three years of bereavement with no perceptible weakening of his beliefs in the tenets of Christianity, but his sister in her Introduction to Grant Richards' memoir says: "In his old age he named his thirteenth year as the beginning of his change of belief."

The ending of this poem, with its mention of St. Paul, who would one day bring to Athens his God, who is also Socrates', may have suggested to the school authorities the subject for the verse-competition next year. But no copy was kept of Alfred's prize-winning poem, "St. Paul on Mars Hill." It was mentioned in the weekly *Messenger* but, alas, not printed; and, according to Laurence Housman, the sole copy in the British Museum was destroyed during World War II.[7] It would have much to tell us of young Housman's increasing knowledge of the ways of God and man and about the beginning of the formation of his ethical judgments. But, lacking the poem, we may safely infer that the latter two, taken together, must have consolidated for him a certain religious security, for there is nothing that strengthens belief like writing eloquently in it. The fact that, five or six short years later, this defense crumbled proves how shattering the experiences of Alfred's last months at Oxford must have been.[8]

III *"The land of lost content"*

The first thirty-six lines of "The Death of Socrates"—it consists of fifty-three heroic couplets in six stanzas of irregular length—are addressed to the theme of Byron's "Fair Greece! sad relic of departed worth!" But the larger portion of the poem is strictly concerned with the philosopher, his death and immortality, and is marked by restraint and a remarkably mature dignity. The passages that follow represent fairly the dual substance of the poem—the setting and the story:

> Though thou art free no more, though every trace[9]
> Of life has faded from thy marble face,
> Though all thy gods are fled, and silence reigns
> For ever in thy desecrated fanes,

Though all that once were thine—the fair, the brave—
Are sleeping in the darkness of the grave,
Though all the light that lit thy dawn has set—
Greece, in thy ruin thou art lovely yet. . . .
Still in the shadow of thy flowery vales
Ceaselessly sing the mournful nightingales,
And round thy shattered altars every tread
Awakes the voices of the deathless dead.
Still thou art lovely, lovely in decay,
With purple hill and rippling azure bay,
And ocean girdling all thy shores with light,
And temples on thy headlands flashing white. . . .

But though thy empire in the dust lies dead,
And strength and courage from thy land have fled,
The shades of those who made thee great and fair
Throng every breeze that stirs the sunny air. . . .
'Twas here, where yonder columns front the sea,
That Wisdom lingered, Socrates, with thee.
Best of the Grecians, seeking to explore
The realms that never had been searched before,
From which the bravest shrank with bated breath—
The great unknown that follows after death.
Men spoke of plains where happy spirits dwell
Amidst the dreamy fields of Asphodel,
Yet little did they love from life to flee
Into the depths of what they could not see. . . .

What wonder then, that men like these should prize
Lightly, the solemn accents of the wise? . . .
But why should they, for shame, for pity, why?
Condemn the good, the innocent to die?

Yet it is done. The hour is come at last
When all his life of virtue must be past;
At last the chilly hemlock bowl he drains,
The subtle poison shivers through his veins. . . .
Though death and he are met in deadly strife
Still he speaks on, and still he speaks of life,—
Of endless life, of life beyond the tomb,
Where Socrates, emerged from earthly gloom—
A new-born soul with wings of thought unfurled,
Shall find the threshold of another world. . . .

The glories of the unveiled heaven stand bare—
A thousand stars gleam out upon the air. . . .
For as that sun into the deep descends,
O, Socrates, thy mortal being ends.
As yon clear stars shine forth from sky and sea,
There dawns another, brighter life for thee—
Where heaven its everlasting fields unfolds,
And streams of knowledge in its valleys holds,
Where melody of joy to earth unknown,
And never-dying gladness is thine own. . . .
And so, a life more wondrous far than this,
A life of unimaginable bliss
Is veiled, till death from off the mortal eye
Has drawn the cloud that covers immortality.

Thy weeping followers on the earth stand dumb
With sorrow; unto them no dawn has come,
On them no lifted veil has shed the light;
With lisping thought, and visionary sight,
They wait in twilight. But the day shall be
When a frail bark shall bear across the sea
One, in the wisdom of whose solemn eyes
A deeper, clearer well of light shall rise,
And on the hill thy feet so oft have trod,
He shall in fulness preach thine Unknown God.

After "St. Paul on Mars Hill" (1875), the springs of serious poetry ceased to flow for a time, and other sources were opened. During the latter half of his first year (1877-1878) at Oxford, Alfred contributed a considerable quantity of humorous and satirical verse and prose to an undergraduate magazine. Two poems he published in an Oxford poetry magazine in 1881 indicate clearly that he had abandoned his belief in Christianity as well as the afterworld of Socrates. The first, "Parta Quies" (later, number 48 of *More Poems*), is addressed to one dead—his mother? himself?—to whom the unbreaking sleep has come. (The opening three lines of the poem are now over his grave by the Ludlow Parish Church.) The other poem, "New Year's Eve," (now *AP* 21) was written, so Laurence Housman opines,[10] under the influence of Swinburne. It describes an imaginary church service signaling the collapse and end of the Christian faith, its divinities and dignitaries in retreat: "We were gods and implored and immortal/Once; and to-day we die."

[30]

The fourth piece in Housman's first poetry notebook—"When Israel out of Egypt came" (now *MP* 2)—dating about 1887, perhaps earlier, completes the story of his decline from the betrayal he felt in his mother's death to deism which rejected the idea of divine intervention in human affairs and thence to atheism. In his 1874 prize-poem he had described Socrates' bereft disciples, who "stand dumb/With sorrow; unto them no dawn has come." This foretells young Housman's mental state three or four years later, when he wrote the despairing lines of stanzas three and four of the poem we now read as *More Poems* 2, describing his abandonment by God: He had been the guide and salvation of others, of the children of Israel fleeing the wrath of their enemies; He had brought them safely home, but no such saving guidance, the poet laments, was ever granted him, certainly not in the time of his greatest need. The tokens that came to Israel did not come to him.

The reasons for Housman's religious disillusionment thus become clearer: he had learned from his mother a faith that was severely shaken by her death, for which he found no reason or consolation at the time of the event or later. The culminating disaster of his fourth year at Oxford found and left him without spiritual support, in a state of tragic despair that was saved from chaos and suicide only by the strictest self-discipline. Asceticism became his uncomforting substitute for religion that sustained him through the rest of his life.

Sarah Jane Housman was only forty-three when she died, March 26, 1871, prematurely aged from the strain of child-bearing and the endless vexations of coping unsuccessfully with the financial burdens of her growing family and the ineptitude and irresponsibility of her husband. Alfred, in his precocity, must have divined the main causes of his mother's tragedy, her immolation before her husband's unrestraint, the hopeless misalliance of their married life. He saw the fatal link between procreation and death, and in his revulsion, condemned the sex act and all that it implied, thus raising the first barriers that shut him away from heterosexual ties.

Two years later the sharp edge of his bereavement was to some degree blunted by his father's marriage to Lucy Housman, a cousin, and one of the family's closest associates; she had nursed Mrs. Housman in her last illness. Assured of Lucy's sterling qualities, Alfred from the beginning of her new responsibilities pledged her his full support when she entered the motherless family, the youngest of whom was not yet three. He continued his schoolmastering of his brothers and sisters with Lucy's approval, finding in her strong and devoted nature, if little to love, much to admire. His attachment to his stepmother, who might have been expected to arouse in the stricken boy precisely opposite feelings, was one of his few friendships with women that strengthened with time. Over the years his letters home were sent to her and, with no infidelity to the dear memory, he addressed Lucy as "My dear Mamma" and signed himself "Your loving son."

Many a sensitive lad, shaken by the losses and changes Alfred had to cope with, has survived them safely and inherited what he later (and scornfully) called "the birthright of multitudes": found his mate and begot sons and daughters with society's blessing. Others have not been so fortunate. In Alfred's nature the main impulses and tendencies were from his earliest childhood set in the opposite direction. His predisposition toward sexual aberration, first aroused by the close affection of his mother and not balanced by any compensating masculine activities growing boys need to share with their fathers, was augmented by an instinctive early dislike of females of his own age[11] and by his aversion to the tug and tussle of schoolyard sports. His native pride and sensitivity kept him from reaching out for companionship among young persons he knew, and the deadly silence of his elders on matters sexual left him without guide or direction in understanding his adolescent perplexities, now exacerbated, by his mother's death and his alienation from his early faith, to a degree that would have overtaxed the soundest and best-advised. Thus constituted, Alfred at the end of his seven years at Bromsgrove School in 1877, was, as he perhaps darkly knew when he looked ahead to Oxford, already in the grip of the "cursed trouble" that soured the wells of his life, produced his poetry, and urged him to the topmost heights of scholarly renown.

CHAPTER 2

Oxford

ALFRED matriculated at St. John's College, Oxford, on October 13, 1877. He had won an open scholarship that afforded him a handsome stipend of one hundred pounds per year. Now, with his immediate educational future seemingly assured, he may have welcomed the trials and responsibilities that he knew would be arduous but not too formidable for the Bromsgrove boy who had consistently led his class. He struck a note of cool detachment in his first letter home,[1] addressed to his stepmother, describing the momentous ceremony of matriculation. He reported his feelings of supercilious amusement at the ceremonial "farce," in which the Latin, he complained, failed to meet his standards. He discovered similar defects of this nature a few days later in the classroom lectures, at which his attendance, optional by custom, became less frequent than it should have been for a first-year man. Thus, at the very outset of his college career, were planted the seeds of scholarly arrogance whose bitter harvest he reaped with due increase four years later.

I Ye Rounde Table

During the last two terms of his first year at Oxford, Alfred spent much of his time and energy in the founding and editing of *Ye Rounde Table*, an undergraduate periodical ambitiously subtitled *An Oxford and Cambridge Magazine*. One of the co-founders, also a St. John's man, was A. W. Pollard, just Alfred's age, who had taken a room near his in the second quadrangle of the College. The two saw much of each other and were invited together to join the staff of the *Table* as contributing editors. Such was the beginning of a life-long friendship, in the course of which Pollard performed for his friend the same memorable service Hippolyte Babou rendered to Baudelaire: he suggested the right and memorable title for his first book of poetry, which the author had awkwardly christened *Poems by Terence Hearsay.*

Like most collegiate literary ventures, which their backers' enthusiasms invariably endow with an assured immortality, *Ye Rounde Table* was destined to an early death; it survived through only six issues, from February 2, 1878, to the Commemoration Number, dated June 22. Of the six founding editors, Alfred was one of the most talented, certainly the most diligent. All of the literary energy that had come out in the family exercises, and later in competitive writing in Bromsgrove School, now found a fuller outlet in the columns of the new periodical. Under the appropriate *nom de plume,* Tristram—all the contributors took Arthurian names—he produced copy for more articles than did any other staff member; and with the editor-in-chief, A. P. Poley,[2] he wrote more than half of the forty-seven main pieces that filled the six numbers of the magazine.

Now for the first time in his nineteen years, Alfred savored the intoxicating pleasure of writing what and how he pleased, with the assurance of seeing it in print—perhaps not the best training conditions for a young man of proved literary skill who was feeling more and more disdain for authority and its power to strike back—but what fun it was! Versatility of attack was his main forte: he wrote humorous verse in the manner of his schoolboy exercises, including a witty parody of the poet-laureate, "Tennyson in the Moated Grange." He lampooned Oxfordian institutions in his two audacious "Varsity Ballads," the first of which was a satirical thrust at the hated University Proctor, the other a mock warning against the Roman Church, said to be plotting a take-over of the University. In "Under the Clock," he twice reports with a jaundiced eye the argumentations of the Oxford Union Society. His well-nourished scorn of Oxford scholarship breaks out in "The Eleventh Eclogue," in which two widely reputed professors are mercilessly ridiculed. The personal nature of some of these pieces recalls the blistering satire of Swift, and in the accuracy of some of his lashes, Housman is at no disadvantage by reason of his youth.

Because Alfred's *Rounde Table* contributions are so valuable an index to his literary development during the first year of his Oxford period and because the magazine is so rarely found,[3] I cite what might be otherwise called an over-lavish selection: five

of his thirteen pieces. The first, which appeared in the second
number of the magazine (February 2, 1878) has to my knowledge been reprinted only twice: in a garbled version of only
four stanzas, recalled from memory by Laurence Housman, that
appeared in the *Manchester Guardian* (February 5, 1957); the
other, giving the full six stanzas, was printed by me in *The
Journal of English and Germanic Philology* (October, 1962).

THE SAILOR-BOY

There was a gallant sailor-boy,
　　He crossed the harbour-bar,
He sailed on board a gallant ship,
　　In fact, he was a tar.
He leaned across the good ship's side,
　　Into the deep looked he;
When a skimpy little mermaid
　　Came swimming through the sea.

Her form was very scaly,
　　She sang in every scale,
And then she cried, "Encore, encore!"
　　And wagged her little tail.
But when she came where leant and looked
　　The sailor-boy above,
A pang shot through her little heart—
　　She found she was in love.

She opened conversation
　　Very cleverly, she thought:—
"Have you spliced the capstan jib, my boy?
　　Is the tarpaulin taut?"
She was a very naughty girl,
　　And naughty still would be;
But ah! she was not nautical
　　By any means, you see.

The sailor-boy was candid,
　　He let his mirth appear,
He did not strive to hide his smile,
　　He grinned from ear to ear.
She noticed his amusement,
　　It gave her feelings pain,
And her tail grew still more skimpy
　　As she began again.

"Oh, wilt thou come and dwell with me?
   And thou shalt have delight
In catching limpets all the day
   And cracking them all night;
And oysters are abundant
   In the palace where I am,
And I will come and be thy bride
   And make thee seaweed jam."

The sailor-boy did one eye shut
   And then did it unclose,
And with solemnity he put
   His thumb unto his nose.
He said, "Be bothered if I do,
   However much you sing,
You flabby little, dabby little,
   Wetty little thing."   TRISTRAM.

TENNYSON IN THE MOATED GRANGE

This parody on Tennyson's "Mariana" (1830) appeared in the third number, March 16, 1878:

With whittl'd sticks the Laureate's plots
   Were thickly cover'd, one and all;
The Yankee pilgrims loung'd in knots
   Expectorating o'er the wall.
Their general air was sad and strange,
   They'd cross'd the seas one glimpse to catch
   Of Him; and now they kept their watch
Upon the lonely moated grange.
   They only said, "This waiting's dreary,
     Calc'late that's *so*," they said;
   "Reckon that we're aweary, aweary:
     Guess the ole coon's in bed!"

His hair was just as rouhh [*sic*] as ever;
   His tie was just as much untied;
He never brush'd or tied them, never,
   Either at morn or eventide.
After the flitting of the bats
   He drew his casement-curtain by,
   And with his hair brush took a shy;

It glanced athwart their glooming hats.
   And then they said, "This ain't so dreary.
     He's riled up *some*," they said;
    "Let's liquor up! this looks more cheery;
     Wake snakes! was that his head?"

All through the midnight he would sit
   Remarking how the night-fowl crow'd:
A telegram from Downing Street
   Inquiring "How about the Ode?"
Came to him: and he stamped upon it,
   And set about his weary work:—
   A panegyric on the Turk,
To match the Montenegro sonnet.
They said, "He wrote quite slick when Marie
   Alexandrowna wed;
'Tis *kewrious* how they shift and vary,
   These Britishers," they said.

All day he walk'd from room to room,
   Perusing, till his nerves grew weak,
The Ministerial threats of doom,
   Or someone else's post-card shriek—
"Don't write!" The Yankees walk'd about
   Carving their names (their temper rose),
   Quoting his poems thro' the nose,
And saying he was written out.
   "Why ain't the Swan of Avon here, eh?
    Reckon that fowl's gone dead,
   Wal, Avon's no tall estuairy
    To Ohio," they said.

"Ring out, ring out, my mournful rhymes!"
   They wouldn't ring; he loath'd their sound
As much as those propos'd at times
   By Beaconsfield: he said "Confound
Them all!" but most he loath'd his work
   When the dim sunrise came this way,
   From Stamboul, and Besika Bay,
And various places, mostly Turk.
    He said "This must stop somehow, clearly;
     I'll smoke a pipe," he said;
    "And, if you're waking, call me early,
     For now I'm going to bed."   TRISTRAM.

PUNCH AND JOUIDA
A NOVEL

"Punch and Jouida," which also appeared in the third number, declares in its title that it is a parody on the lush style of Marie de la Ramée, known under her pen name Ouida. Her popular novel, *Under Two Flags*, was published in 1867. I quote about one-half of the first installment of Housman's burlesque; a second appeared in the fourth issue of the *Table* (May 11).

I.

Beneath its sinister and voluptuous marble smile, a man lay sleeping in the hot, swooning afternoon. The lamp of day, Hêlios, the beautiful, heartless, godlike Greek divinity, was yielding his tired tarnished chariot to the passionate and crimson arms of Pelops.

. . . .

The marble spires and gilded columns wavered and bowed their tremulous heads beneath the light Etesian gale, as it wandered wearily on through the luxurious ceilings and empurpled floors of the leading upholsterers' shops; while on the breeze the dying sunbeams floated bewildered over gorgeous draperies of Ormuz and silks of Samarcand, where the cochineal of the Indies trailed in reckless profusion over the priceless Brussels and Kidderminster carpets. High above all else into the purple and palpitating heaven, the Olympus of the Greeks, towered the two mighty theatres, the immemorial glories of the city.

. . . .

Outside its palpable walls and terraced undulations stood twelve august and variegated statues.

It was beneath the sinister and voluptuous marble smile of one of these, that a man lay sleeping in the hot, swooning, etc. It is an inscrutable smile. No man yet has drawn the fierce dark secret from the marble lips. Some tell me it is the face of the implacable rose-crowned Nero as he watched the burning of Rome. Some say that it is Judas Iscariot. Some that it is the third Sorceress in Macbeth. But when they tell me this, I smile, for I know that they are wrong. I know that it is the face of Diogenes, the Cynic tyrant of Syracuse, his lips wreathed with the same cruel smile with which he might have sat in his tub in that artfully wrought and artistically decorated chamber, in which he could hear all the bloodless whispers and scorching shrieks of the prisoners in his dungeon; with that same smile with which he might have doomed the fragile and floating Europa to a fiery death within that brazen bull which she had wrought with her own rich creamy hands and dewy-petalled finger-tips.

Here the man lay sleeping. His face was brown; his dark eyes flashed a red lustre through his closed eyelids; his head was concealed by a multitude of raven locks, which uttered a warning croak at intervals.

. . . .

At a quarter to four he opened his melting eyes and sat up. . . . He had in his hands violets, primroses, roses, lilies, poppies, dahlias, chrysanthemums, and amaranths, which gleamed many-coloured in the light of the falling sun.

. . . .

At last he rose and turned to a mystic and exciting stage or sentry-box which reared its oscillating height at his side. An eager and gesticulating crowd had even now gathered around the marvellous alien; for his figure indeed attracted them.

. . . .

They cried out with quivering lips and pleading eyes. "Begin," they said.

He swept aside with a haughty sweep of his fine aristocratic hand the Tyrian folds of the curtain; and as he proudly withdrew his olive form into the Phoenician recesses of the sentry-box, there appeared on the miniature stage two passionate and divine existences.

They were Pulcinello and Jouida.

II.

They were locked in a dreamy and tempestuous embrace. The long lithe creamy arms of Jouida wooed the amorous breezes as they extended over the Herculean shoulders of her Amoeboean lover, while over the snow neck of the maiden shot out the rose-tinted nose of Punch. Of all his splendid and glittering countenance no portion shone like this.

. . . .

It was not the calm clear logical feature of the fine and carefully varnished Greek. It was rather the full, robust, resonant Roman, swollen with the wantonness of empire, and rushing forth from the face in a grand and gracious swoop as the eagle darting from its eyrie upon the doomed hare who vainly leaps towards her burrow to find shelter in the bosom of the earth from this thunderbolt of the Uranian and celestial heaven. The thoughtful brow of Pulcinello rose like a beetling crag above the twin Vesuvii or Actnae of his eyes, between which, with the tense and vigorous curve of the cataract from the rock or the chased silver bow of the god-like archer Phoebus, leapt forth that mighty feature and descended with fierce and insatiable desire upon the upward rushing chin, like the surging tides of the seas that beat upon the crowned Acropolis of the grey-eyed goddess whom the ruthless Turnus slew. Above the embracing lovers hovered in the air a dim and tremulous canine form. Pulcinello gazed at it with hot eyes dimmed with passion, and as he dashed his imperial hand across them he murmured the immortal words sung so long ago by the blind bard beneath the walls of Ilion:—

"Toby, or not Toby? that is the question."   TRISTRAM.

JONES HIS REPARTEE

This, the first of Tristram's two "Varsity Ballads," was printed in number four, May 11, 1878. "Jones His Repartee" is a stab at the University Proctor, age-old foe of the Oxford undergraduate. The "shop" in stanza nine is the print-shop where *Ye Rounde Table* was published.

Years, centuries had vanished
    Since Proctors first were made,
Yet they, without repression,
    Plied their nefarious trade;
For no man yet had hurled at them
    A scathing, sharp reply—
When asked "Are you a member of
    This University?"

Not yet: for Vengeance lingers,
    And Doom, though sure, is late:
But after Crime come flying
    The fiery feet of Fate;—
In this case, Jones of Jesus
    Was Fate:—one evening, he,
Just after Hall, invented
    A crushing repartee.

Fast through the shaken city
    The fearful rumour spread:
The Vice was told the tidings,
    And he went straight to bed:

The Dons, at the idea
    They doubled up with groans:
The Undergrads presented
    A vote of thanks to Jones.

The Proctors twain they trembled
    And smiled a sickly smile;
With tottering steps to Jesus
    They walked in single file:
They waited on the Principal,
    They cried, in awe-struck tones:—
"If there's a heart within your veins—
    Oh! tell us, which is Jones?"

The Principal was helpless
    To succour their distress:
He said that he had quite an
    Embarras de richesses,
As almost all the Fellows—
    And half the scholars too—
And every other commoner—
    Were Joneses,—that he knew.

But Jones,—our Jones,—foreshadowed
    The hour of his delight:
He pictured writhing Proctors
    In visions of the night,
Prospectively beholding
    Their anguished bosoms heave,
Seeing them tear their hoary hair
    And rend the velvet sleeve.

About the time when sunset
    Occurs, and sunbeams flee,
He went in quest of Proctors,
    He and his repartee.
He traversed all the districts
    Which Proctors most frequent,
But still he never met them
    Whichever way he went.

To Ritualistic churches
    He always used to go,
And hang about the porches
    To catch the Proctors; no!—

No use! whene'er the Proctors
  Caught glimpses of a man
Who *might* be Jones of Jesus,—
  They gat them up and ran.

At last you might have seen him
  One night in raptures stop
To purchase this unrivalled work
  At Mr. Shrimpton's shop:
He issued forth: he noticed
  A dim form standing by:
He heard—"Are you a member of
  This University?"

He merely turned: the Proctor
  Fell prostrate on the stones;—
He clasped his hands in torture,
  He knew it *must* be Jones:
There played on Jones's features
  A smile of fiendish glee—
—Then froze:—for Jones of Jesus
  Forgot his repartee.

The moon, 'mongst other objects,
  Shone on a festive cup
Where the exultant Proctor
  Had gone to liquor up;
She shone on Vice triumphant
  And virtue overawed;
She shone on Jones of Jesus
  Expiring in the Broad.   TRISTRAM.

TEMPORA MUTANTUR

"Tempora Mutantur" signaled Tristram's first appearance with
a lead-article. It was one of three signed contributions from him
to the final, the Commemoration, number of the magazine. At
the date of the writer's "letter," the Ashantees and New Zealanders have taken over England, and one Coffee Calcalli is
now Vice-Chancellor of Oxford. His garbled quotations from
Shakespeare make this one of Housman's most amusing prose
compositions.

Oxford

Letter to the Editor of the *Times*, June 27th, A.D. 2078.

Oxford.

Sir,—The evening sun was now sinking over Shotover, when the learned and venerable Vice-Chancellor, Coffee Calcalli, heading a company of the rank and beauty of the land, and attired in his academical robes of strings of sea-shells, approached the interesting ruin of the Martyrs' Memorial.

"This," exclaimed the Vice-Chancellor,

.   .   .   .

"is the state of man! I allude to the Martyrs' Memorial, not my umbrella.

> "This is the state of man: to-day he puts forth
> The tender leaves of hope, and nips his root,
> And when he falls he falls like Lucifer
> Into a lean and slippered pantaloon.

.   .   .   .

It was here remarked by a by-stander, that the Vice-Chancellor had not got slippers, and certainly not a vestige of the other article of clothing mentioned.

.   .   .   .

The Vice-Chancellor then proceeded to explain how the Martyrs' Memorial was erected to the memory of the martyred King, Charles I., who was barbarously beheaded on the same spot.

"Still," cried the Vice-Chancellor, lifting up his umbrella for a sounding-board,

> "There's a divinity doth hedge a King
> Rough hew him how we will!

"How true are these words of the immortal Bird. How wondrous the divinity that *doth* hedge every King, be his name Charles or Cole!" When the Vice-Chancellor had said this, he facetiously secreted himself behind the ruins, and emerged tattooed with a new pattern, and stained with woad, like an Ancient Briton: a race which inhabited this island some years before the victorious incursion of the combined New Zealanders and Ashantees. He had also flung some scarlet paint into one eye, intending, as he expressed it in the words of the Swan, to "make the green one red." He then slowly threaded his way through the prostrate bodies of that large majority of his audience which had been overcome by his last remark, and proceeded absently along the Broad, immersed in thought.

.   .   .   .

[43]

As this prevented him from being able to see where he was going, he stumbled over some one who had succumbed to his last remark, and was now engaged in going to his long home in the middle of the pavement. It was the Senior Proctor. The Vice-Chancellor, seeing that he was coiling up in his last agonies, wished to shake hands with him, "Because," said he, "the Bird of Avon remarks that this mortal coil must give us paws." This turned out to be too much for the Proctor's vital spark of heavenly flame, and next morning friends were requested to accept this intimation. The Vice-Chancellor immediately observed to the decorated official who habitually precedes him,—

"He was a man: take him for all in all
We shall not look upon his like again."

The official, however, remarked that it was no good taking him for 'all in 'all, as 'all had taken place at six o'clock that evening; though he had no doubt he could get him something cold out of the kitchen. The Vice-Chancellor has quoted the Bard less often since this. As I sat down, Sir, to write to your columns this faithful account of the proceedings of the evening, I heard him observe in a faint voice that he was going to sleep,—perchance to dream. He then exclaimed that *there* was the rub. I looked out of the window, but not seeing the rub, I posted my letter.

Your representative,

TRISTRAM.

II *The Youthful Humorist*

Housman placed on his family, sometimes without avail, strict limitations on the circulation of his humorous skits in prose and poetry. His sister Katharine, one of the most obedient, remarks in her chapter "Boyhood" in the Holt memorial volume that his nonsense prose "could be delightful; but no publication of that is to be permitted to come into contrast with his scholarly writings."[4] Nevertheless, she quotes "with bated breath"—as if fearful of a touch on her shoulder from the spirit-world—the opening lines of "A Morning with the Royal Family," written for family delectation only, but published without permission, probably by Basil,[5] in *The Bromsgrovian* in 1882. The same magazine also later printed Alfred's now-famous Aeschylean parody, "A Fragment of a Greek Tragedy," signed by the poet himself.

So it has turned out that the *Rounde Table* pieces from Housman's Oxford period, together with others of their kind that have long been well known, provide enough to allow a fair estimate of his developing skill as a satirical parodist. If we had the first fifty-odd pages from his first poetry notebook, it might be possible to trace a well-marked line of descent from his first amusing pieces written at home to his devastating scholarly criticism which he produced so abundantly during his professorships at University College, London, and Trinity College, Cambridge. But still another significant bit of verse written about 1900, while he was at University College, remains from his second notebook (p. 199) that links his cutting "Eleventh Eclogue" of the last number of *Ye Rounde Table* with the brilliant introductions to his editions of the Latin poets and his fifty-year presidency of the Classical journals:

> Gross weighs the mounded marl
> On Nicholas and Karl;
> Dance on their graves, and they will never rage.
> Now 'tis the turn of men that cannot think
> And yet delight to wet the pen in ink
> And watch the goosequill, all the worse for drink,
>   Pursue ancestral instincts on the page.
> They must lift their voice
>   And teach their grandmothers and prattle rules:
> This neither is their courage nor their choice,
>   But their necessity in being fools.

The unusual word *prattle* in this envenomed pass at Nicolas and Karl and their successors suggests that it may have been delivered about the time of Housman's adverse review of Breysig's edition of the *Aratea* of Germanicus since he also used this word in it.

His critique was published in the *Classical Review* (February, 1900). By this time he was a master in the thrust and parry of academic controversy, for which prose is of course the proper weapon. But satirical poetry often serves to temper the blade; and the later Professor of Latin had only to give an edge to what Tristram had employed twenty-two years before in producing his contributions to *Ye Rounde Table*.

These activities of young Housman's first year at St. John's set and deepened the grooves of his critical judgments on the academic world he was just entering, and in which he was to make

for himself a place of almost unrivaled eminence. As a critic of
things about him in his first year at Oxford, he knew he did not
speak with authority, but it pleased him to speak as if he had it.
He desperately wanted it or something like it—some utterance
by which he might avenge himself for the blows he had suffered
at the hands of the seen and unseen enemies who had hurt him.

His flight to deism had left him with no counselor beside his
own high ambition, which was constantly demanding performance to match it. But he still felt in his soul the gnawing sorrow
of bereavement, the semi-poverty in which his schooldays had
been spent and which his brothers and sisters were still endur-
ing, the mismatched school clothes, the taunts and shoving-about
he had silently taken from his philistine comrades, and the
crushing humiliation of their accursed nicknames for him:
"Mouse" and "Stinky."

All these indignities and rejections he had taken from the
unworthy were now in some tiny measure being repaid, he felt,
in this outpouring of his frustration and resentment. So it may be
fairly said that the arrogant scholar Housman later became,
whose devastating critiques made the leading Classicists of
Europe pale when they unwrapped their literary journals, was
coming to life in the jibing, idol-shattering "Tristram" of *Ye
Rounde Table.*

III   *Failure at Oxford*

The reasons for Housman's academic failure in the "Greats"
(the final examination for the B.A. in classics) and his sorry retreat from Oxford in the spring of 1881 are not easily identified
or described. One reason lay in his highhanded disregard of the
required courses of study, which included not only the Greek and
Latin classics, in which he was proficient—he had earned a "First
Class" in Classical Moderations in 1879—but ancient history and
philosophy as well. His neglect of lectures that did not interest
him was not a fatal dereliction, but his unwillingness to swallow
his dislike and make on his own account an adequate preparation in some alien fields, albeit unworthy of his attention, where
he knew he would be examined, could not have led him down a
surer way of ruin. When he faced the final examination lists at
the end of Trinity term, he had no answers to write for many
of the questions. His naïve, untempered confidence in his own

program of reading, which included a long and absorbed perusal of the love-poetry of Propertius, had let him down disastrously; and this he must have realized with burning clarity as he handed in his papers.[6]

Another reason for his failure—and a far more serious one—lay in his emotional involvement with one of his classmates, Moses Jackson, also a scholar of Alfred's college and but one year older than he. Jackson was a handsome, well-built man, one who would stand out in any college assembly, devoted to athletic sports and keenly interested in the St. John's rowing crew. His academic interests lay entirely in scientific fields, and as his acquaintance with Alfred developed, he took a jovian delight in scoffing gently at his friend's devotion to things literary and at his lack of gusto for the playing-fields. What words could Alfred employ to defend himself or to rebuke this paragon of manly strength to whom he felt himself so closely drawn? From his schooldays an admirer of the athlete-soldier ideal, he found in Moses Jackson the living fulfillment; and, as admiration grew into affection "passing the love of women," he became trammeled in a net of emotional complexes from which he could not extricate himself.

In their fourth year at St. John's, they, with A. W. Pollard (like them, required to seek lodgings outside their College), took five rooms together, setting up a study schedule that left Pollard much out of the company of his two classmates. Details of this close companionship, recorded presumably in Alfred's diary, may be told in the publication of the British Museum (Add. MS. 45861. [See Preface, note 20]). Whatever hoarded evidence may be forthcoming, we are in no great need of further data concerning the unhappy crisis into which Housman found himself irresistibly drawn and which culminated in public disgrace and inner ruin during the final year of his Oxford residence. It is not exaggerating to say that the remainder of his life was a controlled reaction to the events of his twenty-first year. This year and the preceding are the ones he means in "When I was one-and-twenty" (*ASL* 13), describing his arrogant self-sufficiency ("no use to talk to me") at twenty-one (1880-1881), and the "endless rue" he had been forced to accept as the bitter savor of his life one year later. This poem, so clearly a cry from the heart, is not now represented in his notebooks by a complete draft; but the first line of it (on A 216) is deeply trenched below with a heavy underscore; above it is the date, "Jan. 1895." In this poem, and very frequently elsewhere, Housman speaks of his Oxford crisis: the full surrender of his affections, the reflex of guilt and the unbearable loneliness that came with it, the impulse of suicide.

How near Housman came to self-destruction is indicated in the chaotic draft of a poem—later *Additional Poems* 15—that sprawls over page 180 of his first poetry notebook. The draft dates from the time he was living alone in London at Byron Cottage, Highgate, where he wrote most of the poems of *A Shropshire Lad.* The first line begins " 'Tis six years since, 'All's lost.' " Immediately a fitter phrase came up, and he wrote "An end, thought I." Then more alternative phrases begin to swarm over the top of the page: "Good night, Stop here," and a couplet: " 'Tis over; now's high time to die,/There's no more living . . ." But he stays his hand for the same reason given in another poem (eventually *More Poems* 34) where the same debate is described. Of this poem we have only a late-written ink draft on pages 121-22 of the fourth and last notebook. The next-to-last stanza, as first written, shows significant variations from the text printed by Laurence Housman:

> And if so long I carry
>   The life that season marred,
> 'Tis that the child of Adam
>   Is not so evil-starred
>   As he is hard.

Housman's strong dramatic sense appears in his frequent preference for the dramatic monologue and in his skill in creating characters and situations that compose his tragic plots. His circle of acquaintances in Bromsgrove and its environs was small, and he did not enlarge his knowledge of English country folks while at Oxford. The rustic people in his poetry are therefore not drawn from life, and this fact may have been the one he had in mind when he said that very little of his poetry was autobiographical.[7] But the jewel outshines, as it should, the casket: what the Shropshire reapers and dancers say and do is far less important than their feelings, which are the poet's own: his anguished reaction to the realization that his unlucky liaison with Moses Jackson had forever made him in his own eyes a loveless misfit incapable of normal desires and normal satisfactions.[8] His thwarted and corrupted self he divided among the condemned culprit, the soldier bleeding to his death, the jealous fratricide, the ploughman speaking up through the sod. The fortunate die young; the brave, sometimes by their own hand. All reach for our pity and tolerance as victims of a blind, intolerant fate. Since our post-war era has registered a vast modification of the public mind toward sexual aberrations, we are fortunately able to regard clear-eyed and unprejudiced the experiences which made Housman a poet and at the same time estimate, over the perspective of three-quarters of a century, the price he paid in almost unbearable suffering.[9]

But when Alfred turned away from Oxford in the spring of 1881, he was well aware that there was no such understanding awaiting him at Bromsgrove, not even in his family circle, but his pride would have rejected it if it had been offered. He told his family nothing; no explanations for his debacle were asked and none were given. When a disgruntled relative cut off a small allowance, he made no protest. He concealed his self-loathing behind an impenetrable mask and set himself to reading, in the midst of the buzz of family chatter, for the Civil Service examinations. Perhaps he thought that the way to an academic career was barred to him forever, although he did return to Oxford in the autumn for his bread-and-butter pass degree. During the eighteen-month period at home he found some temporary employment, thanks to his old headmaster, Herbert Millington, in teaching the sixth-form pupils in Bromsgrove School, which he and some of his charges had attended together four brief years earlier. This was the land of lost content. What were his thoughts when he saw sitting at his old desk, construing passages he had memorized there, a bright-faced lad who reminded him of his unspoiled innocence?

CHAPTER 3

London and Cambridge

HIS Civil Service examinations safely passed, Housman obtained a position in the London Patent Office. Moses
Jackson, already a government employee there, had probably
been a major influence in interesting Housman in preparing for
the examinations and doubtless had exerted some influence in
expediting his friend's appointment. The beginning salary of Her
Majesty's clerk was a scanty hundred pounds a year—the same, as
he may often have ironically recalled, as his annual stipend at
St. John's. At Jackson's invitation he shared quarters with him
and his younger brother, Adalbert, from 1882 to 1886. Mixed
motives urged Housman to resume close acquaintance with his
former roommate: economy may have been one; desire to be
near the man who had changed his life may have been another.
Housman's feelings of idolatry for Jackson never lessened; whatever he may have thought of his own predicament, he laid the
blame for it upon himself alone. In his early years in London he
developed a warm affection for Adalbert Jackson, a Classics
student at University College, whose death in 1892 he commemorated in "A.J.J." (*MP* 42), one of the most moving tributes
he ever wrote. After four years' lodging with the Jackson
brothers, Housman moved to 17 North Road, Highgate, where
he lived alone for nineteen years. His desire for a change of
residence probably arose from the wish to spend more uninter-
rupted time on his self-assigned reading at the British Museum.
To this end, he retreated into almost impenetrable seclusion:
his brother Laurence and sister Clemence, whose long period of
residence in London overlapped most of his, paid only one visit
to Highgate, on an invitation to tea.[1]

I *A Clerk in Her Majesty's Service*

As a clerk in the Patent Office Housman found that his duties
were largely matters of routine and the working day short

enough to allow the scholar in him ample time to pursue his studies in Classical subjects, his main literary interest for so long a period; perhaps he could find there a means of recouping his academic failure. Once again, as in the days of his carefree skylarking with *Ye Rounde Table* and his dilettante reading as fancy called, he was exploiting his mental equipment, finding out where his fortes lay, and learning under his own direction where he could set his mark. But there was this difference: now he was reaching for fame, grimly resolved to achieve, by unrelenting labor, levels of attainment as high as the rim of the deep pit into which he had fallen.

Housman's first efforts attracted the notice of textual experts of high standing.[2] Before his ten-year "purgatory" as a government clerk ended, he had published, or was readying for publication, four papers on Horace, a thirty-five page article on his Oxford idol Propertius, two on Ovid, four on Aeschylus, one on Aristotle, two on Euripides, one on Isocrates, one on Persius, three on Sophocles, one on Virgil, and four other smaller miscellanea. His output was as timely as it was abundant, for when, in 1893, vacancies were announced in the Greek and Latin chairs in University College, London, Housman applied for the opening in Latin; he also requested that, if unsuccessful there, he might be considered for the Greek professorship. As if to taunt fate to do its worst now or surrender, he stated in his application that eleven years before, he had failed his final University examinations in the Classics. By way of offsetting this confiteor, however, seventeen testimonial letters arrived with it from top-ranking Classical scholars in England, the Continent, and the United States.[3] This bold strategy, which must have shaken the College authorities, was crowned with success: he was unanimously elected to the Latin chair, his first choice.

After he had assumed his duties, it was observed that his publications on Greek topics began to fall off. Asked the reason, he said, "I found I could not attain to eminence in both." This reply casts an illuminating beam upon his character: for him, in this stage of his private war with nemesis, eminence in one literature and not in the other would not do. It had to be eminence all the way, and this he would attain, now that he had selected his Everest. Few greybeards could have believed the solid productions of his scholarship before his taking the chair had been the work of a man of thirty-three. How could he have mastered so much so early? The brisk acerbity of his style, that made the most recondite subjects stir to life and the convincing rightness of his textual emendations, coupled with pervasive evidence of the depth and breadth of his reading, served notice to the grand masters of Classical scholarship that a new Daniel was come to judgment.

His professorial duties at University College were not burdensome although his pupils were not of high caliber. He regularly spent about ten hours a week in class work, and gave to his graduate students each year a course of lectures based on the research he was pursuing at the time. Once again, he fortunately had much "after-hours" time to carry on his chosen investigations in the Latin classics and, far more important, to begin filling his first notebook with the pieces that were to go into *A Shropshire Lad*, which appeared in 1896.

Throughout the colorless labor of his clerkship and the distracting renewal of his ties with Moses Jackson, his pent-up feelings had found no relief in the unburdening that sometimes comes with the act of composition. The very presence of the man with whom his emotional self was so inextricably tied may have served to repress his impulse to write. This surmise seems to be borne out by the fact that Housman wrote perhaps no more than ten pieces of his serious poetry until after he had left the Jackson brothers and begun to live alone in Byron Cottage, Highgate, in 1886.[4] About that time he began writing his lyrics in a notebook once used for Classical miscellanea, later interspersed with nonsense verse. This chiding soliloquy is his first surviving entry of the "new" poetry:

> Nor break my heart with hoping any more,
>   Tomorrow you shall have the grave to wife:
>   Now, in the accepted time, make friends with life.
>
> To have missed no chances when you come to die
>   Haste, for the heaven is westered since you came:
>   Day falls, night climbs, the hour has lost its name;
>   Quick, quick! the lightning's pace were weary, slow,
>   And here you loiter spelling gravestones: go.[5]

This fragment, written in ink now faded to mauve and later heavily inked over, occupies the upper two-thirds of Notebook A, page 60. It tells us much of Housman's state of mind during the trying years of the late 1880's, his uneasy footing between despair and hope, his self-adjuration to be constantly on the climb. Here, as ever afterwards, he finds himself behind the hour.

II   *Beginning of the* Shropshire Lad *Lyrics*

Three pages later he entered the first poem that we can recognize as belonging to *A Shropshire Lad:* "Into my heart an air that kills" (*ASL* 40), one of the most poignant lyrics he ever wrote, full of the sense of irremediable loss:

> Into my heart an air that kills
>   From yon far country blows:
> What are those blue remembered hills,
>   What towns, what shires are those?
>
> That is the land of lost content,
>   I see it shining plain,
> The happy footpaths where I went
>   And cannot come again.
>
>   (The original version, on A 63.)

The second *ASL* lyric, Number 14 to be, "There pass the careless people," is on pages 82-83. Reading it in the notebook context is to hear anew and with a new clarity the cry of tragic hopelessness that runs through the four notebooks. I quote the ink-and-pencil draft as Housman copied it:

> There pass the careless people
>   That call their souls their own:
> Here by the road I loiter,
>   How idle and alone.
>
> No, past all plunge of plummet,
>   In seas I cannot sound,
> My heart and soul and senses,
>   World without end, are drowned.

His folly has not fellow
In all the ken of day
That gives to man or woman
His heart and soul away.

There flowers no balm to sain him
From east of earth to west
That's lost for everlasting
The heart out of his breast.

Beside the labouring highway
With empty hands I stroll:
Sea-deep, till doomsday morning,
Lie lost my heart and soul.

The full chorus of despair—abandonment, disillusion, self-contempt—has probably never been more movingly uttered in twenty lines.

Page 84 contains the third *Shropshire Lad* poem, the mysterious "Bring, in this timeless grave to throw" (later *ASL* 46), copied here under the heading "A Winter Funeral." Since these three pieces, like others in these opening pages, are written in ink, it is safe to assume, after a careful study of the contents of the four books, that they were not composed here but copied from other drafts. So the pages run up to A 106. None are dated, but A 66 provides a valuable clue as it contains one or two lines that later went into "1887" (*ASL* 1), thus giving us a terminus post quem for dating the surviving poems of Notebook A.

Housman's self-analytical manner is revealed in a few other poems in this early section; on page 88 is "Yon fire that frets the eastern sky" (*MP* 25), written of an anniversary of his birthday, on a day when he says he is departing into death, "not to be born again." Another, on page 89, "Like mine, the veins of these that slumber" (*MP* 20), contemplates a burial field whose occupants, once warm-blooded as he, he will soon join "with ice in all my pulses." Thus his preoccupation with the grave stands out in the first entries in Notebook A.

On page 106 the book ceases to be a copy-file and becomes a depository of the poet's first efforts to give form to his emotions and bring them into something like a completed utterance. This section opens with a not-unhappy pastoral, "The Merry

Guide" (*ASL* 42), two successive drafts of which fill pages 106-9, and a third was entered on A 114-15. All are dated "Sept. 1890." By this time it is clear Housman had gained a considerable measure of relief and self-possession—if not the "exceeding great relief" that Coleridge experienced from a similar exercise of his mind, certainly something more than the long evenings at the British Museum could have afforded him. He had pacified his inner tumult to a state that allowed him to view it with some objectivity, and the very real enthusiasm and zest shown in the hurried but meticulously written drafts of "The Merry Guide" prove that he had entered a road which, if it did not lead immediately upward, would at least help him escape some of the despondency that lay about him in the black years of the early and middle 1880's.

In his Preface to his second book, *Last Poems* (1922), Housman stated that the greater part of *A Shropshire Lad* was written in the early months of 1895. But it is evident from the dates scattered through Notebooks A and B that eighteen of the sixty-three pieces were completed before that time and that about one-third more were entered in B *after* the months he said were so prolific. This fits with other evidence to indicate that the commencement of Housman's real poetic activity was not a sudden freshet but more like a sustained, controlled welling-up. He denied, in answer to a questionnaire a few years before his death, that he ever had any such thing as a "crisis of pessimism."[6] He may not have considered the "continuous excitement" he mentions in his Preface to *Last Poems* as a crisis of this or any kind; but the notebook record plainly shows that the first five months of 1895 were not as rich as he would have us believe. Nor did they see the completion of three-fourths (so read the first draft of his *LP Preface*) of the lyrics of his first book. As a matter of fact, the month of August, yielding ten poems, was the most productive of the year.

The explanation for these high tides of poetry—not forgetting the most obvious one, his permanent estrangement from Moses Jackson in 1886 or thereabouts—is probably beyond our seeking; but we know Housman confessed that his most fruitful periods were induced or accompanied by feelings of unrest. Outward events, tragedies read in the daily press as well as the deaths of relatives and friends, smote him deeply. Shortly after he gave his Introductory Lecture at University College, the death on November 12, 1892, of Adalbert Jackson may have helped to build up the feelings that overflowed into his notebooks.

Another poetic impulse, distressful in itself and more so for the train of earlier unhappiness that memory added to it, probably came with his father's death, November 27, 1894, from which he may have derived "Now hollow fires burn out to black" (*ASL* 60) and the gloomy "In midnights of November" (*LP* 19), where the poet hears the "dead call the dying/And finger at the doors."[7] Robert Louis Stevenson's death, coinciding with his father's, inspired him to write "R.L.S." (*AP* 22), which, contrary to his habit at the time, he submitted for publication and it appeared in *The Academy* of December 22, 1894.

His poetic imagination had ample scope for much more than the images of his own misfortunes, for the trial and condemnation of Oscar Wilde in the spring of 1895 called forth in the autumn the burning verses of "Oh who is that young sinner . . .?" (*AP* 18).[8] Housman felt a profound sympathy for Wilde in his public disgrace and imprisonment; and, after the unfortunate's release and death in Paris in 1900, Housman followed his sad story—not only in the public press but in the books of detraction and defense that began to appear after the turn of the century.

III *Editing the* Astronomica *of Manilius*

During his tenure of the Latin chair at University College, Housman's main scholarly occupation was the editing of the first of the five books of the *Astronomica* of Manilius. A herculean task not completed until 1930, it demanded the full exercise of his hard-won expertise in the high art of emendation of Classical texts. The fact that Manilius was a third-rate poet, who, "when he came to write his fifth book, no longer possessed even so much astronomy as had sufficed him for writing his first"— so Housman complained in his Preface to Volume V—did not blunt his attack on his self-set chore. Its performance, as successive volumes appeared and were approvingly reviewed, began to give weight to the growing opinion that the new editor of Manilius was "the first scholar in Europe." Perhaps of primary interest to us is the fact that Volume I contained a dedicatory poem in Latin elegiacs to Moses Jackson, a rough draft of which

can still be read on pages 145-46 of Notebook B. Its purport may
be gathered in these concluding lines of the translation by
Edmund Wilson:

> From human hand to hand, I give—
> To thee who followest away
> These rising signs, to seek the day—
> This present from a western shore:
> Take it: to-morrow runs before,
> With those whom life no longer owns
> To lay our flesh and loose our bones—
> To dull with all-benumbing thrust
> Our wits that wake not from the dust,
> Nor spare, with learning's lettered leaf,
> The bonds of fellowship as brief.

Jackson was teaching in India when Book I was published, and
Housman, after sending to his publisher the list of persons to
whom presentation copies should be given, ordered two moroc-
co-bound gilt-edged exemplars and insisted on dispatching
"Mo's" copy himself.

Another professional exploit—the work of one year only—performed during the University College period was Housman's
editing the Satires of Juvenal, which, published in 1905, was
provocatively subtitled "for the use of editors." He concluded his
preface with another gesture of the arrogance that was becoming
his second nature: ". . . it is an enterprise undertaken in haste
and in humane concern for the relief of a people sitting in darkness." Such acerbities as these, multiplied in his other prefaces,
and his long-drawn-out duels in the *Journal of Philology* and
elsewhere were of a piece with his satirical writing in *Ye Rounde
Table* and with the dark broodings of much of *A Shropshire Lad*.
Laurence reports (memoir, pp. 77-78) that he found among his
brother's papers several pages of choice vituperation, a kind of
critical arsenal on which he could, and did, draw when engaged
in his favorite sport of slaying false reputations.

After he had spent eighteen years at University College, the
prospect of greener pastures at Trinity College, Cambridge,
opened to him when the Kennedy Professorship of Latin became
vacant in December, 1910. Housman's candidacy, once he was
prevailed upon to have it known, was by no means an assured

thing. Though there were few to deny his lofty reputation in the domain of Classical scholarship, there were more whose ruffled feelings sought ways and means to oppose his expansion of it at Cambridge. But he had active friends both within and without the citadel, and about the first of the new year its governors threw open the gates and announced his election. *The Oxford Magazine,* remarking that it was an "uncommon event" for an Oxford man to be called to a Cambridge professorship, sagely praised—how could it do otherwise?—the judgment of the electors: "Cambridge has invested in genius, and that, after all, is of all investments the safest." The Cantabrigian investors obviously had no doubts about the wisdom of their choice, for they added to it another coveted distinction: a fellowship in Trinity College.

Housman's residence at Cambridge by his own choice did not begin until October, 1911; and, during his last months in London, he completed his work on the second Book of Manilius, wrote his Inaugural Lecture (which he delivered in the Cambridge Senate House May 9),[9] and attended to the many minutiae of an extended leave-taking filled with the inevitable misgivings that arose with the contemplation of leaving his comfortable privacy in his London quarters and his easy routine at University College. The divided judgments of his family, informed of his new prospect after his election, did not add to his composure: Laurence and Katharine were congratulatory; but Basil, whose counsel Alfred much respected, expressed strong concern that the move might not be a wise one.[10]

Knowing Housman's expert judgment in food and wine, his University College associates had elected him to the office of Treasurer of the Professors' Dining Club; and, before his leavetaking, they gave him a rousing farewell banquet at which, as if to make amends for his two decades of taciturnity, he laughed and joked with the gayest, striking off with glass held high one of his best sallies: "Cambridge has seen Wordsworth drunk and Porson sober. Now I am a greater scholar than Wordsworth and a greater poet than Porson; so I fall betwixt and between." At another leave-taking his students, acknowledging his connoisseurship in poetry as well as wine, came bearing tributes; among these was a huge silver drinking-cup on which was engraved his already notorious epigram: "Malt does more than Milton can/To justify God's ways to man."

[58]

Housman's prescribed instructional duties at Trinity were not onerous; as at University College, they left him a comfortable daily margin for his research and writing. As the Kennedy Professor, he was required to assist in the examinations of candidates in various University courses and "give lectures in every year." His stint regularly consisted of two lectures each week throughout the three terms of the academic session. Outside the classroom he had practically no contact with his students—an arrangement that probably suited both sides as Professor Housman must have appeared as one of the least approachable of mentors to the awed but attentive students that sat in his small classes.[11] As he neared the end of his service at Cambridge, he once expressed regret that he knew few if any of the younger members of the instructional staff at Trinity. Some of them had been his students, but that went for little: his air of frigid reserve discouraged all approach within the lecture-room or without. Only on rare occasions would he accede to invitations to meet with the Trinity College Classical Reading Society and spend an evening discussing a Greek or Latin author. "One commonly came away from the meeting," so Gow reminisces, "with the feeling that so would the recording angel on the Judgment Day read his scroll, and so would faults be amended beyond appeal or dispute."[12]

There was another side, but one rarely shown. Before leaving London Housman had wryly confessed his ambition to become a member of the Wine and Garden Committees of his new College. His many-vestured fame had gone before him, and he obtained both of these appointments. Gow bears testimony[13] to Housman's unrivaled knowledge of vintages. He was particularly fond of Madeira, "that noble but deleterious wine"; and once, when its cost exceeded what the committee thought prudent to pay, Housman bought it himself and presented it to the College. His own cellerage was carefully selected over the years, and after his death it was discovered that in his will he had bequeathed it to the Family Dining Club, a group of a dozen colleagues who used to dine together every two weeks. There he was at his convivial best, responding "with bursts of silvery laughter" to the elevated witticisms of his friends and contributing choice specimens of his own.

But beyond the strict circuit of these intimate groups Housman withdrew into himself and on his solitary walks about the city might pass, without saluting, a club member he had exchanged jokes with the evening before. Strangers showing the least sign of familiarity were invariably floored by his stony reserve, and many were put off with the choker as harsh as that inflicted on an unfortunate who, hopefully introducing himself as an acquaintance of Laurence Housman, was met by the curt, "Knowing my brother is no introduction to *me*."

This Olympian distaste for casual meetings was carried to almost unbelievable extremes. During a stroll with Dr. Percy Withers, a person who shared Housman's confidence as much as anyone else outside his family, his host and he were approaching one of Withers' neighbors of whose merits he had just been speaking to his visitor. Withers stopped to greet his friend, expecting Housman to stop also and perhaps submit to an introduction. But he did not stop: "He walked steadily on, as though the lane were vacant, and when a few minutes later I overtook him, his face was clouded with—was it merely annoyance, or was it superciliousness? I don't know; it was glum enough for either."[14]

Housman's main professional enterprise during his Cambridge period was the editing of the last three books of the *Astronomica*. The third appeared in 1916, the fourth in 1920, and the last—postponed by a variety of interruptions accompanying the aftermath of the War, his family anxieties, the publication of *Last Poems* (1922), and the retardations that kept pace with his increasing years—did not see the light until 1930, six years before his death. All five books of the *Astronomica* were published at the editor's own expense and offered for sale considerably below the cost price. "But," he whimsically says in his Preface to Volume V, "this unscrupulous artifice did not overcome the natural disrelish of mankind for the combination of a tedious author with an odious editor."

During the war years he published some pieces which, later collected in *Last Poems*, served to give the volume the definitely soldierly character that distinguishes it from *A Shropshire Lad*. The most famous of these was his "Epitaph on an Army of Mercenaries" (*LP* 37), which appeared in the *Times* October 31, 1917, an anniversary of the First Battle of Ypres (1914). This sinewy poem was much sought for, and Housman was beset with requests for permission to reprint it. Granting this favor in 1929 to Harold Monro, he took occasion to utter his old complaint against careless editing and perversity of printers: "I express the hope, which experience forbids me to cherish, that it may be printed as it stands in my book." The "Epitaph," after its edged irony was apprehended, lifted Housman into a public esteem not far from that enjoyed by Kipling as a "national" poet.[15] It had much to do with his being offered the laureateship some years later in MacDonald's ministry, an honor which Housman declined—as he also declined on his seventieth birthday the Order of Merit, one of the most coveted distinctions bestowed by his government.

These offers, together with many more than are recorded, began to flow in upon him as early as 1905, when the University of Glasgow asked him to accept its Honorary Degree of Doctor of Laws.[16] Housman's precisely worded letter of non-acceptance mentioned "reasons which it would be tedious and perhaps difficult to enumerate, though they seem to me sufficient and decisive."[17] But there was one badge of merit, and only one, that he did not refuse: an Honorary Fellowship at St. John's, Oxford. He could accept with pleasure and gratitude this token of esteem from his own College, where the great crisis of his life had occurred, where he had met Moses Jackson, the man who stirred the depths of his being and unknowingly helped him lay on the rubble of defeat the foundation of his supreme achievements in poetry and scholarship.

A few months before the "Epitaph" appeared he had published in *The Blunderbuss* (March, 1917), a Trinity College magazine, the poem "As I gird on for fighting," which was collected as *LP* 2. *The Edwardian*, the magazine of King Edward's School of Bath, where his brother-in-law E. W. Symons was headmaster, published in December, 1915, two war poems: "The Conflict" (later *LP* 3), a memorial to Housman's nephew Lieutenant C. A. Symons, and another memorial poem, "Illic Jacet" (*LP* 4). By a curious turn of circumstances, the latter poem, which, as Mrs. Symons says, anticipates the death of the family's youngest brother, killed in the Boer War in 1901, had appeared in *The Academy* (February 24, 1900). Housman sent this poem to his sister not long after her son's death in the Battle of Loos in the early autumn of 1915, with the comment that the "business of poetry is to harmonise the sadness of the universe." *The Edwardian* of April, 1916, also printed "The Sage to the Young Man" (*MP* 4), another poem in tone and subject somewhat like the others just mentioned; it was among the first pieces Alfred entered in Notebook A, and he returned to it in four later drafts from September, 1890, to the summer of 1894. But, to him, it was not good enough to make *Last Poems*.

IV *"The Application of Thought to Textual Criticism"* and Last Poems

The year 1921 was marked by Housman's reading, before the Classical Association at Cambridge, of his famous "The Application of Thought to Textual Criticism." It was published a year later in the *Proceedings of the Classical Association*. More than any other document, this lecture is his apology for the scholarly side of his life and is therefore of outstanding interest. Housman began by defining what textual criticism is: ". . . the science of discovering error in texts and the art of removing it." He continued with seeming ingenuousness to explain that there is no mystery about this double process; it is based on nothing more than reason and common sense. It has no claim to be called an exact science: "A textual critic engaged upon his business is not at all like Newton investigating the motions of the planets: he is much more like a dog hunting for fleas. If a dog hunted for fleas on mathematical principles, he would never catch a flea except by accident. They require to be treated as individuals; and every problem which presents itself to the textual critic must be regarded as possibly unique."

But there are some restrictions inherent in the exercise of this function so genially introduced: not a few find it dull, and far fewer know how to practice it. Proficiency in the physical sciences is comparatively easy to attain, for they provide broad, easy avenues to the identification of what is clearly right and of what is clearly wrong. But the way of the textual critic, Housman declared, is always hard. Then, with his matchless knowledge of the history of the recension and emendation of Classical texts, he pointed out some of the pitfalls of criticism, where so many stragglers have lost their footing: the problem of evaluating manuscripts, the failure to recognize the possibility of error

when all signs point, or seem to point, to one inevitable conclusion, the vagaries of scribes, and the unthinking argument
from the supposed validity of numbers. Having behind one,
Housman declared, all the knowledge of the older and newer
criticism will not of itself make a man a superior critic; and he
ends: "... one thing beyond all others is necessary; and that is to
have a head, not a pumpkin, on your shoulders, and brains, not
pudding, in your head."

Housman had long been beset by inquiries as to when he was
going to bring out a successor to *A Shropshire Lad*, and to all
he had usually given a testy "never." No one could have been
more surprised, therefore, than Grant Richards upon receiving,
early in September, 1920, a letter ending with the question:
"Suppose I produced a new volume of poetry, in what part of
the year ought it to be published, and how long would it take
after the MS left my hands?" Housman's publisher did not then
know what only an examination of the poet's notebooks would
have disclosed: that the reason for his persistent stand-off lay
in the simple fact that he had not, during the long years of his
professional involvements, found inspiration or taken time to
produce a second volume of poetry.

Housman in his pride wished to conceal from everyone the
secret of his long poetic aridity and, as has already been shown,
took some liberties with the truth when he stated in his Preface
to *Last Poems* that "about a quarter of this matter belongs to
April of the present year." Actually sixteen pieces redrafted into
Notebook D, the finishing-ground for *Last Poems*, were carried
over from completed or near-completed earlier drafts in the three
other books; and all of twenty others went directly into printer's
copy from A, B, and C without being transcribed at all.[18] Thus
the agreeable fiction of a new poetic flurry in 1922, twenty-seven
years after the high tides that brought in *A Shropshire Lad*,
must be abandoned in its literal sense although it may be accepted that the excitement of reworking some of the old poems
passed over in 1895 may have acted as a very real stimulus on
Housman's creative energies and inspired the production of a
few—but only a few—of the finest poems in his second volume.
"The night is freezing fast" (*LP* 20) and "Tell me not here, it
needs not saying" (*LP* 40) are up to the level of his finest.

While engaged with the fifth book of the *Astronomica*, he

turned aside to bring to a conclusion his edition of the ten books of Lucan, published in 1926—another apex stone of the monument he had designed and begun to erect forty years before. In December, 1926, he wrote to Percy Withers: "My new edition of Lucan sells just twice as fast as *A Shropshire Lad* did."[19] We may surmise what feelings lay hidden behind this comparison: pride? irony? regret? It was not something said lightly.

Housman's *Last Poems* and his impressive scholarly output enhanced his reputation as poet and editor but did little to swell the enrollments of his lecture courses. Gow agrees with Professor Whatmough's "usually eighteen or twenty at the most, including a don or two" (See note 11, this chapter). But Gow goes on to say that the dons were among the faculty who "knew best where to learn," and he comments of the undergraduates thus: "it was impossible to listen attentively to Housman without becoming aware that one was in contact with a mind of extraordinary distinction; and it is not only, or even chiefly, to professional scholars that such a contact is fascinating and exhilarating."

Housman never sought the platform and often refused, when he could, invitations to address student and professional groups. He yielded perhaps most frequently to the requests from the Cambridge Philological Society, whose *Proceedings* (1919-1923) records a nice variety in the subjects he brought to their meetings: a poem by Horace; a passage from Dryden's "Heroic Stanzas on the Death of Oliver Cromwell"; a quotation from Byron's *Journals*; two lines from D. G. Rossetti's "The Orchard-Pit"; a quotation in a letter from R. L. Stevenson to Henry James; on a line in Shelley's "I arise from dreams of thee"; and passages chosen from Seneca.

When persuaded to undertake a lecture, he invariably laid aside work he considered more important and occasionally expressed his regret beforehand at having so easily become a victim. Such were his feelings about the preparation of the Leslie Stephen Lecture in 1933, which he delivered from the same rostrum he had occupied when he had read his Inaugural Address in the Senate House exactly twenty-two years before. Now he deliberately chose a subject in which he had often professed a lack of competence: "The Name and Nature of Poetry." At the beginning of his talk, he characteristically deplored the judgment of those who had urged him to the platform: "I have not so much improved as to become a literary critic, nor so much deteriorated as to fancy that I have become one." Having taken this safe stand, he went on to discourse at length on some of his favorites among the English poets: Shakespeare, Arnold, Chaucer, Milton.

In the course of his lecture he read a definition—or a description—of poetry that has since become one of the select touchstones: "And I think that to transfuse emotion—not to transmit thought but to set up in the reader's sense a vibration corresponding to what was felt by the writer—is the peculiar function of poetry." But the really memorable part of his lecture was a report on his own experiences in the writing of poetry, which will be more fully described in the next chapter.

V *"Soon will evening's self be gone"*

Housman's generally abstemious habits, his love of walking, and the vigor of his native constitution enabled him to surmount until the last few years of his life many of the disabilities of old age. His frame, though spare, was well set and erect, and his face usually showed the ruddy tinge of health. He once wryly complained to Percy Withers, "It is one of my grievances against the Creator that I always look better than I am . . . , and consequently receive fewer tears of sympathy than I deserve."[20] Cyril Clemens, whom Housman had invited in August, 1930, to be his guest at dinner in Hall at Trinity, has left us this photographic portrait of the man:

On my reaching his chambers overlooking Whewell's Court a few minutes late, he was awaiting me with a perceptible degree of impatience, and dressed in cap and gown.

In appearance Housman was a striking man—one who would stand out in any crowd—five feet, nine inches tall, with hair turning grey at the temples; a fine Roman nose; keen, piercing, kindly, grey eyes; and seventy-one years of age. His smile was of rare sweetness, and the twinkle in his eye gave evidence of a keen sense of humor. I shall always remember the stately manner in which he walked across the quadrangle to the dining hall.[21]

Housman ignored most modern conveniences although he was an enthusiastic air-traveler. He scorned the typewriter—"it makes things look repulsive"—and never mastered the intricacies of the telephone. Although he keenly enjoyed good food and drink—he had one of his favorite dishes named in his honor by the head chef of the Tour d'Argent in Paris—and was, when he could afford it, expensively fastidious about his clothing, he kept to a Spartan simplicity in choosing and furnishing his lodgings, which usually provided little space except for books and manuscripts.

The few visitors who found their way to his Cambridge rooms in Whewell's Court over the gate of Sidney Street, reported on the dark and uncomfortable atmosphere of his living quarters. "There could have been no undergraduate in college who did not have at least as great a degree of comfort" is Grant Richards' summing-up. In the last three years of his life, when his heart showed signs of failure, the two long flights of stairs between the street and his rooms presented a dangerous threat to his daily round. At first Housman scoffed at his physician's counsel to change his address; and, when mentioning this to Laurence, he added jestingly that he still ascended the forty-four steps two at a time—in the hope of dropping dead at the top. Only in his final illness did he condescend to take rooms on the ground floor of another court nearby.

The first serious physical crisis occurred shortly after the publication of the last book of Manilius. It was as if he had simply by an effort of the will staved off the enemy until his work was finished. A long period of varying depression followed and in 1935 he wrote to Grant Richards, "The continuation of my life beyond May 1933 was a regrettable mistake. . . ." Dr. Withers records that Alfred once confided to him: "The greatest blessing and the one undiluted bounty of this life is a sudden and painless end." A year before his death he suffered another depleting heart failure but persisted in his determination to make his annual journey to France. In the autumn he spent some weeks in a nursing home, where he was again confined during the Christmas vacation. He summoned enough energy to rebuke his doctor's protests and at the end of the college term assured a member of his family that he had fully kept up to his standards in the classroom.[22] On April 24, 1936, he dined with his colleagues at the Family Dining Club—it was his last appearance there. He died at his nursing home one week later.

Eleven years before, in January, 1925, Housman had written

on page 112 of his last notebook a twelve-line poem headed: "For my funeral, to the tune of Brief life is here our portion." The hymn, now *More Poems* 47, was sung at the brief ceremony on May 4 in Trinity College Chapel, and it appeared in the leaflet issued by the Cambridge University Press containing the Order of Service for the funeral.[23] Then and later Housman's poem may have caused some conscientious misgivings, for the three stanzas are full of Lucretian overtones and, except for a few archaic words, have very little to do with traditional Christian associations. The poem is addressed to an unidentifiable deity, referred to by *thou* and *thee*, denies the Resurrection, and describes the hereafter as a place of darkness. Housman's funeral poem, when all is said, fitted the man as he had lived. He said categorically that he became an atheist at twenty-one when he was an Oxford senior. He only repeated, perhaps to unhearing ears,[24] this declaration in his hymn. It was the final and unanswerable summing-up of his view of the human condition, the end of all things mortal in darkness and insentience.

His ashes were buried outside the wall of the Ludlow Parish Church in Worcestershire soil taken by loving hands from beneath the trees of Perry Hall and the Clock House, family homes where he had played as a boy. Above the grave is a tablet with this inscription:

IN MEMORY OF ALFRED EDWARD HOUSMAN

M.A. OXON.

KENNEDY PROFESSOR OF LATIN AND FELLOW OF
TRINITY COLLEGE IN THE UNIVERSITY OF CAMBRIDGE.

AUTHOR OF 'A SHROPSHIRE LAD'

BORN 26 MARCH, 1859. DIED 30 APRIL, 1936.

GOOD NIGHT. ENSURED RELEASE,
IMPERISHABLE PEACE,
HAVE THESE FOR YOURS.

Nor was Cambridge unmindful of her chief scholar: a commemorative tablet in Trinity College Chapel, engraved in the language of the Roman writers whose poetry and shaping thought he had so entirely made his own, testifies to his deft but severe editorship and to his assured fame as a poet.

CHAPTER 4

The Poetry:
A Shropshire Lad, Last Poems,
and Translations

SCARCELY more than a glance has been given to Housman's scholarly prose, that portion of his work least susceptible to the fluctuations of critical opinion, because his level of performance is so high and the number of those qualified to judge is consequently so small. He said he wrote as a textual critic for the two or three scholars, yet unborn, who would be able to appreciate his labors; but his poetry he addressed to the common reader, and he wanted it to be widely known. He published his first book at his own expense and asked his publisher to apply his royalties to reducing the cost of reprintings. In this incident lies a striking paradox: the taciturn, unsociable Latin professor disclosing so unreservedly, so eagerly, to all comers the innermost secrets of his heart.

Housman detested hypocrisy and untrue presentments of all kinds. His profession, as he saw it, included the slaying of false reputations and in this pursuit he never relaxed. But in his self-revelations to the world he was as unsparing as in his judgment of others. He must have adopted wholly the sombre advice of Hawthorne in the conclusion of his greatest novel: "Be true! Be true! Be true! Show freely to the world, if not your worst, yet some trait whereby the worst may be inferred!" These traits were in his letter of application for the professorship in University College, London, confessing his failure in the Oxford examinations; they were in his nefarious *Praefanda*, a potpourri of choice ancient pornography published (in *Hermes* LXVI) five years before his death; they were in his poetry throughout, especially in the poems declaring his spiritual cowardice.

A Shropshire Lad, Last Poems, *and Translations*

As to the actuality of his own experiences, he knew they were in the fiber and grain of every one of the lyrics of *A Shropshire Lad*. He was not self-deceived, and his denial of the existence of himself in his poems can be nothing but willful confusion of the facts. This confusion is a basic crux in Housman's dimly understood personality, perhaps another outgrowth of the devastating inner struggles of his early twenties, when his mind became the battleground of the rival impulses that, throughout the remainder of his life, reached no better settlement than an uneasy truce.

I *Oustanding Features of Housman's Poetry*

The main characteristics of his poetry are its formal simplicity, its emotional thrust, and its pessimistic tone. All three of these are, in varying degrees, present in his numerous ballad-lyrics. A reader looking for the first time through a volume of Housman's poetry cannot help observing the frequency of the ballad stanza of four short lines and alternating rhyme. Many of the other short poems also suggest that the writer was trying for ballad compactness rather than for the expansion of his poetic idea. But the impersonality of the folk singer is poles apart from Housman's attitude and method. Even before the meaning of the poem is apprehended, the reader might surmise the poet's involvement by his frequent use of the first personal pronoun, which occurs, by the way, in the opening line of forty-eight (more than one-fourth) of the pieces in the *Complete Poems*. Housman's mastery of the resources of the ballad and his expansion of it go far to make the reader feel the presence of the writer in his story and hear the accents of his lyric cry, which almost invariably sounds a note of sadness and defeat.[1]

But these generalizations must be illustrated and qualified, particularly since they relate to poetry as carefully fashioned as Housman's. Consider his language. It is a richly varied texture woven of many ancient and modern literatures and employed with masterly skill. Echoes of Classical mannerisms, for example, may be seen in his many compounded words: *amber-sanded, rainy-sounding, steeple-shadowed, silver-tufted, many-venomed, death-struck, light-leaved*—a list that could easily be tripled. The chief prompter in verbal coinages of this kind may be Lucretius,[2]

whose influence is a vital element throughout Housman's poetry.

Another Classical borrowing is seen in such phrases as these from "When Israel out of Egypt came" (*MP 2*): *"The realm I look upon and die"* and *"the heaven that I/Perish and have not known."* These lines sound un-idiomatic to the English reader—and they are because they are intentional transfers from Greek syntax. Peculiarities of this nature abound in Housman's famous "Fragment of a Greek Tragedy," first published in *The Bromsgrovian* (June, 1883).[3] One of the great parodies in English, it mercilessly exposes the grating faults of Aeschylus and at the same time reveals something of the critic and poet in Housman, then only twenty-four.

An independent element in the language of Housman's poetry, one from which its tone of simplicity derives, is his large stock of provincial and dialectal words; *shaws, haulms, mayhap, liefer, tun, hap, tedded, sprack* ("brisk"), *hie, amidmost, thorough* ("through"), and *frore* are among the more familiar examples. A much larger group consists of colloquial expressions common to the man of the street and the lane—speechways that contribute most effectively to the realism of the sayings and doings of Housman's characters. This element in his poetic language may, because of his artful use of it, pass without notice, as in real life his Ned Lears and his Rose Harlands may pass unnoticed by us; it is seldom perceived by those who think of "Loveliest of trees . . ." as Housman's finest lyric. But his poetry would lose much savor without the salt of expressions of this kind: *guts in the head, and sure enough, as I hear tell, miles around, no heart at all, free for nothing, never fear, man, lay me low, no use to talk to me, luckless aye, no harm in trying, the like on earth, lads for the girls, enough as 'tis, till they drop, long time since, little 'twill matter, for all they try, 'tis truth you say, what's to pay, 'tis little matter, learned me the way to behave, look the other way* ("ignore"), *dressed to the nines, more's the pity, any wind or weather, want the moon, as like as not, for ever and a day, let's home, man alive, ale's the stuff, faith, 'tis pleasant, what's to show, most like* ("probably"), *fits and starts, her Sundays out, 'tis many a year, for all they say, a deal of pains, muse for why, no heed at all, nothing much to lose, the livelong day, the land's alive, see the record cut,*[4] *the good old time, God knows where.* Even out of context, each of these expressions speaks from the

[70]

page with something of the still, sad music of humanity—un-lettered and unspoiled.

But while perceiving this dominant feature of his poetic diction, we should also take note that such expressions, homely and natural as they are, were for the most part as much derived from Housman's reading as were the echoes from the Classical poets. In the above lists the antecedents of some terms and phrases may immediately declare themselves: *frore* from Milton or Shelley and *shaws* perhaps from the English ballads. Unlike Thomas Hardy, Housman owed little or nothing to his ear and notebook; firsthand association in collecting his store of dialectal or rustic speech was a minor factor although playground talk and the chatter of the servants in his boyhood homes may have left in his mind some memorable phrases. Whatever these sources lent, they blended with literary gleanings to provide as a dress for his thought, not a single-fashioned garb, but a coat of many colors, from homespun gray to royal purple, to fit his changing scenes and different personages.

A poet with these resources at his disposal, believing lucidity to be an excellent thing, has it within his power to achieve a style that is succinct, unmystical, and unmistakably clear. This style is the essence of Housman's poetry, but it was not easily come by. The labored pages of his poetry notebooks show at what cost clarity was attained. He considered it among the prime virtues of his art, and often rebuked his brother Laurence for leaving "that man of sorrows" (his reader) the task of finding out what he meant.[5] Housman has nothing in common, therefore, with the aims and methods of that segment of modern poetry that consists of abstract musings which the reader is invited to endow with what intelligibility he will or can. Clarity meant to Housman the poet what accuracy meant to Housman the scholar; and one main reason for the scantiness of the selections made by him from his four notebooks can be attributed to the fact that the standard of clarity in some of the lyrics he passed over was not—could not be—satisfactorily met.

Housman declared in his "Name and Nature of Poetry"[6] that his test of poetry was the emotional disturbance it produced in him, an effect accompanied by certain physical reactions. These reactions were also present during the composition of his own poetry. Emotion, then, was at the heart of the poetic experience, and his lyrics strike home to the hearts of his readers because of their power to transfuse emotion: we are led to feel his griefs and resentments as if they were our own. The volcanic turmoil within him was the generating process, objectifying in his Shropshire creations his disgust at himself and the blind fate that, in the words of Thomas Hardy, made the human condition "a general drama of pain."

It has already been mentioned that not all of Housman's poetry is dominated by the somber tone that marks his best-known pieces; a sizable proportion of his earliest verse is humorous, and even after 1881 there were occasional interludes of gayety. It is illuminating to read the poetic exercises and juvenilia published by Laurence Housman in *John O'London's Weekly* (October, 1936), in his memoir of his brother published in the same year, and also in the "family poetry" included by his sister, Mrs. Katharine E. Symons, in her chapter "Boyhood" in *The Bromsgrovian: Housman Memorial Supplement*, edited by F. Wallace-Hadrill (1936). Mrs. Symons writes enthusiastically of the wit and high spirits that Alfred released into his nonsense verse, of which only a small part is known to the public. Wistfully, she speaks of "the-brother-that-might-have-been if learning had let him alone." This protest, naïve though it is, deserves better than a sneer. The facts behind Alfred's Oxford debacle were probably unknown to her, and it is also likely that she shared to some degree the layman's distrust of the academic arcana. Be that as it may, if the influence of Alfred's sister, who had begun to take the place of his mother as a confidante, had lasted a few years longer amid the family surroundings, he might have been a far happier man. But a poet? Who can say?

Beside his sister and his stepmother (Alfred's allegiance to her has already been described), Basil, a brother five years his junior, of whom he was particularly fond, was the recipient of many of Alfred's humorous pieces. From the first Housman was touchy about the circulation of these poetic skits outside the family circle, and he once replied testily to an inquiry by Witter Bynner: "I shall not do anything to enable you to get hold of the nonsense verses you mention, and if they dwell in Laurence's too retentive memory I shall not authorise him to communicate them to you."[7]

A rich depository (mentioned in the Preface) of Housman's

light verse was the guestbooks of the Wise family of Woodchester, a brother and two sisters he visited frequently as long as
the family existed. The manuscripts of these poems are now
among the chief treasures of the Lilly Library of Indiana University in Bloomington. Another visitor at the Wises' has preserved an enchanting glimpse of Housman on leave from his
London professorship, entertaining the guests by reading his
absurd "Fragment of an English Opera," chanting it, and "making the Father's voice deep and gruff and the daughter's high
and squeaky." The "Fragment," on pages 242-44 of Laurence's
memoir, is worth reading if only to correct the impression that
Housman lived immersed in a swamp of unrelieved gloom after
his late-adolescent unhappiness.

Although keeping a tight rein when he could on his too-eager
family, Housman during his years at University College contributed—anonymously, of course—three of his best facetious
poems to the student *Union Magazine*: "The Parallelogram"
(1904), "The Amphisbaena" (1906), and "The Crocodile"
(1911). These poems, collected in 1935 in a University College
pamphlet, were reprinted six years later—for the first time in the
United States—by William White. The scarcity of these reprints
puts them unfortunately beyond the reach of the average reader,
but they are worth the search to find them, as three couplets
from "The Amphisbaena" may show:

> It has indeed a head in front
> (As has the Indian elephant),
> But then, to our alarm, we find
> It has another head behind;
> And hence zoologists affirm
> That it is not a pachyderm. . . .

Poetry, even Keats's "ditties of no tone," is for many readers
primarily an address to the ear, and critics have found harsh
things to say about the aural effects of Housman's serious poetry.
It cannot be denied that many of his pieces—and some of his
most popular—are burdened with lines that are distressingly
heavy. This unhappy effect is sometimes the result of Housman's
fondness for alliteration that invariably puts an extra weight on
the accented syllables. Perhaps his plodding line, with its strong
iambic rhythm, is a carry-over from the ballad stanza.[8] He had

an invincible fondness for these formal simplicities, and his note-books show repeatedly how, after jotting down his alternatives for a line that would not come out right, he often—but not usually—fair-copied into it an alliterative phrase. For example, *The blood of all this noteless number* (*MP* 20) first read *The blood of this dissolving number* (A 89). The same kind of sub-stitution is illustrated in the following phrases: *With mien to match the morning* (*ASL* 42) began as *With gallant mien of morning* (A 114); *Nor yet disperse apart* (*ASL* 32) developed from *An instant, and depart* (A 145); *Whatever brute and blackguard made the world* (*LP* 9) superseded *Whatever sturdy blackguard . . .* (D 45). *While the hive of hell within* (*LP* 31) replaced *And the city far within* (D 70); *This luggage I'd lief set down* (*ASL* 50) first read *The luggage that wearies him down* (B 41); and *All the land's alive around* (*AP* 11) was first *All the shire's at work around* (B 80).

Housman's ear was acutely tuned as he wrote, and he seems often to have anticipated—sometimes even with a grotesque in-accuracy—an alliterative sequence even before it was set down by the hand. On page 213 of Notebook A, for example, he im-pulsively wrote *Fast in the foundless* [*sic*] *snare* in the second line of "R.L.S." (*AP* 22). Finally, it should be said that one of the two minor changes Housman introduced into the text of *A Shropshire Lad* in 1923 replaced *long since forgotten* in Poem 52 with the alliterative *no more remembered.*

Housman was aware—as keenly as some of his captious critics, we may believe—of his predilections for certain rhythmic and metrical effects. His brother relates that Housman turned thumbs down on "Atys" (*AP* 1), one of his finest "derived" poems, when he was assembling the contents of *Last Poems*, "because it was written in a metre he was so fond of, that he always doubted the merit of any poem in which he had succumbed to its attraction."[9] It is improbable that many readers share the poet's oversensitive-ness about this finely etched lyric, so full of Herodotean clear-ness and simplicity.

But a nearer view of Housman's ballad stanzas shows that they may not be summarily dismissed as a military parade of simple iambics and nothing more. They are filled with numerous varia-tions that break the pace of the rhythm—as in the third line of stanza 5 in *ASL* 1: "And the Nile spills his overflow." Here the first two syllables, unaccented, run swiftly into *Nile*, which leads into an unregulated flow of syllables that carries on to the end of the line. This broken run neatly suggests the idea of an uncontrolled torrent. "Reveille" (*ASL* 4) contains its own kind of sonic niceties. Written in the rhythm of "Atys," the strong trumpet-note—"Wake" and "Up, lad, up"—in the odd-numbered stanzas of "Reveille" was devised to fit the mood and marching pace of the poem. And, as if to placate the hypercritical reader, there are these anapestic variations:

> And the ship of sunrise burning (1.3)
>
> . . . .
>
> And the tent of night in tatters (1.7)
>
> . . . .
>
> Were not meant for man alive (1.20)
>
> . . . .
>
> There'll be time enough for sleep (1.24).

Several others of Housman's lyrics describe stages of march or flight that are rhythmically simulated by skillfully placed sounds and motions in the line. The reader moves along with the rapid measure in the light-footed verses of "The Merry Guide," where Hermes, Conductor of Souls, is leading his mortal charge over the wide highways of the air:

> Once in the wind of morning (1.1)
>
> . . . .
>
> There through the dews beside me (1.5)
>
> . . . .
>
> With the great gale we journey (1.45)
>
> . . . .
>
> Borne in the drift of blossoms (1.47)
>
> . . . .
>
> Buoyed on the heaven-heard whisper (1.49).

Reading the poem aloud amply shows how much of its charm is owing to the gliding and surging movements achieved with the anapests, dactyls, and trochees stationed among the even-paced iambics.[10]

Housman is almost unmatched in his ability to create lines that just break the barrier of silence. These lines breathe of themselves—breathe and no more:

> Halts on the bridge to hearken
> How soft the poplars sigh (*ASL* 52, 7-8)
>
> . . . .
>
> My soul that lingers sighing
> About the glimmering weirs (*ASL* 52, 15-16)
>
> . . . .
>
> Its rainy-sounding silver leaves (*ASL* 26, 14)
>
> . . . .
>
> And the darkness hushes wide (*ASL* 4, 10).

In contrast, Housman can make his lines as unmusical and harsh as Milton's description of the opening of the gates of Hell. Such are the sounds the criminal in "Eight O'Clock" hears as his death-hour approaches. There he stands cursing his luck with the rope around his neck: "And then the clock collected in the tower/Its strength, and struck" (*LP* 15). Reading aloud *clock collected* is to hear the metallic rattling, the turning of the gears and levers; and then, weighted with two of the heaviest words in our speech, down drops the ponderous final line: *Its strength, and struck.*

Laurence Housman in his *Unexpected Years*[11] tells how the family routine at home was adjusted to the sound of clocks and bells, great and small, inside the house and without; every chime and stroke must have left a distinct, ineradicable impression on young Alfred's memory.[12] Later there were the bells of Bromsgrove and the sounding towers of Oxford. His poetry shows that ordinary words describing such sounds would not do for him: bells and clocks have individuality and must be dealt with distinctively. Bells do not merely ring; sometimes they justle, and the belfries tingle.

The second line of "Eight O'Clock" is *Sprinkle the quarters on the morning town. Sprinkle,* with its little echoes of the rising and falling notes, seems exactly right, as it is; it was so written in all three of the notebook drafts of *LP* 15. But line four has a different history. It now reads *It tossed them down.* The softer *tossed* seems quite inevitable, but Housman did not find it until he had tested and rejected all of the too-noisy or off-tune *dropped, cast, flung, told, dealt, loosed, spilt,* and *pitched.*

Housman's best-known bell poem is "Bredon Hill" (*ASL* 21) in which the clang and boom of bells sound through every stanza. A realistic repetition throughout most of the seven stanzas occurs in line two, which sounds the stroke of the clapper; in line four, the echo; in line five, the fading after-chime. The opening line of the sixth stanza—*They tolled the one bell only*—is as perfect in its concord of vowels and consonants as Tennyson's famous "mellow lin-lan-lone of evening bells." This effect reaches its climax in the final stanza, which is resonant with the word *hum* and its rhymes—and which ends with a remarkable long-sustained echo. And Housman could also imitate bell-dissonance; for this line cannot be read pleasingly: "The bells rang, ringing no tune . . ." (*AP* 21, 4). Here sweet bells are jangled, out of tune and, if not harsh, certainly flat and toneless—as he had planned. The same atonality is in the last line of the poem: *Ringing their own dead knells.*

II *The Poetry Notebooks*

Housman abhorred obscurity, intentional or not, as a mark of incapacity that no literary virtues could atone for. He wanted his poetry to be widely read, indeed; but, above all, he wanted it understood. To write such poetry was not always easy. One of the early drafts of his lecture, "The Name and Nature of Poetry," contains a sentence which ought to be better known than it is, for it is the key to understanding his poetic method: "Not only is it difficult to know the truth about anything, but to tell the truth when one knows it, to find words which will not obscure or pervert it, is in my experience an exhausting effort."[13] It is on this plane, to repeat, that Housman the poet and Housman the scholar come together: their common business is to find the truth and properly relate it. Housman would have concurred with Alexander Eliot's declaration: "The greatest poetry, it seems to me, is always spontaneous and invariably precise. It occurs where the meaning and the music merge; it stands clear as mathematical equations. . . ."[14]

Housman's four poetry notebooks illustrate on page after page the persistency of his struggle for clarity; from first draft to printer's copy, they record many a hard-won victory over the dubious and the second-rate in which approximations and generalizations had to give way to the lucid and the exact. Thus there are no "layers of meaning" honeycombing his poems; he has filled all the rifts. He would have been annoyed—perhaps *amused* is the better word—to know that any two competent readers could disagree on the essential meanings of one of his lyrics. How far a reader might carry his interpretation, or how far its applications might be expanded, is another matter; and it is none of the poet's concern. His sole business is to make his point unmistakably clear, and, he does so, not by tossing down a stream-of-consciousness deposit, but by the strenuous shaping effort of the intellect and the imagination.

Consequently, Housman's poetry requires only the scantiest editorial servicing—perhaps much less than Mr. Carl Weber provided (fifteen pages) for the Jubilee Edition of *A Shropshire Lad* (1946). The few poems based on actual events, such as "1887" (*ASL* 1), "Epitaph on an Army of Mercenaries" (*LP* 37), "R.L.S." (*AP* 22), and "Shot? so quick so clean an ending?" (*ASL* 44) do mean a bit more to the reader if he is aware of the personalities and circumstances involved. And a few words and phrases such as *cut* in "To an Athlete Dying Young" (*LP* 19), which Housman himself explained to a reader puzzled by it, *Dead Man's Fair* in "In midnights of November" (*LP* 19), and *Dressed to the nines* in "The First of May" (*LP* 34)—these, if annotated, may smooth the reader's approach. But even these editorial aids are not essential, and the reader may be better left the fun of providing them for himself.

Equally worthy of study as the tonics of Housman's poetry is how he wrote it: how he felt and seized the first offerings of inspiration; how he revised and perfected his first, second, third drafts. This exciting, instructive story is revealed in the poetry notebooks in which he composed and copied all but about twenty of his collected poems. His final notebook, designated "D" by Laurence after taking over his brother's papers, had received its last entry some eight years or more before Housman described in his Leslie Stephen lecture the poetic process as he knew it. His moments of inspiration, he told his Senate House audience, usually came during his walks after his pint of luncheon beer. Then there would suddenly drift into his consciousness "with sudden and unaccountable emotion" some lines of a new poem and with them a shadowy idea of the theme. Then, after an hour or so, there might "bubble up" other parts of the poem. These he wrote down when he got home, leaving gaps to be filled by the unsought increments of another day. Sometimes the fount of inspiration was plenteous; again, it ran dry, and he was obliged to call to his aid his lay-servant, the brain, to complete the poem, if it could. This teaming-up sometimes did not work well, he said; and such was the case in the making of "I hoed and trenched and weeded" (*ASL* 63), which he brought home one day short by two stanzas. One of them came in the afternoon, but one still-needed stanza he "had to turn to and compose"[15]; so getting the poem finished was a "laborious business," running through thirteen drafts and many months.

In this poetical confession the most remarkable aspect is the crowding together of idea, language, and emotion during the creation of the poem. Housman's poetry did not originate in idea, to which words later gave communicable form; instead, words and idea arose together out of the subconscious mind, and with them came simultaneously the emotion. The theme of the poem "accompanied, not preceded," emotion and language. That is to say, the first stages of the creative act were not designed: they did not occur in the area of consciousness, stimulated to produce the created thing; but the line, the quatrain, sometimes the poem itself, arose ready-made; syntax, rhyme, meter all broke surface together in the bubbling of the spring and presented themselves to the conscious mind at the same moment.[16] A little earlier in his lecture Housman had referred to Wordsworth's well-known definition of poetry as "the spontaneous overflow of powerful feelings" and had implied that Wordsworth's experiences were not unlike his own. But he did not go on to quote the elder poet's corollary about the origin of poetry in emotion *recollected in tranquillity.* This omission of the second half of the process is significant. For with Housman, it seems, the origin of poetry, its language and its theme, was not in emotion recollected but in its very onset, unexpected and unevoked.

Housman's account ought to be accepted at face value, and it is valuable to the student of poetry even though the matters he is describing will always be better felt than told. In his Leslie Stephen lecture he did not say all that he knew about the writing of poetry or all that he might have said about his own habits of composition: he chose to illuminate the very end of his lecture with a brief glimpse into his private workshop—and these insights, added to what may be learned in the notebooks, tell a fascinating story.

When, late in 1939, the remains of the notebooks were shipped to New York to be sold, they were accompanied by a letter containing this glowing introduction: "The interest of the collection is almost beyond description, for any admirer or student of Housman himself or the poetic mind and method in general. Familiar and famous poems can be seen taking shape on the page—a line will be rewritten 3 or 4 times; epithet after epithet will be jotted down and superseded; and so on. Here is, in short, a plain view into the workshop of a great poet." This statement does not exaggerate; for, as was remarked in the Preface to this volume, the notebooks, although sadly depleted by the erasure and cutting to which Laurence treated them, are still the most valuable of the several manuscript collections associated with Housman. Indeed, enough remains in the Washington manuscripts to provide not only a glimpse but a leisurely survey of the poet at work. Dates in his hand make possible a revealing insight into his development from year to year and from draft to draft over a period of more than thirty-five years.

Correctly interpreted, the notebook entries also tell as much about the man as about the poet. One of the most poignant revelations of the emotional accompaniment of his writing, as he described it, comes from the manuscript record of "Epithalamium" (*LP* 24), begun in January, 1895, on A 216. This poem, commemorating the marriage of Moses Jackson, was not begun until six years after the event. The first draft shows only three scattered couplets written over the upper half of the page:

> Friends and comrades lovers yield you o'er
> To her that hardly loves you more. (ll. 7, 8)
>
> .   .   .   .
>
>   breed   nursed
> And leave the land that reared your prime
>   rear
> Sons to stay the rot of time. (ll. 37, 38)
>
> .   .   .   .

[80]

The thoughts of friends keep silent ward,

Armoured sentries
Harnessed angels, hand on sword. (last two ll., 43, 44)

As I have already mentioned, the entry in the middle of the lower half of this same page, below the date January, 1895, is only the line *When I was one-and-twenty,* underscored by a long heavy pencil stroke. As Housman wrote this line beneath the opening of his poem intended to congratulate Moses Jackson on his marriage, what must his feelings have been as he thought of Oxford and of 1881, the bitter year of his double failure? The juxtaposition of the two entries (A 216) is at once grotesque and pathetic, bringing together as they do in a strange disharmony his defeat and his renunciation. According to Laurence's analysis of the notebook, Housman returned to "When I was one-and-twenty" on the following page and wrote out a rough draft of the lyric. But that page was one of the few that he himself cut from his notebooks and destroyed before his death: the world would not have all of him.

Twenty-seven years passed before Housman resumed "Epithalamium" (D 19), but the work on that page did not greatly advance the poem. As if to re-inspire emotion, he wrote the original three couplets again in the upper lefthand quarter of the page and then filled the remainder with twenty more rather feeble lines. It required two more sessions, filling five pages, to complete the poem. He did, however, get his long-delayed "Epithalamium" into print while his friend was still alive to read it. His book was published October 19, 1922; Moses Jackson died January 14, 1923. George L. Watson surmises from Jackson's autographed copy that he "might have turned the pages inattentively, but could not overlook from 'a fellow who thinks more of you than anything in the world' the blunt protestation that 'you are largely responsible for my writing poetry and you ought to take the consequences.' "[17]

The theme of the first poem in *A Shropshire Lad*—to choose a much-discussed example—seems also to have been one of the earliest-inspired productions of Housman's afternoon strolls; for on A 66, only fourteen pages after the serious poems begin, he wrote the line that became number twenty-four of "1887" (*ASL* 1): *The land they perished for.* On the same half-page can still be read, under heavy inking-out, three other lines that fit with the first one: *The weapons of the war, Lies the defended land,* and *The soul you died to save.* There was a lapse of perhaps six years before Housman came to grips with a substantial draft of *ASL* 1, on A 202-3; it was expanded perhaps nine months later on B 18-19. Not one of these pages, unfortunately, has escaped mutilation, and we cannot now read in the notebooks a complete holograph of "1887." The carry-over of the genetic twenty-fourth line cannot therefore be fully traced, but it does reappear on A 203, penciled lightly with its companion line: And fire the beacons up and down/The land they perished for. These labored manuscripts show that repeated visits of inspiration and much thought must have gone into the making of the lyric that was to become the opening poem of *A Shropshire Lad.*

By contrast, the surviving manuscripts of "To an Athlete Dying Young" (*ASL* 19) are uncut and have suffered only slightly from erasure; they therefore illustrate more satisfactorily the stages that Housman mentioned in his Senate House lecture. One interesting thing about the first draft, on A 240, is its look of pell-mell spontaneity. One can see the hand feverishly jotting down lines, couplets, stanzas, grasping at random among the fragments bubbling up. The poet first penciled in the upper-left corner a draft of stanza 1 that does not vary much from the printed text. Then he followed with what became the next-to-last stanza, number 6, of the poem:

> So now with ribboned breast invade,
> First in the race, the sill of shade,
> And hold to the dark lintel up
> The still-defended challenge-cup.

He undoubtedly knew that this stanza would not serve as number 2, also that the first two lines would have to be re-wrought; but without stopping he moved over to the right column and dashed off another quatrain, which eventually became number 3:

> Wise lad, to steal betimes away
> From fields where victory will not stay
> And [?   ] braids
> A garland briefer than a maid's.

The first couplet was nearly right but the second had to go—only to reappear as the conclusion of the poem. Before leaving the fourth line, however, Housman wrote out in front of it *A garland briefer than a girl's*. Only one more line was set down in column two, of which these words are still legible: *that night has shut*. Then turning back to the first column, he wrote the companion-line, *And never see your record cut*. Thus the first couplet of stanza 4 was foreshadowed.

The line including *a garland* may have carried associations that had to be caught at once, for leaving a stanza-space, Housman ran off the complete quatrain, his intellect probably supplying the Homeric echo:

> And round your early-laurelled head
> Will throng to gaze the strengthless dead
> And yet unfaded round its curls
> The garland briefer than a girl's.

Leaving another stanza-space, he wrote near the bottom margin:

> Of runners whom renown outran
> And the name died before the man.

This, with one superfluous word, is the closing couplet of stanza 5. Rereading this page (probably at the same sitting), he subjected every line but five to erasure or cancellation and attempted successfully a revision of the awkward couplet with which his second stanza had begun, producing after at least five false starts—the rhyme-word *shade* was too easy and attracted too many complements—the lines we now read:

> So set, before its echoes fade,
> The fleet foot on the sill of shade.

If the miscellany on A 240 is the deposit of the first bubbling of the spring, the draft on B 10 and 11 is the product of "further inspiration . . . forthcoming another day."[18] Every one of the seven stanzas is present and in its proper position, albeit there is abundant evidence that his intellect was often forced to prop up flagging inspiration. Housman began by copying stanza 1 substantially as he had written it on A 240. Then came a brand-new stanza, evidently the gift of another fortunate afternoon, which went on into print untouched. Below he copied, with a few alterations, the stanza he had attempted on an earlier page: *Wise lad,* etc. But the second couplet still was not right; and, line-canceling it, he wrote toward the right margin:

> And early though the laurel grows
> It withers sooner than the rose.

The second line had to pass the competition of several alternatives, but it outlasted them all, going into printer's copy with only one word changed. The first couplet of stanza 4 was assembled from A 240, and an ending written for it, to produce:

> He whose eye the night has shut
> Never sees his record cut,
> And silence is the same as cheers
> After earth has stopped the ears.

Every line in this quatrain was redressed where it stood or was rewritten in the right margin; number 2 was line-canceled and no substitute proposed. The following stanza was composed of a new couplet (destined to a short life):

> And now you will not join the throng
> Of lads that lived a day too long,

followed by two lines carried over from A 240:

> Runners whom renown outran
> And the name died before the man.

Page B 11 was begun with a quatrain collected from the esquisse of the second stanza set down on A 240, beginning *So set, before its echoes fade.* The last full stanza was also brought over to form, with a few minor revisions, the conclusion of the poem. Before laying down his pencil, Housman turned once again to the refractory fourth stanza left incomplete on B 10. First he wrote, making but few alterations:

> Now the eye that night has shut
> Will never see the record cut,
> And silence sounds no worse than cheers
> Now that earth has stopped the ears.

The figure in the first two lines was still unsatisfactory. Would this be an improvement?

> Eyes the night has filled with smoke
> Never see the record broke.

It was not, and all but disappeared beneath the eraser. Brain again returned to the attack and finally produced three changes that left the stanza ready for the printer: above the beginning of line 1 went the phrase *Eyes the cloudy*; line 2 was rewritten *Cannot see the record cut*; and *After* replaced the two opening words of the last line. Then the opening couplet of stanza 5, left incomplete at the bottom of B 10, was taken in hand again. Housman copied, somewhat wearily we may imagine, the words:

> No fear you now should swell the rout
> Of lads that wore their honours out,

But the beginning would not do; he scoured it out, superscribed an alternative, line-canceled it, and left the crux to another day—which did not arrive until he was shaping up printer's copy more than eight months later.

In summary, the manuscript record of "To an Athlete Dying Young" shows how much the seven-stanza poem owed to second inspiration and second thought. The draft on A 240 produced but three stanzas that closely parallel their final form; only five lines on that page survived revision untouched. However, the germ of the poem is present there in the two quatrains that became the first and final stanzas. The work a few days later on B 10-11 filled in blank spaces and rectified some of the lines turned awry or lost after the first afflatus. Some awkward imagery was pruned out: the ribboned chest and the eyes filled with smoke of night. Housman's fondness for alliteration shows itself in both drafts: on A 240 *dark lintel* gave place to *low lintel*, and *fleet foot* was evolved from an earlier line beginning *Set foot . . .* ; in the second draft *time* was substituted for *day* in the opening line, *The time you won your town the race*, and *fields where glory* replaced *fields where victory* in stanza 3, line 2.

The labor of revision was spread fairly evenly through the stanzas of *ASL* 19; on the other hand, manuscripts of some poems show a concentration of difficulty in a single stanza. An example is found in the unique draft of "The Lent Lily" (*ASL* 29) on B 3. The keen outdoor air that breathes from this poem and its crisp images of natural beauty hint at a brief period between the afternoon walk and the desk. In the upper right corner of the notebook page is the date "April 1895." The firm, precise hand in the four stanzas indicates that this draft was written with the whole poem well in mind, with no misgiving of the trouble that lay in store for the tentative first draft of the opening stanza. Actually, the second and fourth stanzas passed from B 3 into printer's copy without a single change, and the third required but four adjustments, all minor. Now to go back to the original reading of the first strophe:

> 'Tis Spring; come out to ramble
> The hilly brakes around,
> For under bush and bramble
> In [?   ] the ground
> The primroses are found.

Rereading, the poet found nothing wrong in lines 1 and 2; in the next he made but one substitution, *thorn* for *bush*, wisely preventing the echo of the nursery rhyme. But for line 4 there must have been a great deal wrong, for it can no longer be resurrected from the erasure and cancel-strokes that overtook it. Of a substitute written over it, only the last two words, *the ground*, are legible. Seeking the proper opening for the line, the poet tried *Bejewelling*, then *Emblazoning*. These would not do; would *Illumining?* or *Embroidering?* or *Enamelling?* or *Bedizening?* Finally, atop the rising pyramid he set *Apparelling*; then, beyond the end of the line as he had first written it, he penciled hopefully *About the littered ground*—and, extending the long cancel-stroke, obliterated this line also. The seven alternative words were in their turn subjected to the eraser. Not until he wrote the final copy did Housman conclude the stubborn fourth line. His struggles eight months earlier he did not begin again: a single substitution in *About the littered ground* made the line that now reads . . . *hollow ground.*

The record of coöperation between thought and emotion is not confined to those pages of the notebooks that antedate the publication of Housman's first volume; it is continuous through the final notebook. One of the best late examples is the unique draft of "The night is freezing fast" (*LP* 20), written on D 90 in April, 1922, when the material for *Last Poems* was being collected. Stanza 1 was dashed off exactly as we read it in print; the next stanza originally ran thus:

> Fall, winter, fall; for he,
> Quick like himself and clever,
> Has woven a rain proof robe,
> And made of earth and sea
> His overcoat for ever,
> And wears the turning globe.

Dissatisfied with line 2, Housman erased and line-canceled it and wrote out toward the right margin *Prompt hand and head-piece clever.* Over *rain proof* in the next line he tried *harm proof,* struck both out, and superscribed *winter* to produce the stanza as it now stands. This is one of the ten or so poems that went directly into Housman's second volume from original drafts in Notebook D. All the evidence identifies the neatly written draft on D 90 as the first entry of the poem.

The notebooks contain many other examples beside the germinal line of *ASL* 1, *The land they perished for,* that illustrate how the Muses' bounty sometimes was bestowed in short measure in lines that, like fertilized cells, developed in their season into full-blown poems. This process is one of the supreme mysteries of the poet's business, as fascinating to speculate upon as the song the Sirens sang, and probably as far removed from the poet's conjecture as from that of lesser mortals. Each of the expressions in the left column below was at one time the sole representative of the poem it eventually grew into:

Soldier, I wish you well A 162, Spring, 1893	became the last line of *ASL* 22; B 22-23, May or June, 1895.

And she shall lie with earth
  above
And you beside another love.
  A 192, August, 1894
	But she shall lie with earth above,
	And he beside another love.
	 ll. 9, 10 of *ASL* 26 on B 36
	 (destroyed), June, 1895.

Soldiers marching, all to die A 220, January, 1895	became l. 8 of *ASL* 35; B 94, September or October, 1895.

Home for us there's no return- ing A 220, January, 1895	*. . . home there's no returning.* 1.15 of *LP* 25; B 203, about 1900.
the unperished shade of night B 78, August or September, 1895	*The vast and moon-eclipsing cone of night,* *Her towering foolscap of eternal shade* 11.7, 8 of *LP* 36; B 179, about 1900.
Shires where the girls are fonder, *Towns where the pots hold more.* C 3, about 1905	Became 11. 11, 12 of *MP* 33; C 48 and D 87, April, 1922.
When skies at evening cloud C 28, about 1905	*When summer's end is nighing And skies at evening cloud,* 11. 1, 2, of *LP* 39; D 27, early 1922.

III   *A Poem Analyzed*

It may be instructive in a different way—more illustrative of the working together of emotion and the intellect—to examine the growth of a poem that asserted itself from the first in a more-or-less complete draft and was then followed by a second and a third. Such was the metamorphosis of the six stanzas composing "In midnights of November" (*LP* 19). The first draft Housman wrote late in 1894 on A 209. For reasons we can only guess at, Laurence Housman cut from the top of this page an inch-and-a-half strip that may have contained a version of one of the stanzas. Just below the cut margin stands this quatrain:

> In winds at midnight plying
> The leafless poplar roars;
> The dead call to the dying
> And whistle at the doors.

Here, as a glance at his printed poem will show, Housman wrote a prototype of the opening line of stanza one and the last three lines of the second. Before he left the page, he line-canceled *poplar* in line two and wrote *timber* above it, thus producing the present reading. He next superscribed this alternative for the first five words of line three: *And the dead call the—* another unit that would not be altered. Above *whistle* in the next line he wrote *finger*, producing the reading of the text.

Now, moving his pencil to the left margin, he followed with his second stanza:

> I hear my comrades hollo,
> Too long we lads are twinned,
> And I will rise and follow
> Along the snowy wind.

There was not much revision in store for this quatrain: *friends* over *lads* in line two, and *Oh* above *And*.

At this point inspiration lagged; stanza three would not come. So, leaving space for *two* quatrains, he wrote hesitatingly these two lines :"Lie still, my lad, and sleep you/And leave the dead alone." Then, catching at a stray of inspiration, he wrote out after the end of the second line *And cocks crow up the morn.* Finally, he filled the page with what he probably intended to be the closing stanza of his poem, for it adumbrates stanza six, the first two lines of it destined to go unchanged into print:

> The living are the living
> And dead the dead will stay:
> Why will you be giving
> Your soul to such as they?

The first notebook was filled and the second up to page 95 before Housman, about ten months later, wrote his second draft of this poem under the date "Oct. 1895." First he jotted down a new opening: "The brim of Severn freezes/And . . ." The magic of the Shropshire name—twenty-four of Housman's poems have place-names in the first or second lines—did not work; and this effort was never revived. Instead, he went back to his first draft and, as if to start the wheels, copied his original first stanza; but he introduced a slight change in line one and transcribed the three alternatives he had interlined in the stanza. Now it read:

> In windy midnights plying
> The leafless timber roars;
> And the dead call the dying
> And finger at the doors.

Then he began against the left margin of the page one of the
stanzas for which he had left an open space back on A 209. The
four lines ran thus:

> Oh yonder frozen fingers
> Are hands I used to hold:
> Their false companion lingers
> And leaves them in the cold.

He made only one change: *frozen fingers* was too unpoetic; so
frozen was struck out—the first actual replacement in his second
thinking—and *faltering* put above it. Except for one word, the
stanza is now as it stands. But here Housman went astray after
a curious reopening of the stanza, which he wrote out toward
the right margin thus:

> The frozen hands that finger
> Are hands I used to hold,
> And
> But [?   ] I linger
> And leave them in the cold.

Then he turned back to the left column and penciled stanza
three:

> I hear my comrades hollo
> Too long we friends are twinned,
> And I will rise and follow
> Along the rainy wind.

Over line two he wrote this alternative for its first five words:
But friend from friend is: and above *And* he set —*Oh*. This left
the stanza a near copy of its form in the first draft (except for
the long alternative). Again, as with the stanza preceding, a new
(and ineffective) start was made toward the right margin of the
page:

> I hear my comrades hollo,
> And friend from friend is twinned:
> —O I will

In line two, above the second and fourth words, he tried *hand*
as a substitute and above that also wrote *heart* in both places.
The abandoned third line indicates that this stanza was nearing

its vanishing-point. It is easy to see that the trouble with it is the awkward rhyming of lines one and three—a burden taken on in the first draft. He abandoned this rhyme in his revision of the next stanza; and, in so doing, he rid the poem of this tedious feature in the third draft. The next stanza (number four) began as it had in the first draft, but the third and fourth lines were surprisingly new:

> The living are the living
> And dead the dead will stay
> And I will sort with comrades
> That know the night from day.

This version is within three words of the text of the sixth stanza as we know it. Once again, as he had left the stray *And cocks crow up the morn* near the right margin of A 209, he again jotted it down in the same corresponding position on B 95. It proved to be a germinal line of a new stanza, number five in the next draft. But that draft had to wait for twenty-seven years.

The third and final draft was done in the spring of 1922, when Housman was gathering the pieces for his second volume of poetry. This entry, written in ink, occupies D 84 and part of 85. Stanza one now has a brand-new opening, and throughout the poem are scattered several proper nouns—two in the opening stanza. *Dead Man's Fair* is a wisely chosen import from folklore that precisely fits the mood of the poem. The new stanza one, now headed like the rest with a numeral reads:

> In midnights of November,
> When Dead Man's Fair is nigh,
> And storms that seamen drown for
> Are angry in the sky,

Housman may have felt immediately that the nautical allusion was not fortunate, but he tried two alternatives: over the last three words of the third line he wrote *shipwreck seamen*; and to the right of the stanza he sketched an alternative for the recalcitrant last two lines, of which only these fragments have survived obliteration: "And [?   ] and clouds that [?   ] them/Are strong [?   ]." This patchwork was still short of victory, which was not achieved on this page. Stanza two opens with a new line, the only variation from the second draft, except for the punctuation at the end of line two:

> Around the huddling homesteads
> The leafless timber roars,
> And the dead call the dying
> And finger at the doors.

Stanza three now shows the alternatives supplied in the second draft, and the rhyming word *lingers* is replaced by *drowses* to avoid the now-abandoned rhyme:

> Oh, yonder faltering fingers
> Are hands I used to hold;
> Their false companion drowses
> And leaves them in the cold.

The fourth stanza now leads off with two completely new lines, perhaps the chief improvement of the poem as a whole:

> Oh, to the bed of ocean,
> To Africk and to Ind,
> I will arise and follow
> Along the rainy wind.

Stanza five shows the results of the greatest amount of reworking since the second draft; it finally runs:

> The night goes out and under
> With all its train forlorn;
> Hues in the east assemble
> And cocks crow up the morn.

The rest of the story is on the facing page, D 85, which is now in two sections, the middle part having been destroyed, presumably to prevent survival of some scattered fragments on the opposite side of the sheet. The last stanza fills the upper section, and a fortunate emendation of the concluding line achieves an ending worthy of the lyric:

> The living are the living,
> And dead the dead will stay;
> And I will sort with comrades
> That face the beam of day.

The epilogue is on the lower fragment, a tiny half-inch slip where Housman penciled in a small, meticulous hand the two lines he had so long been seeking for the finale of his first stanza. There they are: "And danger in the valley/And anger in the sky." We know this fragment is a part of D 85, for it carries its share of the long downward ink-stroke transecting the top portion of the page (numbered 85), the mark Housman regularly struck through his notebook drafts after writing them into printer's copy.

Reviewing the labor of these three drafts, one may observe, beside the poet's fortunate introduction of place-names, other examples of his workshop practice: his care in preserving a once-established alliteration, *faltering* taking the place of *frozen*; his reluctance to abandon the balladic provincialism *twinned* ("separated"), which survived through the second draft; his recovery of balance in eliminating some of the excesses of his macabre dressing, one of the vital elements of the poem, by providing alternatives for *And leave the dead alone* and *storms that seamen drown for*; and his adroit grafting of this and much more new material onto a poem living in memory for over a quarter-century.

It is tempting to speculate—and there are solid grounds for doing so—on the amount of assistance Housman drew from three of his own poems while working out the third draft of *LP* 19, particularly the vexatious last three stanzas. The three poems are "Revolution" (*LP* 30), "Astronomy" (*LP* 17), and "When the eye of day is shut" (*LP* 33); and all of them were present to his mind during the spring of 1922, when he was shaping the contents of *Last Poems*, although only one of them, *LP* 30, was redrafted into Notebook D (24); the other two went directly into printer's copy from their drafts in B (*LP* 17, 221) and C (*LP* 33, 45-46). All three of the poems broadly resemble *LP* 19 in the cosmological background against which their human events take place. Their verbal similarities to *LP* 19 may best be shown graphically:

LP 19, third draft stanza 3: *bed of ocean*	*beds you made . . ./In the drowned ooze of the sea LP* 33
To Africk and to Ind	*bones in Africa LP* 17 *Safe to the Indies LP* 36

stanza 4: *The night . . ./With* *all its train forlorn*	*Spectres and fears, the nightmare* *and her foal LP* 36
stanza 5: *the beam of day*	*Day's beamy banner LP* 36 *the eve of day LP* 33.

Poets are influenced more by their own writing than by the sum of all other literary contacts; and it is not, therefore, surprising that the three lyrics mentioned contributed substantially to "In midnights of November" when it was being readied for the printer. The most influential was "When the eye of day is shut," its mood and decor so remarkably like what we find in *LP* 19; in both, the suppliant dead are renounced for the living. Pure terror closes in the sullen landscapes of the two poems, steeped in storm and darkness, and darkness within darkness, where ghosts ride the winds seeking the sleeper whose uneasy dreams are assailed by the tap-tap at the door.

A word may be added about the sequence of the poems in the two books Housman published. Nesca A. Robb believes the sixty-three poems of *A Shropshire Lad* form an "ordered sequence";[19] and Ian Scott-Kilvert says the book should be read "as a whole lyrical cycle."[20] I think this is going too far. Housman remarked to Laurence that he had to stand out against designs of this kind urged upon him by Kegan Paul, his first publisher. Some vestiges of the "romance of enlistment" idea do appear in the first four poems of *A Shropshire Lad*; but it is clear that Housman never consented to any straitjacketing in the over-all plan of his first volume, and did not introduce any broad sequential patterns.

There are, it is easy to see, a few blocks of poems here and there that are associated in theme or manner: for example, numbers 13, 14, 15, and 16 tell of the lover's sorrow after losing his heart. (The page of Housman's printer's copy bearing *ASL* 13 carried this introductory notation in the poet's hand: "Another Series.") Further, numbers 25, 26, and 27 are on the theme of fatality overtaking one of two lovers competing for the desired one. There is also a short "homesick" series in 37-39, and this about sums up the serializing.

Flouting the idea of design, the positions of some poems in *A*

Shropshire Lad seem intentionally or inevitably to be awkward: number 63, of course, had to end the volume; but number 62 ("Terence, this is stupid stuff") is where it is because no logical place could have been found for it: it is an oddity, and would have defied any arrangement. This is not to say that Housman threw his poems together at random; in the printer's copy for both books he took care to make numerous changes in position: for example, "The Merry Guide" (*ASL* 42) was first 51, later 40. But this poem, again, is a hard one to find a place for. The same is true of "The Immortal Part" (*ASL* 43); at any rate, Housman first numbered it 59, set it forward to 41, finally to 43. After a careful summing-up of the question of sequence and design, I conclude that, rather than making thematic patterns of his poems —which would tend to subordinate and tone them down—Housman deliberately, for the most part, set his *Shropshire Lad* pieces against each other. If we consider the clash of the grim *Be still, my soul* . . . (*ASL* 48) and the happy-go-lucky next poem, *Think no more, lad* . . . , we have to wonder what the latter has in common with number 50: *In valleys of springs of rivers* —or it with 51, *Loitering with a vacant eye.*

Housman's reluctance to set his lyrics in a schematic arrangement is equally evident in *Last Poems.* Anticipating the necessity of letting his hand show in this task, he asked his publisher to let him see first a full proof of the forty-two poems arranged according to the meters in which they were written. Here, obviously, he was thinking of one grouping he would strenuously avoid where he could. As he set his lyrics in order, he inevitably found that many soldier-poems had to be juxtaposed as they made up over a third of the whole. Only one arbitrary plan is evident, I believe: he wished the opening of *Last Poems* to remind the reader of the beginning of his first book. So the first several poems, like numbers one and three of *A Shropshire Lad,* have a military flavor. Again, there are some inevitable placings: the beautiful final poem is perfect in its place; it and the two just preceding it combine to make something of a summing-up of Housman's life as a poet. But, all in all, there are nearly as many clashes, proportionally, between neighbors as in *A Shropshire Lad*—by the design of the author, who had a flair for the perverse and the unexpected.[21]

IV *Translations*

A small but important group of Housman's poems consists of translations, of which the only pieces so designated in the comprehensive editions are the fifth lyric of *More Poems*, "Diffugere Nives," and the three translations of Greek odes in the concluding section of the volume. His notebooks reveal no trace of his interest in these four pieces, and the exact dates of their composition cannot be determined.

Housman's rendering of the Latin poem, number seven of the Fourth Book of Horace's Odes, was first printed in 1897 in *The Quarto*, a journal devoted to the fine arts.[22] One of his former students at Cambridge relates how,[23] at the end of Housman's lecture hour one morning in May, 1914, after he had completed his explication of the ode line by line, the lecturer surprised his audience by lifting his eyes from the Latin text and "for the first time in two years" looked at the students in front of him and said in a strangely altered voice, something that surprised them even more: "I should like to spend the last few minutes considering this ode simply as poetry." Now the room was still as a church: it was not the master's way, to consider any poetical specimen as poetry; his business was with matters textual and expository. Before his hearers could guess what he was about, he read the poem "aloud with deep emotion, first in Latin, and then in an English translation of his own." Then he added in quick choked accents, "That I regard as the most beautiful poem in ancient literature"; and, gathering up his books and papers, he stepped hastily from the room. But for the presence of one alert observer, the incident might have passed unrecorded; for the event itself was not unusual: Housman's students had no doubt heard other professors read their own translations to their classes. But we can feel, as they did not, the presence of Moses Jackson mediating between Horace and Housman in this scene; we can hear in his tremulous voice another declaration of the old undying passion and his cry of protest at the hopeless inadequacy of all that comradely affection could do when confronting the unfeeling rulers of human destiny.

The three translations from the Greek were, in a different way, also a testimonial to an alliance dating from Housman's Oxford days: they were, practically speaking, an additional means of repaying his old friend A. W. Pollard for coming up with the apt title for his first book of poetry. Pollard was editing about 1887 a volume of odes from the Greek dramatists "translated into lyric metres by English poets and scholars." When he called upon Housman for assistance, he knew his appeal would not go unheeded. Housman's trio of contributions to *Odes from the Greek Dramatists* (London: Stott, 1890) were his versions of sixteen lines from Aeschylus' *Seven Against Thebes*, forty-two lines from Sophocles' *Oedipus at Colonus*, and forty-four from Euripides' *Alcestis*.[24] The tone and substance of the three passages prompt the suggestion that Housman was given a free hand in the choice of his original material. His renderings were among the few additional pieces, beyond *More Poems* and the lyrics Laurence had published in his memoir, that the family chose for the first comprehensive edition of 1939.[25]

Other translations in Housman's poetry are not so easily identified. He acknowledged to a few persons his indebtedness to Heinrich Heine after his career as a poet was over, and not many of his readers recognized the first two stanzas of "Sinner's Rue" (*LP* 30) as a free translation of lyric 62 in the German poet's *Lyrisches Intermezzo*, with the original order of the stanzas reversed in Housman's poem. Housman wrote but one draft (incomplete) of "Sinner's Rue" in the poetry notebooks, and the sheet bearing it (B 188-89) has not survived. However, two holographs remain from the numerous final and near-final copies the poet produced in the spring of 1922, when *Last Poems* was in the making. The first of these is a much-corrected draft on a foolscap sheet which had evidently been intended for the printer. On it are the five stanzas of the complete poem, headed "Sinner's rue," and, below, "After Heine." But, in his final transcript in printer's copy, Housman wrote the heading, "Die Armesuenderblume"; later he drew a heavy line through the title and wrote above it the name we know.

During the comparatively unproductive quarter-century that stretched between his two books of poetry, Housman tried his hand at least twice upon a paraphrase of Théodore de Banville's "Nous n'irons plus au bois, les lauriérs sont coupés." Both drafts were written about 1905 in the latter pages of Notebook C, and neither has survived.

All through the early months of 1922, while Housman was copying into his last notebook the poems intended for his second volume, the scantiness of the late harvest must have impressed upon him the double appropriateness of the title *Last Poems* for his projected volume; and the sentiments in the free translation from Banville that he had sketched years ago in his third note-book must have recurred to him often. There is, then, more than a space relationship between D 27-28, where he completed one of his best "farewell poems," "When summer's end is nighing" (*LP* 39), and D 30, which he headed with the title "Nous n'irons plus aux bois," followed by the first eight lines of the preface poem as they now stand, except that Housman's manuscript for line five shows *In draws the autumn day* instead of *The year draws in the day*. The latter reading went into printer's copy, where were also added the concluding four lines of the poem. It is only in the freest sense of the word that Housman's twelve-line poem can be called a translation of the French lyric (num-ber three of *Les Stalactites*), where the formal park-like setting of Banville's poem encloses a lavishness that is completely anti-thetical to Housman's purpose. No one, therefore, would be likely to see much of Banville in the preface-poem of Housman's second volume were he not reminded of him by Housman's use of Banville's line as the title for his D 30 draft and by the two refrains in the preface-poem: *We'll to the woods no more* and *The laurels all are cut.*

Two fragments from Sappho figure in Housman's poetry. The first, translated, is *The moon has set, and the Pleiades; it is mid-night, the time is going by, and I sleep alone.*[26] He penciled on A 151 a rough draft of his free translation of the lines, then added a fair copy in ink, dated February, 1893. The poem was never recopied, and Housman passed over it[27] when assembling printer's copy for his first book and again when gleaning his early notebooks for *Last Poems*. It first saw the light as number 10, *The weeping Pleiads wester*, of *More Poems* in 1936.

The influence of the same fragment may be seen on page 44 of Notebook B where Housman wrote in July, 1895, another free translation. Only a portion of the last four lines can be deci-phered from his heavily canceled manuscript:

> [?   ] forgot
> Lies in a land where I am not
> And lays to sleep beyond the sea
> The head that will not dream of me.

The next draft of this poem was written on B 225 perhaps five years later; this sheet has not survived. In the spring of 1922 Housman brought forward to D 56 a poem beginning, *The rainy Pleiads wester.* Like the other Sapphic paraphrase, on A 151, this poem did not appear until the publication of his first post-humous volume, in which it was number 11. The last line of the poem in Housman's ink draft is clearly *And 'twill not dream of me,* but Laurence misread it *That will not dream of me.* This error passed unquestioned into the comprehensive edition (Cape, 1929), where it remained through twelve later impressions, being at last recognized and thrown out of the radically overhauled fourteenth impression (1953), in which Housman's line was correctly given for the first time.

But his devotion to the Sapphic fragment did not end with his draft on D 56. Another paraphrase of it, written in two drafts on D 86, he thought well enough of to include in *Last Poems.* It is number 26, "The half-moon westers low, my love." The tone of this fine poem, its two-quatrain structure, the use of *wester* in the opening line—all link it with 10 and 11 of *More Poems,* with the partly legible draft on B 44, and with their famous antecedent.

He also turned into English the well-known fragment from Sappho:

> Ἔσπερε πάντα φέρων ὅσα φαίνολις ἐσκέδασ᾽ αὔως,
> φέρεις ὄιν, φέρεις αἶγα, φέρεις ἄπυ μάτερι παῖδα.

(Evening, thou that bringest all that bright morning scattered; thou bringest the sheep, the goat, the child back to her mother.) These lines are freely rendered by the third stanza of *Last Poems* 24, "Epithalamium." I have described how Housman made three widely separated essays at this poem: the first in January, 1895, on A 216, where he wrote the title and three couplets. Then, over twenty-seven years later, he took the poem in hand again, on D 19 and 20. Finally he wrote two ink copies of the lyric on D 57-61. The attraction of Sappho must have been strongly renewed in Housman's mind as he filled these pages, for he began the first of these two drafts on the verso of the sheet on which he had written his fair copy of "The rainy Pleiads wester." Though some of the manuscript of his second draft has been destroyed, we may surmise that the very first attempt at the free translation of this Sapphic piece was composed on D 57, where we now read it, set apart from the other writing on that page:

> Happy bridegroom, Vesper brings
> All desired and timely things.
> Home return who him behold,
> Child to mother, sheep to fold,
> Birds in air from wandering wide:
> Happy bridegroom, seek your bride.

In the right margin, opposite lines 2 and 3, Housman inserted this couplet:

> All that morning sends to roam
> Vesper loves to lead them home.

On D 60 these eight lines were copied in their proper order, to make the third stanza, but not before *Vesper* was changed to *Hesper* and four other alterations were made.

CHAPTER 5

The Posthumous Poetry

THE latest-entered piece to go from Notebook D (pp. 107-8) into the printer's copy of *Last Poems* was "The rain, it streams on stone and hillock" (*LP* 18). In the remaining portion of his fourth notebook, Housman put his pen to only sixteen more pages (not counting some nonsense verse Laurence mentions in his analysis), of which only ten have survived. These contain his funeral poem (D 112), dated January, 1925; a beautiful little-known lyric, "Here, in the beechen forest" (D 118); copies of five poems brought forward from Notebook C and earlier pages of D[1] (these transcripts, all fair copies, in ink, permit us to surmise that he had not altogether shut the door on the idea of a third volume of poetry); a curious prose fragment;[2] and a few other miscellaneous pieces of verse.

When Housman laid his fourth notebook away, he knew that one poem from among his last entries would certainly be printed after his death: the one headed "For my funeral." But what of the others—eighty or more—the finished and unfinished poems he had passed over in assembling *Last Poems*? Should they be destroyed? Here again we are confronted with a seeming paradox: if he thought they were not good enough for *Last Poems*, why should he wish them ever to see the light of day? Why should he leave them to the arbitration of others? The answer, I believe, is in Housman's inextricable involvement in his poetry —in the very manuscripts of it, in the canceled, erased, rewritten drafts that were to him a living record of his defeat and despair. His notebooks were too full of Moses Jackson to be destroyed by him. Many of the unused poems there, Housman well knew, were more revelatory of his feelings than anything in his first two books. Yet he could more easily put his hands in the fire than burn the notebook sheets where the story of his greatest friendship was commemorated. So he delayed, time ran, and the four books gathered dust in his gloomy quarters in Whewell's Court, intact but for a few pages he determined no other eye should ever see.

I *Housman's Testamentary Directions*

More Poems

Yet, a few years before his death, Housman roused himself to prescribe some definite rules for those who would someday take charge of his papers—testamentary instructions signed and sealed which, in the matters relating most nearly to his deepest desires, were never respected. His will, dated November 19, 1932, contained certain specific directions to Laurence, his literary executor. The pertinent section (number seven) states: "I DIRECT my said brother Laurence Housman to destroy all my prose manuscript writing in whatever language and I permit him but do not enjoin him to select from my verse manuscript writing and to publish any poems which appear to him to be completed and to be not inferior in quality to the average of my published poems and I DIRECT him to destroy all other poems and fragments of verse."

About the time he drew up his will Housman talked with Laurence of its provisions concerning his future editorship; but, with one or two exceptions, he did not name any poems that he wanted his brother either to publish or to suppress. In the *Times Literary Supplement* (March 5, 1954; May 14, 1954), it has been asserted by interested parties without proof (although proof has been asked) that Housman also "vested the authority for choosing between alternative readings, left open in the manuscripts of the posthumously published poems, in his brother, Laurence Housman." This is a fiction. The language of the will clearly indicates that Laurence could publish only "completed" poems, and there is no other known empowering document. Pieces showing open alternatives are by definition incomplete, and such manuscripts Housman commanded his brother to destroy. In this matter, there is no room for shift or evasion.

His brother's unambiguous orders began to plague Laurence when, with the idea of a posthumous volume in mind, he first surveyed the poems, complete and incomplete, in the four notebooks and in other poetry manuscripts among Alfred's papers. But, as the days of choosing and rejecting passed, the restrictions of his brother's will became less and less significant. There were many poems in the condition of fair copy and others within a few words of it—poems Laurence could save from the fire by arbitrating alternatives or by reading meaning into some illegible lines.[3] The pressure of time pushed him through and over delicate decisions; he should have a new book of Alfred's poems—if there were enough to make a book—ready before the end of 1936.

More Poems was published on the same day in London and New York, October 26, 1936. Its incompetent editing showed up on nearly every page, from the frontispiece, where the name of the artist was misspelled, to the last page of the appendix, where in a title *carts* was substituted for *casts*.[4] Even the errors in the two editions lacked consistency, for there were over sixty discrepancies between the London and New York printings, probably the result of Laurence's second-guessing returns to the notebooks and consequent last-minute changes in his text. There is an evil immortality in a misprint, which is never quite overtaken by the pursuing angel; and many of these blunders passed unchallenged into the comprehensive Cape edition of 1939, edited by John Carter. Faults textual and typographical played hide-and-seek with this editor through numerous issues of the *Collected Poems*—even down to the latest reprinting.[5]

The poems of the first posthumous collection, some dating from the extreme time-limits of the four notebooks and therefore representing all seasons of Housman's forty-year vintage, offered little that was new in manner or theme. The reactions of the critics varied widely, among the most enthusiastic being Professor H. W. Garrod, who spoke highly of *More Poems* and declared (perhaps with a finger pointed at the editor) that "most of them [are] better poems than *Last Poems*, even if less well punctuated."[6] On the other hand, the author of the anonymous review appearing on the front page of the *Times Literary Supplement* (October 24, 1926) opined that numbers 3, 10, 11, 25, 29, 30, 34, 37, and 39 of *More Poems* should "on any standard . . . have been excluded." No one remarked or comprehended the revealed passion of number 30 ("Shake hands, we shall never be friends, all's over") and 31 ("Because I liked you better than suits a man to say")—both are poems to Moses Jackson, poems of separation and death.

The forty-nine pieces published in *More Poems* had not exhausted the usable material of the four notebooks, and Laurence returned to them for all but one or two of the eighteen lyrics that composed the section *Additional Poems* that he printed in his memoir of his brother, published by Cape, November 26, 1937. When these pieces appeared in the comprehensive edition two years later, it was found that five more had been added to them; three of these (21, 22, and 23) had been published by Housman himself, and one (19) by Laurence. The new one was 20 ("I shall not die for you").

II *The Comprehensive Editions*

The comprehensive edition had been very much in the mind of the editors of Henry Holt & Co., Housman's "authorized" American publishers, since their failure in 1936 to secure the rights to *More Poems*. It was the poet's sister, Mrs. Katharine Symons, who early in July, 1939, bore the good news to the American firm that the Housman family, now that Laurence's reluctance had been overcome, had decided to bring out their brother's *Collected Poems*. Cape, of course, would be the London publisher, and she herself had nominated Holt as the opposite number in America. Throughout the following months, Mrs. Symons maintained an active interest in the new edition; she decided—with the aid of her sister Clemence and their brother—what poems would be included, and offered her help in running down out-of-the-way material. In her last letter (dated November 18, 1939) prior to the appearance of the *Collected Poems*, she expressed satisfaction that the Cape and Holt editions would be "identical"—the debacle of the error-riddled *More Poems* rankled in her memory—and went on to mention that "a devotee of A.E.H." (she thought his name was John Carter) had been attending to the punctuation of the London edition. Clearly, without fully realizing it, she was in a small way reënacting Alfred's life-long struggle for textual cleanliness. "It [punctuation] was a point that A.E.H. cared for greatly," she soberly ended her letter.

In assuming the editorship, as Mr. Carter later named it, of the new edition, he had much to do beside attend to punctuation. It was generally felt on both sides of the Atlantic that the reissue, in any form, of Housman's posthumous poetry was not something to be undertaken lightly, particularly if any amends were to be made for the sad case of *More Poems*. Nothing less than an extensive and minute reëxamination of the notebook drafts and other determinative manuscripts would be required if the arduous task of preparing a comprehensive edition worthy of the poet were ever essayed. Here a climax in literary history presented itself, one of those rare and fateful opportunities that make or mar an editor's reputation and securely establish or indefinitely delay a *textus receptus*.

The necessary documents were at the new editor's hand, but time and the ability to use them were unfortunately lacking. Since the *Collected Poems* appeared before the end of 1939, it is evident that Mr. Carter could not have spent more than a few months doing what should have absorbed his undivided energies over as many years. Laurence was probably of no practical assistance in the many problems that arose, for he had confessed his inability to tell which notebook was the earliest and had printed "Atys," the first poem of *Additional Poems*, largely from a recollection of a fair draft of it made by Alfred over thirty years before.[7]

It is evident that Laurence had begun to break up the notebooks and to destroy parts of the manuscript before he decided to go ahead with the *Collected Poems*. Otherwise, it is hard to account for the printing of imperfect or superseded drafts in that edition. In scattering the notebook sheets, he could easily have lost track of definitive fair copies and, subsequently, have taken his 1939 text from notebook entries he had used in his first printing of *More Poems* (1936), without asking himself if a better text existed. A mishap of this kind seems to have overtaken "Young is the blood that yonder" (*MP* 34). Housman left an inked fair copy of the six stanzas of this lyric on D 120 and 121. But this draft could not have been the basis of *MP* 34 in its first printing; for stanza five, much different from its reading in the fair copy, was put in the place of number two. Several other variants appear between the D 120-21 draft and the 1936 text. All signs point, therefore, to another notebook source for Laurence's text: a draft on D 94-95, now lost. It must be concluded that Laurence, having mistakenly based his text on this earlier draft, which he afterward destroyed, never took the authoritative later draft into account when he (with Mr. Carter) was fitting *More Poems* into the comprehensive edition. This is an example of the kind of woes that plagued their inventor and his work, and descended upon his co-worker. The London edition of the *Collected Poems* carried Laurence's limping text of *MP* 34 through fourteen impressions, including the "corrected" one of 1953. The new "reset" edition of 1960 showed the stanzas in the proper order but retained some textual errors.

III   *The Sale of the Poetry Manuscripts*

Having seen the manuscript of *Collected Poems* on its way to the printer (and during the preparation of it), Laurence looked ahead to the sale of the notebook remains. The advisability of offering them for sale in New York undoubtedly occurred to him early, and in this he was encouraged by Charles Scribner's Sons, Ltd., whose connections with the American market through its New York office assured highly favorable returns. Under this arrangement, Mr. Carter, an employe of the London office of Scribner's, continued his association with the manuscript remains, sorting and tabulating them as, packet by packet, he received them from Laurence during the late-summer months of 1939.

As Laurence turned once again the pages of Alfred's notebooks —some testifying in their clean, rapid script to the divine excitement poets know, others blurred with the record of inspiration that went awry—he must have felt the inexorable presence of the man who had awed him while living, and whose spiritual record he had been appointed both to preserve and to destroy. He could not deceive himself as to the minimal quantity of these valuable documents he could legitimately save: only perfected manuscripts of pieces that had appeared in Alfred's two books and in *More Poems*, and the pieces that had already been printed in *Additional Poems*, plus a few that might join this section. Everything that author or editor had not thought fit to publish under one or another of these four captions must not be permitted to survive. This restriction meant that all workshop sketching, however valuable; all complete or nearly complete poems that Laurence himself had rejected; practically all drafts prior to

those that had furnished printer's copy—all such materials had
to be destroyed. This was a hard necessity, for Alfred had often
backed the holograph of a final draft with fascinating exercises
that could not by any stretch of imagination or conscience be
edited into complete poetry. How was Laurence to suppress the
contraband and save the prize?

There was only one assembly of notebook sheets that could,
in accordance with Alfred's will, be destroyed without intense
regret, and there were about 140 of these: sheets that were
partly or wholly blank and those that contained nothing but
workshop material. These were torn or cut from the books and
burned. The remainder, about two hundred sheets, were also of
two kinds: (1) about sixty sheets of fair copy that bore no contraband on either side and (2) about 140 sheets that were usually
inscribed with much-corrected drafts, fragments, or other workshop material—all intermixed, on one side of the sheets or both,
with writing that could legitimately be saved. It was obvious
that, under the strict terms of Housman's will, only the first
group of these notebook sheets should be preserved. The mount-
ing-papers now bearing them show, in Mr. Carter's hand, the
notations "And under," "Under," or "Over," meaning that they
were never subjected to the mucilage treatment the others were
soon to receive. This treatment was of course unnecessary where
nothing had to be concealed. Some of these "clear" sheets, when
consecutive, were shingled, the lower one sometimes pasted fast,
but nearly all of them thus designated were tipped in only.

The second and larger group permitted no easy solution:
Laurence knew of no magic way to split a sheet of thin paper.
However, he did attempt to bring the second group to a condi-
tion approximating as nearly as possible that of the first.

In order to eliminate as much workshop manuscript as possible, he dissected the majority of the 140 sheets: some into as
many as four pieces, others to destroy only one or two lines, and
still others to allow but a line or two to remain. As this work was
being done, he kept in mind that each fragment would eventually
be securely pasted to a new mounting-sheet, so that only the
exposed side, containing published poetry, would ever be
viewed, and the existence of workshop writing on the attached
side of many of the sections and whole sheets would not be
suspected. For greater security such material was usually erased

or otherwise canceled, and the same treatment given any passage of this kind that unavoidably remained on the exposed side of any sheet or section. The only uncut sheets of group 2 were a small number that happened to contain only workshop sketching on one side and non-contraband on the other; these he simply glued fast to the mounting-sheets with the canceled workshop side down. As may be imagined, many mid-sheet sections slipped out of position in this process, some may have been lost, and the original order of Housman's four notebooks was radically disturbed.

In this fashion Laurence reduced the four books to 241 pieces of manuscript, large and small. To these were added two other portions: (1) a group of seventeen foolscap sheets copied by Alfred in preparing printer's copy of *A Shropshire Lad* and *Last Poems*, and (2) a group of eight miscellaneous pieces of various sizes, some of them from the early leaves of the oldest notebook. All of this salvaged material finally made a grand total of 165 mounting-sheets, which, when offered for sale, were contained in seven new books that represented the seven envelopes into which Laurence had sorted out the reliquiae of the notebooks as he passed judgment on their contents.

The extent of the losses the notebooks sustained by Laurence's cutting can now be determined with fair accuracy by means of the analysis Laurence himself made of the documents while still intact; this analysis he printed as an appendix to his memoir (256-75). There he provided a table of the contents of the 188 pages of Notebook A, 231 pages of B, 112 pages of C, and 125 pages of D. He may not have been aware of the completeness of his work, but it located fragments, rough drafts or fair copy, or both, of every poem but ten of the 177 now in the comprehensive edition. Short of a reconstitution of the notebooks, Laurence's analysis, interspersed with some notes and publication data, is the best introduction to the history of Housman's poetry. It also provides the unique means by which anyone equipped with a complete set of photocopies of the manuscript remains, and a little more than average patience, may reconstitute Housman's notebooks with a high degree of certainty and completeness.

Shipping restrictions occasioned by the uneasy international situation delayed the shipment of the manuscripts to the New

York office of Scribner's, but they were received before the end
of 1939 and sold to a firm of antiquarian book-dealers. They
came a short time later to the attention of Mrs. Matthew John
Whittall, of Washington, D.C., who purchased them—unseen,
as she told me—and presented them to the Library of Congress,
in 1940. After lying unnoticed for five years, the manuscripts
were, on the advice of Mr. Robert Penn Warren, then Poetry
Consultant of the Library, given a cursory but methodical in-
spection. It was then decided to separate all of the attached
pieces from their mounts, to clean them, and then to re-assemble
the whole corpus in the order in which it had been received,
each piece to be hinged in the remounting so as to permit inspec-
tion of both sides. Each whole notebook sheet and fragment was
sheathed within a nylon envelope, which was later subjected to
intense mechanical pressure, incorporating the nylon threads
with the substance of the paper itself. This operation ensured the
preservation of the aged and brittle pieces but at the same time
obscured the handwriting to some extent. When all this work
was done, 136 new portions of Housman's writing were available.

Contrary to what some ill-informed persons have said,[8] there
was no chemical used in this undertaking, and no "experts" had
a finger in it. The essential step was as simple as removing a
postage stamp from an envelope: the mounting-sheets, with their
manuscript pieces, were laid between dampened paper until the
adhesive was dissolved. When the wet paper came in contact
with the pages carrying ink cancels over writing in ink, the cancels (being from fifteen to fifty years "younger") were often
washed out, with little or no damage to the underlying script.
The original ink on several pages is badly faded, but this de-
terioration may be in part due to the chemical action of the
adhesive. Some pieces absorbed ink stains from the printing and
writing on the dampened sheets between which the mounts were
laid; and there is no doubt that over the past decade the legi-
bility of some of the inked manuscripts has rapidly decreased.

The purpose behind my making during the early 1950's a complete transcript of the notebook manuscripts, after their photocopies had been put in proper order, was twofold: first, to
procure while there was time the text of Housman's drafts, particularly of the posthumous poems, to be used with other quali-

fied drafts and printed texts in providing a sound basis for a definitive edition of his poetry, should it ever be required; and, secondly, to bring to light from the obscurity of the handwriting of the notebook pages—particularly of the 136 newly revealed portions—any unpublished poetry of significance. Eight hundred lines from this source were presented in my *Manuscript Poems of A. E. Housman* (1955).

IV *Poems Recovered from the Notebooks*

New poetry from the scattered and half-obliterated remains of Housman's notebooks would naturally be of prime interest to the lay-reader, and it is for that reason that some specimens are offered here—enough to show the quality and diversity of the unedited pieces remaining in the four notebooks when they left the London office of Scribner's for sale in New York. It will be noted that these recovered poems derive from all four of the notebooks and date from February, 1893, to a short time after January, 1925. Not only are all the notebooks represented in the new poems; most of Housman's main themes also appear in them: the "death wish" and disillusionment (1, 2, 8); the everlastingness of his early fault (3); the harshness of the human condition (4, 6); his tribute to the English soldier (5, 7); and a last testimonial to Moses Jackson.

1

I have desired to die,
  That so this fire might cease,
When you were lost, and I
  Were perished and at peace.

> (Notebook A, p. 156. In pencil; intact.)

2

How many milestones more to pass
  Before the turning road
Shall bring me to my roof of grass
  And steeple-gloomed abode?

> (Notebook A, p. 163. In pencil; slightly faded.)

[110]

3

Then, in the hour when iron is sand
And mountains crumble, this should stand,
Nor falling firmament remove
The landmark of disastrous love.

> (Notebook A, p. 221.
> Nos. 3 and 4 in pencil,
> smudged with an eraser
> and crossed with a large
> X by A.E.H.)

4

The day the child comes to the birth
   He does not laugh, he cries:
So quick he learns the tune that earth
   Will sing him till he dies.

> (Notebook A, p. 221.)

5

Says the grenadier to me,
'Give me half-a-crown,' says he.
To the grenadier says I,
'Very well, my lad, but why?'

'Why,' says he, 'for standing cheer
To a British grenadier.'
So I put the money down
And he took my half-a-crown.

> (Notebook B, p. 88. In
> pencil; lightly erased and
> each line overrun with a
> heavy undula.)

6

If you'll be kind to one another,
   That's the coin would pay me best;
But if man still must hate his brother,
   Hate away, lads, I will rest.

> (Notebook B, p. 93. In
> pencil, much corrected;
> the stanza crossed with an
> X by A.E.H.)

7

Now forms the line and faces
 The lead that spits and rains,
And fleet the red blood races
 Along the soldier's veins.

At all the gates it hammers
 And to heaven [sends a?] shout,
And shakes the bolts and clamours,
 'Ho, jailer, let me out.'

It longs to smell the nitre
 And play in sunshine warm
And paint the soldier brighter
 Than the Queen's uniform.

> (Notebook B. p. 185. In
> pencil, corrected and line-
> canceled, very heavily
> erased.)

8

Hope and fear and hate and lust,
 Foes and comrades, all are slain.
Peace be with them, for I trust
 Never old or young again.

> (Notebook C, p. 17. In
> pencil; heavily erased and
> each line overrun with an
> undula.)

9

Here, in the beechen forest,
 When spring and love were new,
I took my knife last April
 And carved the names of two.

I sealed for years and ages
 What lived a briefer day:
Lost is the letters' meaning,
 The tablet shall not stay.

Still, though the sense is perished,
 Letter and tablet stay.

> So here I bring the auger
>   And in the hole I drill
> I pour out all the evil,
>   The vitriol sure to kill.
>
> Next year in our green woodland
>   Shall stand a naked tree,
> Where spring comes north and islands
>   Turn leafy in the sea.

(Notebook D, p. 118. In ink, much corrected in pencil; three (perhaps four) alternative stanzas and the last 2 lines of stanza 2 erased and line-canceled; the inked lines heavily overrun with an ink undula. Some alternatives in my first publication [1955] have been omitted.)

V   *The Text of the Poems*

Since a number of facts influencing the text and format of Housman's poetry—for example, his change of publishers between the first and second editions of A *Shropshire Lad* and the errors introduced by his editors into the first printings of his posthumous poetry—have been already cited or will be mentioned later, it is necessary to bring into focus this important subject and to review briefly the history of the text of his poetry now read in the comprehensive editions. To begin with the textual history of the two volumes he published is in order.

Housman was a passionate defender of his text; and his long struggle with negligent printers began with the second edition of A *Shropshire Lad*. The type for this book was reset, and the author did not see the proofsheets: ". . . some one played games with the punctuation" was his mild reproach to Grant Richards,[9] who lived to endure chastisements infinitely heavier in the course of his long association with a man who loathed typographical inaccuracy as a mortal fault. When Housman turned through the second edition, he must have been enraged to see on page after page the numerous unauthorized changes in the text and punctuation, broken type, missing letters and other assorted blunders.[10] He saw to it that these errors did not pass into the third edition, which appeared early in 1900. Of this issue he remarked to his publisher that it was "almost exactly correct"[11] and directed him to inform the compositor of the fourth edition ". . . that he had better not put in commas and notes of exclamations for me to strike out of the proof, as was the case last time." Housman's comparatively mild rebuke of this interference may have arisen from detecting that the compositor's aim was to make for easier reading in some stanzas—mainly by adding twenty-five commas.

In 1922, Housman asked for two changes in the text of his first volume: *Loose* replaced *Thick* at the head of line ten of poem 38 to make the line *Loose on the wind are sown*; and line nine of poem 52, which had read *He hears: long since forgotten*, was altered to *He hears: no more remembered*. He gave directions for these two substitutions in the midst of final arrangements for the launching of his second volume of poetry, but his note was mislaid, and the changes did not appear until 1923. Reflecting perhaps on the many textual mishaps that had disfigured the several printings of *A Shropshire Lad*, he remarked hopefully in his Preface to *Last Poems*: ". . . it is best that what I have written should be printed while I am here to see it through the press and control its spelling and punctuation." But his anticipations of textual accuracy were defeated as he opened the pages of his author's copy.

The only change the author made in *Last Poems* was the addition of a title to the thirty-sixth lyric. Asked in 1926 by the headmaster of Winchester College for his permission to include the poem in a school anthology, Housman granted it; and he added for good measure the new title "Revolution," which two years later appeared in the seventh printing of his book.

The history of the texts of the two posthumously issued sections of Housman's poetry, as has been shown, is much more complicated. Even more suspect than the text of *More Poems* is that of *Additional Poems*. In a prefatory note in Laurence's memoir, where eighteen of the poems first appeared, there is a comment (already mentioned, page 105) on the first poem, "Atys," which gives an eloquent hint of the textual insecurity underlying much of the material which Laurence was handling.

The rough draft of the poem, in Notebook B (223-24) has not survived. Destroyed with it were large sections of notebook material containing drafts of other lyrics printed in *Additional Poems*: the unique holographs of *AP* 2, 6, and 7 and parts of *AP* 4, 11, and 14.

It is possible, nevertheless, taking the notebook remains as they are, to pass judgment on the texts of by far the larger number of the seventy-two posthumous poems, the exceptions being a small number of pieces apparently never entered in the notebooks and another group whose holographs perished by erasure or with dissected portions of sheets that were cut in the process of salvage. It is because of these lacunae that the texts of nine poems must be accepted blindly as they stand in the New York or London edition, but printed versions exist for five of these in periodicals and elsewhere, some of them authorized by the poet himself. Furthermore, the seventeen foolscap sheets in the Washington collection, bearing his printer's copy, provide unquestionable authority for collation with the notebook drafts of *MP* 1, 4, 12, 18, 26, 33, 46, and *AP* 18.

There is some evidence in the very first printing of the posthumous poetry that their editor was responsive to both the restraints and the supports of the notebook drafts, for Laurence Housman provided alternative readings—used in the New York edition only—for parts of *MP* 17 and 34 when they appeared in the edition of 1936; he did the same for *AP* 6 and 9 when eighteen new lyrics were incorporated into his memoir, issued by Cape the following year. This recognition of valid alternatives was not, however, expanded and carried into the comprehensive Cape edition; on the contrary, the four apologetic notes were silently passed over as the editor from this time forward accepted Laurence's haphazard arbitration of alternatives left open by the poet in his notebook drafts and fair copies. Even if this arbitration had been permitted by Alfred's testamentary instructions, it would have been an exceedingly dubious practice; for there is nothing in the record of Housman's handling of the drafts that he reworked while collecting *A Shropshire Lad* and *Last Poems* to indicate any principle of selection that his editors-to-be could safely follow when confronted with a line bearing an original and a superscribed reading, both uncanceled. In the notebook drafts of the 105 poems contained in these two volumes, open alternatives may still be read in seventy-four places: of twenty-one of these, Housman sent his original reading into print; of thirty-seven others, he preferred his second reading; and of sixteen others, he abandoned both readings for a third that went into printer's copy or corrected proofsheets.

The first London edition of the *Collected Poems* carried just before the Index an anonymous "Note on the Text," which ran unsigned and without change, except for correction of errors, down to the tenth impression of February, 1948. The fourteenth ("corrected") impression (1953) was actually a new edition; for the editor, having visited the Library of Congress for an examination of the notebook remains, now introduced a number of significant changes in the text of the posthumous poetry: he altered the reading of fourteen lines, made twenty-nine changes in punctuation, five in spelling, turned two quatrains into an eight-line poem (*MP* 9), and relocated a stanza in *MP* 34. There was also a new "Note on the Text" signed by the editor. He was indebted to American research for many of the corrections he brought to the Cape 1953 printing, and the two unexpected innovations he contributed on his own discretion were the only alterations open to question. On the other hand, a much larger number of needed emendations were not made.

The sixteenth Cape printing, called a "New Edition," appeared in 1960. For this, the type was reset and once again a new "Note on the Text" was produced. Once again long-awaited corrections in the text of *More Poems* and *Additional Poems* were passed over; and punctuation, even in the texts of *A Shropshire Lad,* was disturbed by omissions and unwarranted additions. These fluctuations, running over a score of years, had little or no effect on the text of the New York edition which, since its appearance in 1940, was reissued practically unchanged except for a few corrections having no connection with the authority of the notebooks: the restoration of a quotation-mark chipped from the plate for page ten, and the elimination of the hyphen in the second line of the translation from Euripides.

The Complete Poems [of] *A. E. Housman,* the Centennial Edition, published by Henry Holt & Co. in 1959, represented the results of a long exploration of the notebooks and other related manuscripts; and it offers, it is hoped, a text for the posthumous poetry that might not be unworthy of Housman's designation for the third edition of *A Shropshire Lad*: "almost exactly correct." But this is only a temporary aim: the net result of the growing interest in the Washington manuscripts ought to be the concurrence of qualified opinion on a single text for the London and New York editions. It is regrettable that the modest wish of one of A. E. Housman's most faithful sponsors, his sister Katharine Symons, that the texts of his poetry published in the English-speaking world be *identical*, has not yet seen fulfilment—and still seems very far in the future.

The Centennial Edition received flattering reviews[12] and ran through several reprintings. It was however, not approved by the London publisher and others who midway in the preparation of the new edition had demanded and forced acceptance of several changes in its format and contents. Eventually, yielding to continued pressure from parties overseas threatening to take away their license as publishers of Housman's works in the United States, the New York house, some time in 1964, allowed the Centennial Edition to go out of print, and in the *Publishers' Weekly* for January 31, 1966, announced the issuance of *The Collected Poems of A. E. Housman,* which is essentially a reprint of the latest London edition. In this book some of the corrections in the Centennial Edition have been assumed, but others have been ignored, and new errors have been introduced. The entire Index of the 1959 New York edition has been used, but the differences between the London and New York editions have made some of the references in the new printing unintelligible. The texts of some of the poems have been radically disturbed and errors of various kinds appear throughout the book, beginning with the early *Shropshire Lad* poems. Misreadings eliminated many years ago have been sown back into the text of this so-called "authorized canon of the English poet's verse." It is unfortunate that the text of the poetry of A. E. Housman, of all poets, should be made a pawn in publishers' disputes.

CHAPTER 6

Literary Tastes and Influences:
The Bible and the Ballads

AFTER a writer's reputation has been established, everyone wants to know what he read and how it influenced his writing. In the late 1920's John Livingston Lowes' *Road to Xanadu*, showed how Coleridge's reading of books of travel had become transmuted into the substance of his poetry. A new edition of Milton centers on what late evidence has been found of his extraordinarily wide knowledge of history, geography, Classical and biblical literature, and associated subjects.[1] Housman's scholarly excursions in the world of books and manuscripts were wide-ranging, and the energy and thoroughness with which he acquired and employed his knowledge could have gained him eminence in other fields than that of Classical scholarship, had will and fate so ruled. At seventy, he said that Nature had cut him out for a geographer.[2] His interest in that science was lifelong; and in what may be called a remotely collateral field, ancient astronomy, his command was so absolute, thanks partly to his long attachment to Manilius' *Astronomica*, that he was consulted by experts in the subject. All that he gathered in these two natural sciences nourished the poet in A. E. Housman, for some of his finest lyrics—"Revolution" (*LP* 36), "Astronomy" (*LP* 17), "The night is freezing fast" (*LP* 20), "March" (*ASL* 10), "Reveille" (*ASL* 4), "Here are the skies, the planets seven" (*AP* 5), "I wake from dreams . . ." (*MP* 43), "The fairies break their dances" (*LP* 21), "Think no more, lad . . ." (*ASL* 49)—can be read with fuller appreciation when they are seen in relation to the terrestrial and celestial globes.

It has already been mentioned how Alfred as a boy under his mother's tutelage explored his extensive family library—"dating from the time of Caxton," so his sister describes it in the Holt memorial volume. His boyhood reading was wide rather than deep, but the sonorous language of the King James Bible became a part of his thought. Later, in school and college he made and enlarged his acquaintance with the leading English poets of the last three centuries, ripening his enthusiasm for Milton, Blake, Pope, Shelley, Byron, and Arnold. Among his contemporaries that he set high were Thomas Hardy, Walter de la Mare, Christina Rossetti, Alice Meynell, Sir William Watson,[3] John Masefield, Henry James, Robert Bridges, T. S. Eliot, and Oscar Wilde.

There was no trace of snobbishness in Housman's choice of literary fare, prose or poetry, but it cannot be denied that his dislikes for some of his contemporaries was expressed in terms almost as scathing as the criticism he unleashed on unworthy editors of the Classics. He had a standing agreement with Laurence that he would contribute to *The Venture*, of which Laurence was an editor, only upon the condition that it contain nothing by John Galsworthy and Maurice Hewlett.[4] Housman read much for diversion and kept his publisher, Grant Richards, busy supplying him with his favorite light novels and was not ashamed to have it said of him that he introduced to England the frothy *Gentlemen Prefer Blondes* by Anita Loos. Among other American authors whom he liked were O. Henry, Poe, Mark Twain, Artemus Ward, Josh Billings, Sinclair Lewis, Edith Wharton, Ralph Hodgson, and Witter Bynner. He was cool to Robinson and Frost, preferring Edna St. Vincent Millay to either. In his latter years he subscribed to the Sephra Library Service of New York, and we have letters acknowledging his receipt of James Branch Cabell's *The Cream of the Jest* (1917) and *Jurgen* (1919) and of Theodore Dreiser's autobiographical *Dawn* (1931). His feeling for Mark Twain's books ran deep, his favorite being *Huckleberry Finn*. The preposterous elegy in the novel, "Ode to Stephen Dowling Bots," which Housman said he knew by heart, is very much in the vein of his early nonsense verse and may have left its mark on some of the later *facetiae*.

I *The Bible*

What were the chief literary influences on his serious poetry? The only sources he acknowledged were the old English Ballads, the songs in Shakespeare's plays, and the poems of Heinrich Heine.[5] He never spoke of the Bible in this connection, an oversight that cannot easily be explained, for the Bible is by far the dominating literary influence in his poetry—not only in the quantity of quoted and echoed phrases but also in the frequency of mood and thematic elements recurring to Old and New Testament origins, particularly to Job, Isaiah, Proverbs and Ecclesiastes. Housman's silence on the prominence of the Bible in his poetry could not have been intentional and may be partly explained by the fact that he was unaware of the extent of the debt he owed to that omnipresent source—just as so many renowned and humble English writers before and after him have used scriptural expressions without immediate recognition of their origin, so completely have they blended with the common stock of our speech.

Children nowadays get their introduction to the Bible through prettily illustrated books of "Stories Retold," church pageants, and other pictorial and dramatic presentments. Alfred first knew the Bible, not only as a way of life, but as supremely great literature, interpreted by the best of teachers, his mother, who read the Scriptures with him and implanted their sublime language and their subject-matter imperishably in his mind. The reader will recall that, when Alfred was fifteen and a pupil in the fourth form at Bromsgrove School, he wrote a competition poem that ended with a reference to St. Paul; and "St. Paul on Mars Hill" was the subject of his prize-winning poem the following year. Sarah Housman lived her religion: formal prayers and the reading of scriptural texts were a part of the daily routine in the Housman family, and all were regular attendants of their church services, where Alfred, when home from Oxford, occasionally read the lessons in the absence of his father, the usual reader. Even though his faith was severely impaired by the crisis of his boyhood, his mother's influence never lost its hold on him; and the concepts of the Christian faith, passing into later clear-eyed judgment, were constant points of reference when he treated in his poetry of "eternal thoughts."

A mere glance at the Index of Housman's *Complete Poems* reveals several titles of biblical import: "The Carpenter's Son" (*ASL* 47) describes the Crucifixion; "Easter Hymn" (*MP* 1) is poised midway between acceptance and rejection of the Resurrection, which is in the background of "Bring, in this timeless

[120]

grave to throw" (*ASL* 46) and in "Now to her lap the incestuous earth" (*AP* 8). "Half-way, for one commandment broken" (*MP* 35) is about the fate of Lot and his wife. Other biblical allusions are evident in "When Adam walked in Eden young" (*AP* 3), "When Israel out of Egypt came" (*MP* 2), and "Hell Gate" (*LP* 31). The earthly end of the religion of Housman's boyhood is pictured in "New Year's Eve" (*AP* 21). Much of the substance drawn from the Bible, Housman presents in an ironic, even distorted fashion; for example, the Crucified One is made to say ambiguously that he dies "for love," which incidentally is the plea of the rascally galley-slave Don Quixote interrogates in the chain-gang.

Another example of Housman's perversion of a biblical quotation is in lyric twenty-two of *More Poems*, which begins, "Ho, everyone that thirsteth." This is word for word from Isaiah 55:1, which continues, "Come ye to the waters. . . . without money and without price." But Housman's rendering is, to continue, "And hath the price to give." Line 3 of his poem (repeated as line 5) is "Come to the stolen waters." The stolen waters are mentioned in Proverbs 9:17; they symbolize sinful pleasure, the delight of the fool in places of wickedness: "He knoweth not that the dead are there; and that her guests are in the depths of hell." (Proverbs 9:18). Housman's elixir of life, then, is stolen waters sold at a price. "Drink and your soul shall live," so concludes stanza one. The poem, taken as a whole, is perhaps the most extreme example of his warping of a Bible text; it demonstrates with what bitterness his indignation could avenge itself upon the laws of God and man: a far cry from his youthful jibe at religion as in his *Ye Rounde Table* satire, "Over to Rome," and in a short poem he sent to Percy Withers, "It is a fearful thing to be/The Pope. . . ."[6]

Biblical language enters into Housman's poetry in various ways. First there are direct quotations, such as the one just cited from Isaiah, also "swept and garnished" (*MP* 3:11), "A dead man out of mind" (*ASL* 63:8), and "Sleep on now and take your rest" (*LP* 29:16). Standing alone, these would easily be recognized as quotations, but the almost perfect suitability of them, blended into the context of Housman's poems, tends to make them and many others of their kind lose the stamp of their original identity. A much larger group comprises phrases slightly altered to fit their contexts: "my bones within me say" (*ASL* 43:3, 36)—"All my bones shall say" (Ps. 35:10); "When your soul is in my soul's stead" (*ASL* 62:56)—". . . if your soul were in my soul's stead" (Job 16:14); ". . . altered is the fashion of the earth" (*MP* 5:4)—"the fashion of this world passeth away." (I Cor. 7:31); "quit you like stone, be strong" (*ASL* 51:22)— "quit you like men, be strong" (I Cor. 16:13); "We have seen his star in the west" (*AP* 21:52)—"We have seen his star in the east" (Matt. 2:2); ". . . in the grave, they say,/Is neither knowledge nor device: (*LP* 5:18-19)—"there is no . . . device nor knowledge . . . in the grave" (Eccl. 9:10); ". . . the enemies of England they shall see me and be sick" (*ASL* 34:16)—"The wicked shall see it, and be grieved" (Ps. 112:10).

But a parallel display of borrowings and origins is the only way to show how numerous Housman's biblical quotations and echoes actually are, how much or how little he rephrased them, and for what purpose. See the Appendix, pp. 179-193.

It would be an obtuse reader indeed who would not detect a definite biblical flavor in page after page of Housman's *Complete Poems.* The flavor is acrid generally, suiting as it does the poet's taste for the somber and minatory passages of the Scriptures. Housman rated the story of Job over the story of Ruth; the 44th Psalm over the 23rd. His sister Katharine, so Alfred reported to Laurence shortly after the publication of *A Shropshire Lad,* told him that she liked the verse better than the sentiments, which seemed to her to come straight from the book of Ecclesiastes.[7]

Like the "lonely word" of Virgil that Tennyson admired, a single word of Housman's steeped in scriptural associations often strikes the reader's eye and transports his imagination down a long corridor of storied meaning. Such a word is *portion* in "Our only portion is the estate of man" (*LP* 9:19), where the Younger Son says, "Father, give me the portion of thy substance that falleth to me" (Luke 15:12). Again, how immediately the word *vision* in "I wake from dreams and turning/My vision on the height . . ." (*MP* 43:1-2) takes us to "In thoughts from the visions of the night, when deep sleep falleth on men . . ." (Job 4:13). So it is that a reader quick to identify borrowings from the Authorized Version in Housman's poetry will respond to a biblical quotation or echo once in about every sixteen lines. Again it may be said that it is not unnatural that these echoes sound almost invariably the note of sadness and loss, for the author of *A Shropshire Lad* when they came into his poetry had long been an exile from the spiritual country in which for only a few precious years he had held an active citizenship with his mother, who had made it his home, a home which he lost with her. Though he never found his way back to this spiritual domain, its landmarks were never out of view: and the language he had learned there remained forever the language of his heart. His spiritual peace and the loss of it are solemnized in the first *Shropshire Lad* poem (quoted on p. 53) he entered in his first poetry notebook. It is his essential biography in eight lines:

> Into my heart an air that kills
> From yon far country blows:
> What are those blue remembered hills,
> What towns, what shires are those?
>
> That is the land of lost content,
> I see it shining plain,
> The happy footpaths where I went
> And cannot come again.
>
> (*ASL* 40; the original version, on A 63)

II *The English Ballads*

Some correspondents once inquired of Grant Richards about Housman's use of "reach" in *And straight though reach the track* (*ASL* 36).[8] Richards passed the letter on to Housman, who, as his habit was in dealing with letters from persons who had no designs upon him, replied promptly through his publisher. In this case he cited dates and quotations from the Oxford Dictionary showing the meaning of the word *reach*. He then went on to say, "Perhaps your friends are baffled by the subjunctive mood, and think it ought to be *reaches*; but see *Psalm* 138.6: Though the Lord *be* high, yet hath he respect unto the lowly." Housman readily turned to the Bible to illustrate the use of obsolescent subjunctive forms of verbs, but he might just as readily have quoted from one of the English Ballads, for he was thoroughly acquainted with ballad literature and acknowledged it as one of the main sources behind his poetry. From both sources he no doubt picked up the habit of savoring his early poems with archaic verb forms with -*est* and -*eth* endings; and these two literary fountainheads, not widely separated chronologically, combined also to justify and strengthen his taste for provincial and dialectal words. All of the following archaisms—and they fairly represent their kind in his poetry—occur also in Child's comprehensive collection of *English and Scottish Popular Ballads*:[9] *holt* (*ASL* 31), "woodland"; *prime* (*ASL* 24), "early period"; *plight* (*ASL* 41), "condition of being"; *quick* (*ASL* 61), "living"; *sain* (*ASL* 14), "bless"; *shaws* (*MP* 5), "thicket"; *oakenshaws* (*LP* 25); *straws* (*ASL* 4), "strews"; *thorough* (*ASL* 17), "through" (*ASL* 17); *doubt* (*AP* 3), "fear." It may not need to be said that the reader will recognize at least one of these as a common biblical word. And there is the sonorous closing line of the "Easter Hymn" (*MP* 1): "Bow hither out of heaven and see and save." Who can say what or how much it owes to line 57 of "Robin Hood and the Monk" (Ch. 119:54)?*—Ihesus yow saue and se!" Housman's borrowing of the alliterative phrase would be far less remarkable than the coincidence of language.[10]

But the main contribution of the Ballads was not in verbal parallels. Consider Housman's stanzaic patterns. Although they exhibit numerous variants in line length and line number, with patterns of rhyme and accent of several different kinds, a glance into his *Complete Poems* shows that the typical ballad stanza predominates. Forty per cent of the lyrics of *A Shropshire Lad* show this form; and, if we add twelve more pieces consisting of four-line stanzas, with their second and fourth lines moving in iambic tetrameter, we may say that fifty-eight per cent of his poems in this volume fall into the *abab* quatrain pattern. Of his 177 poems in the collected editions, only forty-seven do not conform to the quatrain scheme. One more particularity: the sprung syntax of the Ballads, a prominent characteristic of their folk origin, may have found its way into some of Housman's pieces not often thought of as ballad-like. For example, the dropping of the relative pronoun in "Terence, this is stupid stuff" (*ASL* 62:59), "There was a king reigned in the East," calls to mind many lines like these: "sent it to Sir Patrick Spence/Was walking on the sand" (Ch. 58 A).

---

* References to the Child Ballads are made by the symbol Ch, followed by the number of the ballad. For a long ballad, stanza numbers are added, and sometimes a version (A, B, etc.) is specified.

III *Ballad Themes*

These different examples could be multiplied on a very large scale; but, impressive as such a display might be, it would obscure recognition of the fact that Housman's debt to the Ballads lay, not mainly in the area of language or stanza forms, but in the wealth of themes, situations, and characters they gave him. These rugged tales of danger and violence fired his imagination as they did Walter Scott's; here was a world where both the never-failing juvenile passion for adventure and the mature sense of the tragedy of human wrongs could find ample room to explore. Here was a world peopled with the most pathetic lovers, the most fascinating rogues, and the most gallant soldiers that ever trooped out of the pages of storied romance.

Into this world Housman sent his mythical Terence Hearsay to bring back reports of the strange and wonderful doings of its inhabitants. He met the sturdy renegade defying the laws of God and man, the culprit lying long in jail or making his brief stay at the head of the gallows stair,[11] the suicide, the slayer pursued by conscience and the king's men, the unlucky suitor returned from the grave to visit his sweetheart, the fratricide killing for love, the maiden disgraced and betrayed, and the battle-tempered sworn companions riding together on the lances. In his earliest excursions into the old balladry, Terence Hearsay found much of himself in these stories of lost innocence, the oppressor's wrong, and unavailing courage—gleams of life that shed a somber luster upon Housman's moods and ripening convictions after his Oxford failure and through the long years of expiation.

One word more on a common situation in the Ballads: the rendezvous of two lovers. In a late-written poem (about 1922), "I to my perils . . . ," now *More Poems* 6, Housman rather loftily abjures this romantic staple both in real life and (presumably) in poetry. But this disclaimer, like his denial that very little of his *Shropshire Lad* was autobiographical,[12] is not borne out by his poems. Actually some of his finest lyrics are on the theme of lovers' trysts. Not many of the pieces in the comprehensive editions would be placed by popular assent above "Bredon Hill" (*ASL* 19). In this and others of its quieter kind, as well as those of seduction and betrayal—for example, "On your midnight pallet lying" (*ASL* 11) and "Delight it is in youth and May (*MP* 18)—

the old Ballad spirit is very much in evidence; and the poems are read with clearer understanding against the background of their Ballad analogues: "Earl Brand" (Ch. 7), "Lord Thomas and Fair Annet" (Ch. 73), "Lord Lovel" (Ch. 75), "Bonny Barbara Allen" (Ch. 84), "Clerk Saunders" (Ch. 69), and others of their kind.

For a closer look at some of Housman's ballads, we shall examine two unpublished poems—one about a revenant, the other about the mishaps of Nancy and Ned—to exemplify some of the foregoing generalities. These ballads were written within a few days of each other early in 1895. The first, which Laurence's analysis describes as "an unfinished narrative poem," occupied Page 231 of Notebook A. The upper third of the page, Laurence destroyed; so the first lines now legible take us into the midst of the story:

> How many hopes, how much desire
> Brought these two souls to the mire.

Like the typical ballad sweetheart, Nancy is cast off by her family:

> Her father turned her from the door
> And she, like better folks before,
> She knew not where to lay her head.

She goes through the rain and darkness to her lover's house where Ned is sitting alone by a waning fire, thinking of his sweetheart. But she is ashamed to face him. "Long and speechless and apart," she lingers outside the door. At last Ned is aroused

> When a foot came to the sill
> And a hand afraid to knock
> Fingered faintly at the lock.

He springs to his feet. "The rain blew in, the door swung wide," and Nancy stood weeping before her lover, who embraced her and wept with her. As they consoled each other, "in heaven the world-wide night" dropped its tears upon them. So much may be rescued from the twenty-three surviving lines, now heavily erased and canceled.

The other poem was written on A 234-35.[13] Of the first page only the upper half remains, and the two incomplete stanzas on it are also heavily obliterated. But enough is legible to show that the poem is a dialogue between Terence, who speaks the first stanza, and the ghost of a friend. Terence says:

> Oh man, the news will keep.
> Stay with the dead, man; stop your ears:
> There are worse things than sleep.

The ghostly voice replies:

> Oh Terence, Terence, the long way hither,
> The mist and the crying rain:
>
> Must I go home again?

The middle third of the next page is missing, but none of the ten lines on the two remaining pieces are completely erased. All but two of them are easily read. It is clear that Housman intended this draft to provide a new opening for his story, for Terence speaks, repeating the ghostly summons he has just heard:

> "Hist, Terence, hist! wake up: 'tis I."
> That was a voice I know.
> Up I got and out I looked
> And saw who stood below.

This stanza has the true ballad pace and flavor. Opposite it Housman wrote the second stanza, of which these portions may still be read:

> starlight
> [?   ] the moonlight fell
> [?   ]   clear,
> To look at him you could not tell
> He had been dead a year.

Then at the bottom of the lower fragment is this conclusion: "The dead man in the moonless night/Went back to find his grave."

This incomplete poem, as well as "Is my team ploughing?" (*ASL* 27) and "O is it the jar of nations?" (*AP* 14), may have taken on the color of a number of the old Ballads that have to do with conversations with the returned dead. "The Unquiet Grave" (Ch. 78) and "Proud Lady Margaret" (Ch. 47) are typical of their class. One version (A) of the latter ends thus:

> "For the wee worms are my bedfellows,
>   And cauld clay is my sheets,
> And when the stormy winds do blow,
>   My body lies and sleeps."

This stanza at once calls to mind Housman's

> Fred keeps the house all kinds of weather,
>   And clay's the house he keeps;
> When Rose and I walk out together
>   Stock-still lies Fred and sleeps. (*ASL* 25)

"The Gardener" (Ch. 219) has a theme Housman might have remembered to his advantage in writing "Delight it is in youth and May" (*MP* 18), already mentioned. In the Ballad a young man invites a maiden to enter his garden and to become his bride. But she refuses him and tartly says she will provide a robe for him among the winter showers:

> "The snow so white shall be your shirt;
>   It becomes your body best;
> The cold bleak wind to be your coat,
>   And the cold wind in your breast." (219 B)

With this, something else comes to mind: the twentieth lyric of *Last Poems* in which, for a winter robe, Dick has made an overcoat of earth and sea and "wears the turning globe."

Housman's "The True Lover" (*ASL* 53) in form and feeling is one of his nearest technical approaches to the traditional Ballad. It sketches the outline of a tragic romance in six stanzas of dialogue and three of commentary. Two or three of the Ballads may well have provided some of the details in Housman's poem, besides entering into its plan as a whole. Compare the first stanza of "The True Lover":

> The lad came to the door at night,
>   When lovers crown their vows,
> And whistled soft and out of sight
>   In shadow of the boughs,

with the third stanza of "Clerk Saunders" (Ch. 69 F):

> He's throw the dark, and throw the mark,
>   And throw the leaves o green,
> Till he came to May Margaret's door,
>   And tirled at the pin.

The lovers in the Ballad story are surprised by the girl's brothers, who kill Clerk Saunders as he sleeps. Margaret awakes at dawn and looks at her lover's heavy eyes:

> She thought it had been a loathsome sweat.
>   A wat it had fallen this twa between;
> But it was the blood of his fair body,
>   A wat his life days wair na lang. (69 A)

This matches the question of the sweetheart in "The True Lover":

> "Oh lad, what is it, lad, that drips
>   Wet from your neck on mine?
> What is it falling on my lips,
>   My lad, that tastes of brine?"

In the second stanza of the lyric

> "I shall not vex you with my face
>   Again, my love, for aye;
> So take me in your arms a space
>   Before the east is grey"

the reference to the dawning is reminiscent of the moment of departure often mentioned in the Ballads; and the first two lines may owe something to "Sweet William's Ghost" (Ch. 77 B), in which Margaret asks her lover to kiss her, but he refuses:

> "My mouth it is full cold, Margaret.
>   It has the smell now of the ground;
> And if I kiss thy comely mouth,
>   Thy life-days will not be long."

In the last year of his life, on August 24, 1935, in replying to Mr. Bernard Frechkman's inquiry about a possible connection between the opening line of his "Fancy's Knell" in *Last Poems* (number 41) and Richard Corbet's "The Fairies Farewell," Housman confessed that his poem was an "open imitation,"[14] and went on to add that there many others in his poetry. He cited the line from the fifteenth-century song, "A Lyke-Wake Dirge"— "When thou from hence away art past"—as the original of another line (number 9) in "The True Lover": "When I from hence away am past."

Like all ballad-readers, Housman must have come under the spell of "Bonny Barbara Allan" (Ch. 84). How nearly the first stanza of *ASL* 6 sums up the lover's case in the story of proud Barbara:

> When the lad for longing sighs,
> Mute and dull of cheer and pale,
> If at death's own door he lies,
> Maiden, you can heal his ail.

In the Ballad the servant describes to Barbara Allan his master's sad appearance: "For death is printed in his face,/And sorrow's in him dwelling" (84 B). Housman's second stanza is equally graphic:

> Lover's ills are all to buy:
> The wan look, the hollow tone,
> The hung head, the sunken eye,
> You can have them for your own.

The old Ballad concludes, as everyone knows, with the decision of the remorseful fair, seeing the body of her lover carried into the church, that she will die for him tomorrow. There may be a shade of this idea in the third and final stanza of Housman's poem:

> Buy them, buy them: eve and morn
> Lovers' ills are all to sell.
> Then you can lie down forlorn;
> But the lover will be well.

Two Ballads, "Lord Thomas and Fair Annet" (Ch. 73) and "Fair Margaret and Sweet William" (Ch. 74) begin with two lovers on a hill talking throughout a long summer day. The man, a faithless lover, announces his intended wedding to another sweetheart. "Bredon Hill" (*ASL* 21) opens with the same characters, but they are talking of their marriage. However the sinister element is there too: the girl hears the invitation of the church bells, "But here my love would stay." As the somber theme develops in Housman's lyric, the girl goes to church alone, without her lover:

> Groom there was none to see,
>   The mourners followed after,
> And so to church went she.

In all of the ten full versions of the two Child Ballads, the story ends with the death of the lover, and this is Housman's meaning in his ending, when the bereaved one says, "Oh noisy bells, be dumb;/I hear you, I will come."

The eighth lyric of *A Shropshire Lad*, "Farewell to barn and stack and tree" ranks with "The True Lover" as a narrative poem of passion and tragedy. In the Child Ballad No. 49, "The Twa Brothers," one brother kills another with his knife as in Housman's poem. The printed versions of this Ballad do not indicate any motive for the fratricide—version F blames it on the "hand o accident"—but a canceled stanza in the unique draft of Housman's poem (A 191) points to a love-rivalry:

> Let Lucy sorrow that she was born
>   To set us two to strive:
> If she loves the lad she loved at morn
>   She loves no lad alive.

Housman's poem is concerned with the feelings of the murderer, his farewell to a friend, and especially his thoughts of his mother. All of the seven versions of "The Twa Brothers" end with references to the family of the evil brother. In one the mother's grief is described:

> She turned hersel right round about,
>   And her heart burst into three:
> "My ae best son is deid and gane,
>   And my tother ane I'll neer see." (49 E)

As for his counterpart in *ASL* 8, his thoughts run homeward too:

> "My mother thinks us long away;
>   'Tis time the field were mown.
> She had two sons at rising day,
>   Tonight she'll be alone."

Housman must have set high the Ballad "Mary Hamilton" (Ch. 173), which, incidentally, boasts the largest number of versions in the Child collection. In the poem the queen's maid-of-honor, accused of killing her illegitimate child, speaks from the gallows:

> "Little did my mother know,
>   The hour that she bore me,
> What lands I was to travel in,
>   What death I was to die.

> "Little did my father know,
>   When he held up my head,
> What lands I was to travel in,
>   What was to be my deid.

> "Yestreen I made Queen Mary's bed,
>   Kembed doun her yellow hair;
> Is this the reward I am to get,
>   To tread this gallows-stair!" (173 C)

The mood and the overtones of this Ballad seem to have crept into "The Culprit" (*LP* 14), in which the condemned one addresses the crowd from the scaffold. He, like Mary Hamilton, speaks of the mother that bore him, of his father, and asks for "the county kerchief" (the mask) before the noose is fitted. Mary also pleads

> "And tye a napkin on my face,
>   For that gallows I downa see." (173 B)

The last remark of the culprit in Housman's ballad is that he has no son. Here may be one more link with the Child Ballad, one version of it, wherein the Queen speaks to Mary:

> "For if ye had saved the babie's life,
>   It might hae been an honour to thee." (173 D)

Alfred more than likely came to know the old Ballads before he went to school; he may, like the boy Oliver Goldsmith, have listened charmed to a serving-maid singing them in his parents' house. These romantic poems were excellent nourishment for his boyish love of soldiering and other kinds of adventurous patriotism. (One of our early photographs of him, aged seven, shows a sober-faced guardsman fingering the long hilt of his straight-edged sword.) More than twenty pieces in his collected editions are written in praise or pity of the British soldier; and the presence of two of his best patriotic poems in the first four of *A Shropshire Lad* has already been commented on.[15] Though Housman refused, probably because he did not want to be thought holding a candle to Kipling, to let the patriotic note be as strong as his publisher wanted it in the opening pages of his first book, his love of the redcoat is clear in setting "1887" (*ASL* 1) and in "The Recruit" (*ASL* 3) in key positions. Thus the military spirit of the ballad is quietly declared as a prevalent feature that carries on to very near the end of *A Shropshire Lad*.

In *Last Poems* Housman crowded seven martial lyrics into the first eight places. The first poem, "The West," illustrates his frequent tendency to put himself into the action: he is speaking throughout to his comrade, who is of course Moses Jackson. The same two brothers-in-arms are the principals in "Oh were he and I together" (*AP* 2), which is a lament for his comrade, now absent. This poem, as truly redolent of the Border heather as anything Sir Walter wrote, is ballad romance *pur sang*.

IV *The Contribution of the Ballads*

No one can satisfactorily explain how a poet's reading gets into his poetry, and one who tries it may err in mistaking an echo or a borrowing for coincidence. But there is usually more solid ground than chance on which to found a reckoning of the extent of literary influence upon a writer. How it arrives is another matter, but we may safely begin with the suggestion that the act of composition is the outcome of a conscious association of ideas: for poetry to come, Housman had to be in "a receptive and expectant" state. The theme occupies the center, let us say, and about it plays the as yet wordless flux of images, lights, shadows—all the "forms of things unknown." Things remembered flow in, vaguely shadowed forth, perhaps, in the language of their origins. These presentments would be most vividly and abundantly projected when the act of composition is at its intensest; they enter, now garbed in language, into the new-made poem as elements that impinged on the creating imagination from without and were accepted and absorbed by it: in a word, by its own generating power made a part of itself.

Housman seemed to possess a faculty like Milton's of summoning in an instant to the vital center of his creative consciousness all the resources of his mind. His obituary in *The Times* (May 2, 1936) contained this remarkable passage, which testifies to his ability to bring the sum of his scholarly knowledge to bear upon a given problem:

Manilius, Bentley's greatest memorial, is also Housman's, and not even his Lucan, another brilliant work . . . is to be compared with it. Here also he was working in a field where Bentley had worked. Neither for language nor for method had he studied Bentley in vain. Even where Bentley altered in haste, plying his "desperate hook," Housman would instinctively look for the reason of Bentley's discontent. This attitude of his towards the greatest of English scholars is typically illustrated by his treatment of a passage in Horace: *Rapiamus, amici.* Read *amice,* says Bentley, because the ode is addressed, not to friends, but to a single person. But, adds Housman, that person is not named, as all persons addressed in odes by Horace are: read therefore *Amici,* the vocative of one Amicius. Does the name Amicius exist? See this and that inscription. Even so, is the "i" long? See a Greek inscription where the spelling leaves no doubt.

What Housman the scholar did was also the practice of the poet: all the varied stores that his eager and wide-ranging appetite had gathered were accessible to him when his poetry was taking shape—either on the afternoon walk, or, later, "after tea," when it was being teased into completeness by his faithful intellectual daemon. It is not, therefore, to be wondered at that the Bible and the English Ballads, so intimately known, are so frequently met by Housman's attentive reader.

CHAPTER 7

Literary Tastes and Influences:
Shakespeare, Heine, and Lucretius

IT might be imagined that Housman could have had no more than the ordinary reader's interest in Shakespeare's songs—one of his three admitted sources—if we thought only of some of the most popular ones, such as "Who is Sylvia?" and "Hark, hark the lark." Housman paid his respects to these and others like them by describing them in his Senate House Lecture as ravishing nonsense[1]—a ware he did not deal in. He went on to mention the "greater and more moving poems"—"Fear no more the heat o' the sun" and "O mistress mine, where art thou roaming?"; and to these he might have added "Blow, blow, thou winter wind"; "Come away, come away, death"; "Pardon, goddess of the night"; "No more, thou thunder-master"; and others in this vein. He must have come upon these early; and we may imagine the Bromsgrove boy smiling with wry appreciation at Apemantus' currish grace in *Timon of Athens* (I, ii):

> Immortal gods, I crave no pelf:
> I pray for no man but myself:
> Grant I may never prove so fond,
> To trust man on his oath or bond;
> Or a harlot for her weeping;
> Or a dog that seems a-sleeping;
> Or a keeper with my freedom;
> Or my friends, if I should need 'em.
> Amen. So fall to't:
> Rich men sin, and I eat root.

This extreme misanthropic note does not appear elsewhere in Shakespeare's songs, but it is not uncharacteristic of them as a whole: they savor, all told, more of Feste than of Ariel—whence we may read one reason for their appeal to Housman.

I *Songs from Shakespeare's Plays*

He appreciated the songs as being much more than lyric incidentals in the plays; he relished their indigenous dramatic values, their fidelity to the action of their contexts, their sparse accurate comment on the tragedy or comedy of a crowded scene. Housman's sympathy for "all ill-treated fellows" found congenial themes in many of Shakespeare's lyrics that express, often with typical sixteenth-century excess, the feelings of various unfortunate characters in the action of the dramas. How many of the darker traits of these lyrics and their surroundings may have entered into Housman's working imagination, no one can say; but his poetry, when we begin exploring it, offers many parallels: suicide for love, the ill conscience, innocence betrayed, the longing of age for the years of youth, the lament for the irrevocable dead. Seventeen of Housman's lyrics are devoted to the theme of the rejected lover, who ends in despair or suicide. The "lover sick to death" of *Love's Labour's Lost* (IV, iii) could meet with many of his kind in Housman's poems.

As often as Housman's lovers are their own undoing, they are victims of an unkind fate; and, in their behalf, he makes his appeal or protest to the ruler of the universe as the family of Posthumus Leonatus besought Jupiter's mercy on its son and brother. The opening lines of the poem in *Cymbeline* (V, iv) announce a theme which Housman understood: "No more, thou thunder-master, show/Thy spite on mortal flies." A kind of responsory unfolds itself when we hear the mother of Posthumus say of her son that he "came crying 'mongst his foes"; so Housman in a birthday poem (*MP* 25) says of himself that he "came crying upon earth." This again is the burden of a poem recovered from his notebooks (A 221):

> The day the child comes to the birth
> He does not laugh, he cries:
> So quick he learns the tune that earth
> Will sing him till he dies.

King Lear maunders: ". . . we came crying hither:/Thou know'st the first time that we smell the air/We wawl and cry" (IV, vi).

[136]

The appeal in behalf of Posthumus continues by describing his virtues and ends on this note of defiance:

> Peep through thy marble mansion; help!
> Or we poor ghosts will cry
> To the shining synod of the rest
> Against thy deity.
>
> Help, Jupiter! or we appeal
> And from thy justice fly.

But the prayer is vain, and the petitioners know it, because they do not believe in the justice to which they appeal. If Jupiter had been just, Posthumus would not be in need of intercession. His virtues have not brought him divine favor in the past; they will now avail him nothing. The same note of rebellion against an indifferent or unjust fate is often struck in Housman's lines.

To balance the rigors of man's hard condition, Housman extols the pleasures of the present hour: the delights of youthful love, of morning, of springtime when the cherry is in bloom, or of the autumn when "the beautiful and death-struck year" was a kind companion. But these treasures are few and brief; the more reason, then, to seize them before they pass. Housman was ready for the counsel of Feste; it went straight to his heart:

> What is love? 'tis not hereafter;
> Present mirth hath present laughter;
> What's to come is still unsure:
> In delay there lies no plenty;
> Then come kiss me, sweet and twenty,
> Youth's a stuff will not endure.
>
> (*Twelfth Night*, II, iii)

Breath's a ware that will not keep (ASL, 4) is the Shropshire way of putting it. Housman found the same admonition in the song of the two Pages in *As You Like It* (V, iii), beginning "It was a lover and his lass." These are the last two stanzas (omitting the refrains):

> This carol they began that hour,
> How that life was but a flower.
>
> .   .   .   .
>
> And therefore take the present time,
> For love is crowned with the prime.

The last word in the preceding quotation will serve as a re-
minder that, the more closely Housman imitates the theme of a
Shakespearian lyric, the more likely he is to use Shakespeare's
language, sometimes a phrase of some length. This fact will be
illustrated later in this chapter where language parallels are
more graphically drawn. Here it is sufficient to compare the use
of *prime* in these two passages from poems on the *carpe diem*
theme:

> Say, lad, have you things to do?
> Quick then, while your day's at prime (*ASL* 24)
>
> .   .   .   .
>
> The swift hour and the brief prime of the year
> Say to the soul, *Thou wast not born for aye.* (*MP* 5)

Looking again at the song from *As You Like It*—

> The carol they began that hour
> How that life was but a flower,

—we may find our recollection turning to another of Housman's
poems similar in theme and situation and possibly linked to
Shakespeare's lyric by the use of the word *flower* in stanza two:

> Ah, spring was sent for lass and lad,
> 'Tis then the blood runs gold,
> And he and she had best be glad
> Before the world is old.
> What flowers to-day may flower to-morrow,
> But never as good as new . . .
>
> (*ASL*, 5, second draft, B24)

If the present hour offers no reward worth pursuing, Housman
may counsel the refuge offered by stoicism. This implies a renunciation of society, scorn of love, steady contemplation of the
ills of the universe, and reconciliation with the idea of death.
These points of view lie at the heart and center of Housman's
poetry. He might have chosen Amiens' refrain, "Most friendship
is feigning, most loving mere folly," as a group-title for some of
his most characteristic lyrics. "A great while ago the world began," sings Feste in the Epilog of *Twelfth Night*; Housman's
antiphonal is, *Ay, look: high heaven and earth ail from the prime
foundation* (*ASL*, 48).

The surly petition of Apemantus, the dry wisdom of the Fool in *Lear*, the mumbled catches of the grave-digger in *Hamlet*, even Timon's bitter outcry in his epitaph—all have their analogues in Housman's verse. Let us pause a moment before the epitaph of Timon, even though warned away:

> Here lies a wretched corse, of wretched soul bereft.
> Seek not my name: a plague consume you wicked caitiffs left!
>
> Here lie I, Timon; who, alive, all living men did hate:
> Pass by and curse thy fill, but pass and stay not here thy gait.
> *(Timon of Athens,* V, iv)

The second poem Housman entered in his first poetry notebook (A 61) is an epitaph that, if not as harsh as Timon's malediction, surely echoes his accents:

> Stay, if you must, O passer by the way;
> Yet night approaches: better not to stay.
> I never sigh, nor flush, nor knit the brow,
> Nor grieve to think how ill God made me, now.
> Here, with one balm for many fevers found,
> Cured of an ancient evil, I sleep sound. (*AP* 12)

These parallels summon up lines and phrases that seem to have come from the pen at a moment when Housman had Shakespeare's language in mind. Another example is the first strophe of "In my own shire, if I was sad" (*ASL* 41), which describes a pageant of the seasons and concludes with the springtime "bluebells in the azured wood." Two songs from *Love's Labour's Lost* must have contributed some of their color to the lines. The first, the "Cuckoo Song," begins thus:

> When daisies pied, and violets blue,
> And lady-smocks all silver white;
> And cuckoo-buds of yellow hue
> Do paint the meadows with delight. . . . (V, ii)

We cannot help pausing upon the lady-smocks, the cuckoo-buds, and line 16 of Housman's poem, which is *Lady-smocks a-bleaching lay*. Now the word *bleach* is not a common word with Housman; this is one of his two uses of it. How did it come to his mind and the poem? The answer may be found in the second stanza of the "Cuckoo Song," where we read *And maidens bleach their summer smocks*. It is Housman's use of the words *bleach* and *smocks* that irresistibly takes us back to Shakespeare's poem.[2] The latter word is probably to be read as a bit of characteristic punning—as Housman's *traveller's joy* in *LP* 40 means both the flower and the emotion.

The alliterations "lass and lad" and "lover and his lass" were worn smooth long before Shakespeare increased their circulation in such new mintings as "It was a lover and his lass" (*As You Like It*, V, iii) and "Buy, lads, or else your lasses cry" (*Winter's Tale*, IV, iii). The word *lad* is very common in Housman; he uses it ninety-four times as against three times for the word *boy*. *Ah, spring was sent for lass and lad* (*ASL*, V), *A country lover and his lass* (*ASL*, 26), *The lover and his lass* (*LP*, 7)—all have a familiar chime. So does *Of lovers' meeting* (*MP*, 6), which carries us back again to Feste's song in *Twelfth Night* (II, iii).

But when we come to *What golden lads are low* (*LP*, 2) and *golden friends I had* (*ASL* 54), we again perceive certainly an echo of Shakespearian phrasing, an echo from the lyric which Housman commended so warmly in his Leslie Stephen lecture, the Dirge from *Cymbeline* (IV, ii). Shakespeare's "golden lads and girls" may also have gone into the making of *that heart of gold* (*MP* 42) and *hearts of gold* (*ASL* 37). Definitely, we can see the carry-over of Shakespeare's lyric in "Fear the heat o' the sun no more,/Nor the snowing winter wild" (*ASL* 43). The two lines are very near the opening lines of the dirge, sung by Guiderius and Arviragus:

> Fear no more the heat o' the sun,
>   Nor the furious winter's rages;
> Thou thy worldly task hast done,
>   Home art gone, and ta'en thy wages:
> Golden lads and girls all must,
>   As chimney-sweepers, come to dust.
>
> Fear no more the frown o' the great;
>   Thou art past the tyrant's stroke;
> Care no more to clothe and eat;
>   To thee the reed is as the oak:
> The sceptre, learning, physic, must
> All follow this, and come to dust.

[140]

> Fear no more the lightning-flash,
>   Nor the all-dreaded thunder-stone;
> Fear not slander, censure rash;
>   Thou hast finish'd joy and moan:
> All lovers young, all lovers must
> Consign to thee, and come to dust.

The first three of the four stanzas of the Ode are worth their room in any analysis of Housman's poetry, for their sentiments and language—doubtless encountered in his early reading—must have become to him something like a mirror of life in the days of his adolescence when he pondered the triumph of death over all things earthly—one of the principal motifs of his poetry. The third *Shropshire Lad* poem he entered in his first notebook (p. 84, now *ASL* 46) "Bring, in this timeless grave . . . ," describes a burial; his second draft of it (A 116) carried the title, "A winter funeral." The lyric presents in its choice of flowers and garlands for the grave a studied antithesis to Arviragus' intended ever-blooming offerings for "Fidele": primroses, harebells, eglantine, and mosses. Housman brings nothing that will flower again, only flax and dried grasses: "No spray that ever buds in spring."

The fourth line of the Ode may have slipped into Housman's poetry in these lines:

> And early 'tis for turning home (*LP* 1)
>
> .   .   .   .
>
> Will lead one home to rest (*ASL* 7)
>
> .   .   .   .
>
> . . . pass hence and home (*ASL* 44)
>
> .   .   .   .
>
> And then dost call them home. (*MP* 47)

But the word *wages* means as much to Housman as *home* does. It joins with *dust* and the idea of death in two memorable lines: "Dust's your wages, son of sorrow" (*ASL* 44:15), "And took their wages and are dead" (*LP* 37). (It is surprising that so good a reader as Mr. Richard Wilbur should see in the latter line, from the renowned "Epitaph on an Army of Mercenaries," an echo from Romans 6:23: "The wages of sin is death." The word *sin* alone should have barred the door to this sinister connection.)[3] *Dust* in the meaning it carries in the Ode reappears in Housman's

Lie down in the bed of dust (*ASL* 43)

. . . .

But men may come to worse than dust (*ASL* 44)

. . . .

. . . truth returning/To dust and night. (*MP* 40)

So much for the effect the songs in Shakespeare's plays had on Housman's poetry. His poetic debt to their vast context he never acknowledged, but it cannot be imagined that the non-lyrical part of Shakespeare's plays contributed nothing to his moments of inspiration. To explore this suggestion would require a book in itself; I shall offer a few representative parallels to show from what varied corners and crannies of the great treasure-house Housman drew some of his words and phrases. First, even though it may clash with the mood of the foregoing quotations, there is Housman's prose sentence that deserves to be better known: "Stand on a barrel in the streets of Bagdad, and say in a loud voice, 'Twice two is four, and ginger is hot in the mouth, therefore Mohammed is the prophet of God,' and your logic will probably escape criticism; or, if anyone by chance should criticise it, you could easily silence him by calling him a Christian dog."[4] The flavor of this passage owes a part of its bite to Feste's "Ginger shall be hot in the mouth" from *Twelfth Night* II, 3.

Ophelia's "Pale as his shirt (*Hamlet* II, 1) is in *as white's their shirt* (*ASL* 63:73). The phrase "bringing home/of bell and burial" (*Hamlet* V:1) may be echoed in *Shoulder-high we bring you home,* (*ASL* 19). From "deeper than e'er plummet sounded" (*The Tempest* III: 3) may come *past the plunge of plummet/In seas I cannot sound* (*ASL* 14). "When well-apparelled April on the heel/Of limping winter treads" (*Romeo and Juliet* I:2) must have been in Housman's mind as he wrote, in his translation of an Ode by Horace, *hard on the heel of spring/Treads summer sure to die* (*MP* 5). Falstaff's gibe at his soldiers, "food for powder, food for powder," (*King Henry IV*, Part 1, IV:2) sounds in Housman's *"food for powder/Soldiers marching, all to die"* (*ASL* 35). Iago's "Hell and night" at the end of the first scene of *Othello*, Act II, is echoed in *night and hell* (*MP* 19). It is probable that Shakespeare's *fust* (*Hamlet* IV, 4) is behind Housman's use of the word in *And here fust we and moulder* (*MP* 33); also that *fret* in "fretted with golden fire" (*Hamlet* II:2) gave Housman its meaning (quite apart from *snowflakes*) in the opening line of *MP* 25: *Yon flakes that fret the eastern sky*: and it is undeniable that "The . . . remorseful day" (*King Henry VI, Part 2,* IV, 1) got into the last line of *MP* 16: *Falls the remorseful day.* Finally, Thersites' "his wit in his belly and his guts in his head" (*"Troilus and Cressida* II, 1) is echoed in *AP* 17: *flint in the bosom and guts in the head.*

II *The Sonnets*

But the strongest appeal in Shakespeare is still to be examined: the sonnets, "the most autobiographical ever written,"[5] where Housman could not fail to read, in and between the lines—so obscure to many before and since—the clear story of a predicament so like his own: the poet's anxious love of a man, the paragon of manly virtues, to whom all of his affections and desires were irresistibly drawn. Housman perceived in the poems a sensibility as acute as his own; a mind, like his, at variance with itself; passions seeking outlets he himself had been all too familiar with in his latter Oxford days. The innermost chords of his being must have been stirred by Shakespeare's declaration of his unworthiness, his abnegation of any and all claims on his friend, his despair at long stretches of absence, his assumption of all guilt in their alliance. How burningly such passages as these must have touched Housman's mind as he read or recalled the sonnets during his purgatorial period in London, when most of his poetry was written:

> Weary with toil, I haste me to my bed,
> The dear repose for limbs with travel tired;
> But then begins a journey in my head
> To work my mind when body's work's expired.
> For then my thoughts, from far where I abide,
> Intend a zealous pilgrimage to thee. . . . (Sonnet 27)

'Tis not enough that through the cloud thou break,
To dry the rain on my storm-beaten face,
For no man well of such a salve can speak
That heals the wound and cures not the disgrace:
Nor can thy shame give physic to my grief;
Though thou repent, yet I have still the loss.
The offender's sorrow lends but weak relief
To him that bears the strong offense's cross. (Sonnet 34)

How like a winter hath my absence been
From thee, the pleasure of the fleeting year!
What freezings have I felt, what dark days seen!
What old December's bareness everywhere! (Sonnet 97)

O, never say that I was false of heart,
Though absence seemed my flame to qualify!
As easy might I from myself depart
As from my soul, which in thy breast doth lie.
That is my home of love. . . . (Sonnet 109)

A. E. Housman was a Victorian, not an Elizabethan, and he never addressed Moses Jackson in terms as unequivocal as Shakespeare's. Yet the essence of one of the main themes of the sonnets sounds forth from Housman's "Because I liked you better." I quote from the penciled draft (p. 207 of the first notebook), where the two-stanza poem was written; it is much more explicit than the printed text of the four stanzas of *More Poems* 31:

Because I liked you better
    Than friends in liking may,
It irked you and I promised
    I'd cast the thought away.

And now the headstone naming
    The heart no longer stirred
Will say the lad that loved you
    Was one that kept his word.

This exposition of one of the dominating themes of the sonnets —Time's conquest over friendship and love—is essayed frequently by Housman, again in "Smooth between sea and land" (*MP* 45) and "Stone, steel, dominions pass" (*MP* 24), and with recognizable Shakespearian overtones in *ASL* 57 (the earliest surviving draft):

> You smile today, you hearken now,
>   So sighs and griefs are over;
> You give again the lover's vow,
>   And happy is the lover.
>
> 'Tis late to hearken, late to smile,
>   But better late than never:
> I shall have lived a little while
>   Before I die forever.

The theme of the ravage of time is balanced in the sonnets by Shakespeare's proud declaration that a final victory will be his: he will defeat time and ensure his friend's immortality by enshrining him in poetry that will last forever. Housman knew the lover's anguished hatred of death, the despairing recognition that nothing can save the loved one from the supreme indignity. In *ASL* 33 (A 148, first draft) he is at the nadir of powerlessness as he contemplates the end: all he can do is to declare again his love and ask for kindness:

> If truth in hearts that perish
>   Could touch the powers on high,
> I think the love I bear you
>   Should make you not to die.
>
> .   .   .   .   .   .
>
> Vain care and endless longing
>   And fruitless hope to please,
> Oh, you should live for ever
>   If there were help in these.
>
> But now that all is idle,
>   To this lost heart be kind,
> Ere to a town you journey
>   Where friends are ill to find.

But another day brought another mood. Housman's self-confidence was as great in its own way as Shakespeare's ever was, and once he threw down the gauntlet to the enemy in terms like those we so often find in the sonnets. The poem was written to a youthful suicide,[6] a person Housman never knew. He com-

mends the act of self-destruction and ends his seven-stanza poem
with this prophecy:

> Turn safe to rest, no dreams, no waking;
>   And here, man, here's the wreath I've made:
> 'Tis not a gift that's worth the taking,
>   But wear it and it will not fade. (*ASL* 44)

So much for anonymity: Housman's lyric has endowed the unknown dead with everlastingness. But that flight was not attempted again, never at his heart's supreme behest. Fancy had
its limitations beyond which even love could not rise. His re-
morseless honesty to himself would not allow him the comfort
of dallying with the surmise that he would confer immortality
on Moses Jackson by engrafting him new. No wonder Housman
said of his poetry that the satisfaction it gave him was something
like—no more than—a mattress between him and the hard
ground.

Perhaps the chief effect of the sonnets on Housman was that
they encouraged him to entrust his experiences to poetry, to
reach for the relief from spiritual stress that such writing often
brings. What other relief offered itself to him? He must have
sensed the benefice, the victory that Shakespeare, despite his
prevailing pessimism, earned for himself in the reiteration that
his lines, which he believed to be immortal, would endow his
friend with everlastingness. Here was pride indomitable; here
was certainty. It was good to study the details of another man's
success, won on a hard-fought field and under conditions not
unlike his own. What more natural that, when A. E. Housman
unlocked his heart, Shakespeare's sonnet story, already a part of
it, left its traces in *A Shropshire Lad* and the later poetry?

III *Heine*

Heine's influence on Housman was deep and long-lasting because of the commonality in their natures of certain emotional
attitudes and points of view. Many details of Heine's temperament—his reactions to homesickness and a feeling of estrangement from his family, an extreme devotion to his mother, a
hounding sense of fated affliction—must have struck Housman's
imagination as keenly as if he were reviewing memories of his

own. Heine's poetry exhibits many varying strains, from the moving love poems of the 1820's to the Job-like lamentations of his last anguished years. They were the two voices of his protest against the laws of God and man, uttered in lyrics of matchless charm and power. They both aroused and consoled the spiritual rebel in Housman; and, as he once penciled opposite a particularly self-revealing passage in T. E. Lawrence's *Seven Pillars of Wisdom* the note "This is me,"[7] so he might have inscribed many a page of the *Buch der Lieder* and the *Vermischte Gedichte*.

The way to an understanding of Heine's poetry lies at the end of a study of his divided personality. For his was indeed a nature at war with itself: Jew against Christian, Greek against barbarian, artist against philistine. Heine was all of these by turn and, throughout his life, never one completely; for his life was a series of ascendencies and revolutions in which the antagonistic elements alternately exploited and exhausted each other. This conflict influenced the picture of the human cockpit as he saw it; his microcosm was a model of the universal plan. Thus he comments on the visions of his famous dream-poem:

> O, dieser Streit wird enden nimmermehr,
> Stets wird die Wahrheit hadern mit dem Schönen,
> Stets wird geschieden sein der Menschheit Heer
> In zwei Partein: Barbaren und Hellenen.
>
> —"Für die Mouche," *Liebeslieder*, 75

> (O never will this conflict end,
> Forever will truth quarrel with the beautiful,
> Forever will the human race divided be
> In two factions: barbarians and Hellenes.)

Out of this civil war of the spirit also came Heine's sense of irony, his bent toward paradox and antithesis, his contempt for simple natures (except where his heart was concerned), his pessimism, and his mordant wit. Housman had these same elements in his blood; he was to describe these same conflicts in the soul of his Shropshire Lad, for example:

> Here the truceless armies yet
> Trample, rolled in blood and sweat;
> They kill and kill and never die;
> And I think that each is I. (*ASL* 28)

Other lines from this same poem—particularly "They cease not fighting, east and west,/On the marches of my breast"—bear an impressive resemblance to these lines from Heine's *Nachtgedanken,* in which the exile thinks of his fatherland and of those who have died there: "Mir ist, als wälzten sich die Leichen/Auf meine Brust—! (*Zeitgedichte* 24). It is as if the corpses were thronging over my breast!"

Die Heimkehr 22 illustrates Heine's tendency to conduct a kind of dialogue with himself or to describe his emotion as if it were moving in a second self:

> Still ist die Nacht, es ruhen die Gassen,
> In diesem Hause wohnte mein Schatz;
> Sie hat schon längst die Stadt verlassen,
> Doch steht noch das Haus auf demselben Platz.

> Da steht auch ein Mensch und starrt in die Höhe,
> Und ringt die Hände vor Schmerzensgewalt;
> Mir graust es, wenn ich sein Antlitz sehe—
> Der Mond zeigt mir meine eigne Gestalt.

> (Quiet is the night, the streets are noiseless,
> In this house once dwelt my sweetheart;
> Long ago she departed from this city,
> But the house stands there yet on the selfsame place.

> A man stands there too and looks toward heaven,
> And wrings his hands, overpowered with grief;
> I shudder when I see his face—
> For the moon shows me my own self there.)

The third, and last, stanza is addressed to the poet's ghost and double. Housman's early habit of introspection might have been confirmed to some extent and turned into Heine's divisive trick by the time he began writing his serious poetry. Housman and his double appear together often in the two books he published, as well as in his posthumous verse. In *ASL* 9, he is both the watcher by the gallows and the imprisoned culprit lying in jail; in *ASL* 20, he is the lad gazing into the pool and also his own image; in *ASL* 41, the Shropshire exile amid London's unfriendliness contrasts himself now with his happier past self; the same debate is staged in *ASL* 51, where he is at once the statue in the gallery and the sad loiterer it addresses. In *ASL* 56, he is both the coward and the courageous soldier going together into the fire of the guns; in *LP* 35, he is the money-scant youngster at the fair and the man grown wiser and sadder; in *MP* 1, he is thinking of Easter and the Resurrection both as a non-communicant and as a communicant; in *MP* 16, he is not only the stronghearted maker of the vow but also its faithless abjuror. Many other examples could be cited.

So Housman joins hands with Heine in this objectifying of an alter ego, and this practice may indicate a common cause for their pessimism, born from a sense of disunity and unsettledness that arose from such vain questioning of the unseen governors of human destiny as in the German poet's "Zum Lazarus" I:

> Woran liegt die Schuld? Ist etwa
> Unser Herr nicht ganz allmächtig?
> Oder treibt er selbst den Unfug?
> Ach, das wäre niederträchtig.
>
> Also fragen wir beständig,
> Bis man uns mit einer Handvoll
> Erde endlich stopft die Mäuler—
> Aber ist das eine Antwort?
>> "Zum Lazarus," I; *Vermischte Gedichte,* 58

> (Where, then, lies the blame? Can it be
> Our Lord is not quite almighty?
> Or does he the wrong himself?
> Ah, how underhanded that would be.
>
> So we ask unceasingly,
> Until with a handful of dirt
> They stop our gab at last—
> But is that an answer?)

Perhaps one verse from these was echoed in "The lad that hopes for heaven/Shall fill his mouth with mould" (*MP* 22).

Housman would not have rejected the extreme of Heine's pessimism, expressed in such lines as

> Der Tod is gut, doch besser wär's,
> Die Mutter hätt' uns nie geboren.
>> "Ruhelechzend," *Vermischte Gedichte,* 60

> (Death is good, better still our fate
> If our mothers ne'er had borne us.)

and in

> Gut ist der Schlaf, der Tod ist besser—freilich
> Das beste wäre, nie geboren sein.
>
> "Morphine," Vermischte Gedichte, 59

> (Sleep is good, death better—in sooth,
> Not to have been born is best.)

It may be recalled that the lyric which Housman translated from Sophocles' *Oedipus at Colonus* (ll. 1211-48) expresses a conviction similar to Heine's—and the idea appears also in the forty-eighth lyric of *A Shropshire Lad*:

> Then it was well with me, in days ere I was born. (l. 8)
> . . . .
> Oh why did I awake? when shall I sleep again? (l. 16)

The romantic outbursts which overflow Heine's *Junge Leiden* and his other early volumes must have left a definite imprint on Housman's mind, although his early maturity, we may believe, enabled him to view with some detachment Heine's parade of mournful lovers. Still, many of the German poet's favorite themes and not a few of his passionate excesses can be paralleled in Housman's poems: farewells to untrue love, fratricides, lovers returned from the grave, youthful criminals and suicides. Heine's reiterations on the theme of the transitoriness of human affection, couched in his favorite four-line stanza, would have deepened Housman's flair for the ballad and the ballad stanza. Such lines as these must have become a part of his settled thought:

> Schattenküsse, Schattenliebe,
> Schattenleben, wunderbar!
> Glaubst du, Närrin, alles bleibe
> Unverändert, ewig wahr?

> Was wir lieblich fest besessen,
> Schwindet hin, wie Träumerein;
> Und die Herzen, die vergessen,
> Und die Augen schlafen ein.
>
> "Seraphine," Verschiedene, 9

(Spirit-kisses, spirit-love,
Spirit-living, oh how fine!
    Think you, fool, that all endures
    Never altered, always real?

The loveliness we held securely
Vanishes like dreams away.
    And our hearts will lose the memory,
    And our eyes be shut in sleep.)

Ach, es wird so kalt und dunkel!
Um die Sonne flattern Raben,
Und sie krächzen. Lust und Liebe
Ist auf lange jetzt begraben.
                    "Hortense," *Verschiedene,* 5

(Ah, it grows so cold and dark,
Across the sun the ravens flutter
And caw. Joy and love
Have long been buried.)

And these lines would seem to have become a part of Housman's
poetry:
                    alles rollt vorbei,—
        Das Geld und die Welt und die Zeiten,
        Und Glauben und Lieb' und Treu'.
                    Die Heimkehr, 38

                    (everything passes away—
        Wealth and the world and the season,
        And faith and love and loyalty.)

Compare:

        Stone, steel, dominions pass,
            Faith too, no wonder. *MP* 24

Also:

        Deutsche Treue, deutsche Hemde,
        Die verschleisst man in der Fremde.
                "Lazarus," *Lamentationen,* 4

(German loyalty, German shirts,
Become spoiled away from home.)

Compare:

        Homespun collars, homespun hearts,
        Wear to rags in foreign parts. *MP* 24

Heine habitually set tag-poems at the head of his separate volumes; Housman did this only for his second volume, *Last Poems*. We do not know whether he selected the prologue piece that Laurence placed at the head of *More Poems*, but it serves its purpose well: (I use the earliest notebook version of the first stanza, D 26):

> They say my verse is sad: no wonder.
>   For he that spells it scans
> Tears of eternity, and sorrow
>   Not mine, but man's.

This passage may be a distant echo of Heine's famous quatrain:

> Meine Qual und meine Klagen
> Hab' ich in dies Buch gegossen,
> Und wenn du es aufgeschlagen,
> Hat sich dir mein Herz erschlossen.
> > *Vermischte Gedichte*, 22

> (My pain and my lament
> Have I poured into this book,
> And when you open it,
> My heart unlocks itself to you.)

Rhetorically the first two lines of the fifty-first double quatrain of the *Lyrisches Intermezzo* (repeated in the second stanza) are nearer Housman's poem:

> Vergiftet sind meine Lieder;—
> Wie könnt' es anders sein?
> (Poisoned are my songs;
> How could they be otherwise?)

Speaking of these details, I may mention here that it is not improbable that Housman's title *Last Poems* was borrowed from Heine's *Letzte Gedichte*—a title found in some editions of his poetry. The name of one of Housman's few entitled poems, "God's Acre" (*AP* 11), may be another echo from Heine; and it has already been pointed out that the first two stanzas of "Sinner's Rue" (*LP* 30) had their origin in Heine's sixty-second poem in the *Lyrisches Intermezzo*, which opens thus:

Am Kreuzweg wird begraben,
Wer selber sich brachte um;
Dort wächst eine blaue Blume,
Die Armesünderblum'.

Am Kreuzweg stand ich und seufzte;
Die Nacht war kalt und stumm.
Im Mondschein bewegte sich langsam
Die Armesünderblum'.

(At the cross-road is buried
Whoever takes his own life;
There grows a blue flower,
The Poor Sinner's Flower.)

(At the cross-road I stood and sighed;
The night was cold and silent.
In the moonlight stirred gently
The Poor Sinner's Flower.)

Compare the opening stanzas of Housman's lyric in the earliest foolscap draft:

I walked alone and thinking,
When faint the nightwind blew
And plucked on mounds at crossways
The flower of sinner's rue.

Where the roads meet they bury
Him that his own hand slays,
And so the flower of azure
Springs at the four cross ways.

It may be that Housman's "son of sorrow" (*ASL* 44) is carried over from Heine's "Sohn des Unglucks" ("Der Mohrenkonig," *Romanzero*); and the striking phrase "his finery of fire," describing the infernal sentinel in line 40 of "Hell Gate" (*LP* 31), may owe something to Heine's "Feuerlivrei" ("Traumbilder," *Junge Leiden* 7).

Once these echoes are sounded, others declare themselves:

Es bleiben todt die Todten,
Und nur der Lebendige lebt.
            "Die Ilse," *Aus der Harzreise*

(The dead remain dead,
And only the living live.)

Compare:

The living are the living
And dead the dead will stay. *LP* 19

On a similar theme are these lines:

Ich lebe und bin noch stärker,
Als alle Todten sind!

Die Heimkehr, 21

(I am living and am still stronger
Than all the dead.)

Compare again:

A lad that lives and has his will
Is worth a dozen dead. *ASL* 25

Heine's third poem in his "Nachlese" (*Vermischte Gedichte*, 21)
may have left its influence on two or three of Housman's lyrics:

Ich will mich im grünen Wald ergehn
Wo Blumen spriessen und Vögel singen;
Denn wenn ich im Grabe einst liegen werde,
Ist Aug' und Ohr bedeckt mit Erde,
Die Blumen kann ich nicht spriessen sehn,
Und Vögelgesänge hör' ich nicht klingen.

(I will go into the greening wood
Where flowers are opening and birds are singing;
For when one day I shall lie in the grave,
My eye and ear will be covered with earth,
I shall not see the opening flowers,
And the ringing bird songs I shall not hear.)

These verses bring to mind the tone and some of the phrases of
the ninth lyric of *More Poems: When green buds hang in the elm
like dust/. . . Forth I wander, forth I must,/And drink of life
again.* Perhaps the last two quatrains of *ASL* 2 are even more
apposite:

And since of threescore years and ten,
Twenty will not come again,
And yet, of all the springs in store,
I shall see but fifty more.

[*154*]

> And since to look at things in bloom
> Fifty springs are little room,
> About the woodlands I will go
> To see the cherry hung with snow. (B 34)

Here the idea of mortality is softened, but Housman was capable of Heine's bluntness, as for example in *After earth has stopped the ears* (*ASL* 19), which sounds like an echo of *Ist Aug' und Ohr bedeckt mit Erde*. The same macabre note is struck in Terence's adjuration to the revenant: *Stay with the dead, man; stop your ears* (*Manuscript Poems of A. E. Housman*, p. 55).

IV *Lucretius*

Housman's liens with the Latin poet Lucretius are a part of his long connection with things astronomical, which began in his childhood and culminated in his greatest scholarly achievement, the editing of the *Astronomica* of Marcus Manilius, a labor of nearly thirty years. Turning away from his beloved Propertius,[8] the delight of his Oxford days, must have been something of an act of penance for Housman, who was poles apart from the stoical credo of Manilius and his belief in "heavenly reason" as the governor of the universe. Housman, who carped at the tediousness of the Latin poet, declared that the best parts of his five-volume didactic poem were those in which the author was solving problems in elementary arithmetic. It is likely that, when he began, Housman had no intention of editing the complete *Astronomica*,[9] but, after Book I appeared in 1903, pride kept him at his self-appointed task until it was finished.

Lucretius shared Manilius' breadth of vision, but from his roof-top to the flaming ramparts of the world he beheld nothing but space and the ceaseless tides of matter aggregating and dissolving by the whim of chance through endless time. Before Alfred's Oxford days his imagination must have been quickened by the splendid descriptions he found in Lucretius of the celestial worlds. No less would he have been moved by the poet's exploration of the endlessly fascinating earth, doomed to sure and imminent destruction. Many of Housman's poems are tinged with Lucretian turns of thought and language. His allusions to the human person, considered metaphorically or otherwise, commonly are placed against a terrestrial or cosmological field. Thus the earth has taken his dead friend to her lap (*AP* 8); Dick now "wears the turning globe" (*LP* 20); for another, the sea is his "everlasting tent" (*MP* 41); another comrade was "braver than the heavens are high" (*AP* 6). The lyric "Astronomy" (*LP* 17) describes the poet's dead brother on his passage to Africa as heaving the Southern Cross to the heavens and sinking the polestar underground. The heart and soul of the despairing poet are sunken "sea-deep, till doomsday morning" (*ASL* 14); the unfortunate finds no comfort in the fact that, as he dies, the "stars of heaven are steady" and the "founded hills remain" (*MP* 21); the intending suicide warns that at his death the sky will fall and "earth's foundations will depart" (*MP* 26); the "immortal part" of man, the "eternal seed"—his bones—will last as long as earth (*ASL* 43). It is only the "feather pate of folly" that "bears the falling sky" and "spins the heavy world around" (*ASL* 49).

Housman would have needed no teacher to point out two of Lucretius' most effective stylistic traits: his fondness for alliteration and compound words—features often encountered in Housman's poetry from his very earliest to his last. Certainly, in their use of ingenious compounds, both poets have left their marks on their respective languages; and the reader of Housman pauses upon such terms as *serpent-circled, far-beholding,* and *light-leaved* with as much appreciation as on the older poet's *anguimanus, omnituentes,* and *levisomna.* Lucretius' taste for compounds is usually taken as archaistic; in this tendency, as in others, he harks back to Ennius and Aratus. This sense of the past would merge with Housman's affection for the Bible, the English Ballads, and the songs of Shakespeare. Housman's language, as I have shown, is replete with old-fashioned turns of language, and his notebook drafts show many more archaisms than he allowed to survive in print.

Housman had little respect for those who attempt to improve the human race, but he must have applauded many of the tenets of the *De rerum natura* devoted to the correction of the errors of mankind. His poetry, correspondence, and recorded conversations frequently show accord with the Lucretian views about the mortality of the soul, the indifference of the gods and nature to mankind, the frailty and corruptibility of all things, distrust of love between the sexes, and contempt for women generally. For

Housman, perhaps the strongest attraction of the Latin poem lay in the sense of personal disaster that overcasts it like a cloud, an invincible sadness that had entered and overcome the author and had driven him, some said, to his death. After his disastrous experience at Oxford, Housman would have viewed in a new and intense light the dedication of the poem to Memmius. The idea of a poet addressing himself so generously and unreservedly to an admired, aggressive friend, a man of action, would have been entirely congenial to Housman during the late 1880's, when, with the figure of Moses Jackson in mind—an absent but a still-worshipped idol—he was writing the poems that were to compose his *Shropshire Lad* and in which he expressed his soul-sickness, his betrayal by the gods he had trusted, the insecurity of all physical and spiritual defenses.

Both writers also prefer the pleasures of the country: the rural landscape, though disenchanted, is the place for ideal companionship. With Housman, this choice was literary rather than empirical, for we have seen that he had little or no workaday experience in country living. And it may be that the strong pastoral strain in his poetry owes something of its persistence and some of its trappings to Lucretius, particularly his fine passage beginning with 5.1392: *saepe itaque inter se prostrati in gramine molli.* . . . (and so often, lying in friendly groups on the soft grass).[10] The idyllic crowd gathered there, amusing themselves with dance and song, may have lent some of their music to "Fancy's Knell," the closing lyric of *Last Poems.* Here Housman's keen nostalgic note resembles that of the Roman poet: each foresees the end of an era in his summoning up scenes of earlier happier days, scenes that soon will be—if they have not already been—replaced by others of a different kind. The revels of Lucretius were drowned out by the flood of war (5.1435). As for Housman, tomorrow he and his song go their respective ways to oblivion.

If Housman follows Lucretius in his preference for the countryside and simple pleasures, he is no less in agreement with the philosopher's warning that pleasure anywhere is fleeting. Both poets are haunted by the apprehension of a radical fault in the universe, which was flawed in the making and will never be a fit habitation for man because not made for him. The *tanta culpa* of 5.199 bulks large in Housman's poetry: he curses "whatever

brute and blackguard made the world" (*LP* 9); laments that all
the toil of nature "helps not the primal fault" (*MP* 7); cries in
More Poems 19 his contempts for the maker of the world (for
him become hell), declaring no such infamy ever soiled his
hands.

These lines express the extreme of his revolt against the creator, or creators, of the universe. The laws of the gods and those
of man, are again condemned in *Last Poems* 12, which, read as
the outburst of a youthful Epicurean, "a stranger and afraid,"
sounds the age-old protest against the oppressors who plague
him with threats of "jail and gallows and hell-fire." But his conclusion here, as elsewhere, is that the taskmasters are too strong;
there is no escape to another universe; hard necessity must be
accepted.

Another expression of Housman's dissent arises from his strong
distrust of life viewed in contrast with the calm that preceded
it. This is of course but another fallacy, implying knowledge and
sensation where there was no union of body and soul to provide
them. But it is a respectable fallacy, exploited by Lucretius in
one of his finest passages (3.972-5):

> respice item quam nil ad nos anteacta vetustas
> temporis aeterni fuerit, quam nascimur ante.
> hoc igitur speculum nobis natura futuri
> temporis exponit post mortem denique nostram.

> (Look back again to see how the past ages of
> everlasting time, before we are born, have been
> as nought to us. These then nature holds up to
> us as a mirror of the time that is to come, when
> we are dead and gone.)

The Roman poet argues from the repose of preëxistence to the
repose of death; similarly, Housman in his forty-eighth poem of
A Shropshire Lad colloquizes with his soul on their present unrest, contrasted with their past and future states. The days of
rest were long:

> Men loved injustice then, but shapeless
>   in the quarry
> I slept and saw not; tears fell down, I
>   did not mourn;

> Sweat ran and blood sprang out and I was
>   never sorry:
> Then it was well with me, in days ere
>   I was born. (A 146)

Housman's view of the past closely parallels that of Lucretius: for both, the past was an age of violence; and each rejoices he has not lived in such an age. The next, and final, stanza of *ASL* 48 repeats another of Housman's familiar themes: "high heaven and earth ail from the prime foundation." This stanza, and the one just quoted, should be read in the light of the older poet's contention (5.195 ff.) against the idea of the creation of the earth by gods: *tanta stat praedita culpa*. The list of faults is a long and impressive one, and man is unique among earth's creatures in that he suffers most from her obduracy and caprices. Housman's lyric ends true to his argument: "Oh why did I awake? when shall I sleep again?"

Lucretius saw the earth and its other companions of the universe as the products of blind chance. The earth was aging and soon its roof and foundations would be overthrown:

> sic igitur magni quoque circum moenia mundi
> expugnata dabunt labem putris <que> ruinas. (2.1144-45)

> (Thus then even the walls of the wide world all
> round will be stormed and fall into decay and
> crumbling ruin.)

In the meantime, what supports the great vault of heaven? Housman replies (*AP* 15) that it is the perdurable heart of man, all other supports having been found too weak to bear the strain. *More Poems* 43 is a Lucretian treatise in parvo read against the concluding seventy lines of the second book of Lucretius, where he had declared:

> quam tibi iam nemo, fessus satiate videndi,
> suspicere in caeli dignatur lucida templa!
> (2.1038-39)

> (Yet think how no one now, wearied with satiety
> of seeing, deigns to gaze up at the shining
> quarters of the sky!)

But Housman is one of the few lonely observers; he wakes and looks at the "fields of night" (I quote from his first draft of *More Poems* 43, on A 113);

> Each in its steadfast station
> Embracing heaven they flare;
> They crowd with conflagration
> The empty gulfs of air. St. 2

Here he follows Lucretius' use of *in statione* (4.388, 396; 5.518; 6.193), and the equally frequent expressions meaning "fields of night" (last line of stanza one). Housman's poem concludes

> The signal-fires of warning
> I breathlessly regard
> As [drunk?] from eve to morning
> The world runs ruinward. St. 3

The ominous mood of this stanza is heightened by a fourth, originally intended to form the conclusion of the poem:

> What world-appalling message
> Illegible and high
> Is yon that [showeth?] presage
> The gazer of the sky?

The message is the same as the warning conveyed in the powerful lines of 5.91-109, in which Lucretius, speaking with more than his usual earnestness and clarity—face to face with Memmius, as it were—describes the coming destruction of the universe: *exitium caeli terraeque futurum* (the destruction of heaven and earth that is to be).

Again, with perhaps a fuller sense of detachment, Housman is contemplating this end when in *Last Poems* 29 he calls upon the dead fighter not to awaken—not even at the summons of thunder and earthquake presaging the end of all. Writing these lines, he may have had in mind the great passage—great for its mingling of terror and consolation—that expresses the indifference of the dead to the ruin of the earth's frame:

> ubi non erimus, cum corporis atque animai
> discidium fuerit quibus e sumus uniter apti,
> scilicet haud nobis quicquam, qui non erimus tum,
> accidere omnino poterit sensumque movere,
> non si terra mari miscebitur et mare caelo. (3.838-42)

> (when we shall be no more, when there shall
> have come the parting of body and soul, by whose
> union we are made one, you may know that nothing
> at all will be able to happen to us, who then will
> be no more, or stir our feeling; no, not if earth
> shall be mingled with sea, and sea with sky.)

Finally, Housman speaks, the more eloquently without praise, of the army of "mercenaries" who fought when all was lost and, dying, turned a name of contempt into a synonym for glory. To paraphrase his poem, *LP* 37: They bore up the falling sky on their shoulders and stayed the fall of earth's foundations; they stood fast and saved the sum of things when all seemed lost. The last line repeats one of Lucretius' oftenest-used phrases: *summa rerum*. This poem is one of Housman's most impressive statements: he never exceeded the compacted power of its eight calm lines; and the important thing is that, when he was palming infinity, he turned to the well-known idioms of Lucretius: the familiar allusions to the cosmological scenery against which men play their parts, or attempt to escape them.

In 1.716 ff., when Lucretius praises the Sicilian philosopher Empedocles, he declares that of all the marvels of the island he is the foremost, and that his poetry would seem to set him above those of mortal birth. Empedocles probably came into Housman's ken by way of Matthew Arnold's poem, which he read in his late teens at Oxford. "His favorite English poet in those early days," writes his former roommate A. W. Pollard, "was Matthew Arnold, whose 'Empedocles on Etna' he recommended to me as containing 'all the law and the prophets.' "[11] Housman may have forgotten Lucretius' refutation of the theories of Empedocles regarding the composition of matter, but a figure employed in the same passage to describe the Sicilian thinker and others like him was of a kind poets remember:

> ex adyto tamquam cordis responsa dedere
> sanctius et multo certa ratione magis quam
> Pythia quae tripodi a Phoebi lauroque
>   profatur . . . (1.737-39).

> (and gave answers as from the shrine of
> their hearts in more holy wise and with reasoning
> far more sure than the Pythian priestess who speaks
> out from the tripod and laurel of Phoebus.)

It can hardly be doubted that Housman had in mind the full twenty-five line passage, and particularly the lines just quoted, when he composed "The Oracles" (*LP* 25). One way to an understanding of the context of the poem in the thought of Housman is to read it as spoken by a newly converted Memmius. The first stanza announces that the oracles of Dodona and Delphi are dead: Zeus and Apollo no longer deceive men with their untruths. Second stanza: If I want to know my fate, I ask the true priestess, my own heart, which replies inspired by reason. She tells me that she and I shall die forever. Third stanza: Since I have accepted the fact of the soul's mortality, I am less disturbed than you, oh priestess, for your saying has been heard and accepted by many before me. Fourth stanza: It was heard by the Spartans at Thermopylae, facing the Persian's unnumbered hosts; and, knowing there was no retreat, they "on the sea-wet rock sat down and combed their hair." The verbal analogy, which is very close, comes in the second stanza: It was to the shrine that always speaks and always speaks the truth— "the heart within"—that Housman took his question. The revolt of reason against fear and superstition is also the subject of *Last Poems* 3: the queen of darkness, Hecate, is overthrown by her disillusioned slayer, who will die tomorrow but no longer a slave.

A few of Housman's poems that, like some of those just cited, deal with intimate personal association have been reserved for final analysis. Some have to do with the meeting or parting of friends, for example number 32 of *A Shropshire Lad*, which can be understood only in terms of Lucretius' atomistic theory. Here are two mortals for a moment face to face. The poet says:

> From far, from eve and morning
> And yon twelve-winded sky,
> The stuff of life to knit me
> Blew hither: here am I.

The bonds of life are firm and good, the *concilium* that gives him being is unbroken. He knows that his body, however, is fated to sustain some day the blow from without or the internal malady that will dissolve and disperse it and his soul like smoke on the winds. So, he continues, let us vow friendship and not delay: "Take my hand quick and tell me,/What have you in your heart." The reply, if it is to be heard, must be given soon before the *discidium* breaks and silences all, and the speaker's corporeal and spiritual parts rejoin the unending atomic flow:

> Speak now, and I will answer;
> How shall I help you, say;
> Ere to the wind's twelve quarters
> I take my endless way.

Lucretius describes figuratively this assault on the *anima* (1.414-15). He fears that before he can explain his atomic theory to Memmius "per membra senectus/serpat et in nobis vitai claustra resolvat . . ." (sluggish age may creep over our limbs and loosen within us the fastenings of life). This trope of the bonds or fastenings of life, repeated in 3.808-9, may have had something to do with Housman's

> . . . fleet the red blood races[12]
> Along the soldier's veins.

> At all the gates it hammers
> And to heaven [sends a?] shout,
> And shakes the bolts and clamours,
> "Ho, jailer, let me out."

An appeal similar to that of *ASL* 32 is made in the opening lyric of *Last Poems*, "The West." The title names the vast deep of atomic substance, from which, he says, we were taken and in which we shall drown. The poet entreats his comrade not to send his thoughts onward into this immensity that holds for every man a mortal attraction. The body will return all too soon. Let us forget the land of our beginning and its claim on us, for friendship ends when the breath leaves the body. Writing this poem and *ASL* 32, Housman must have had in mind many passages from the middle of Book 3 of *De Rerum Natura* describing the separation of the soul and body:

> et nebula ac fumus quoniam discedit in
>   auras,
> crede animam quoque diffundi multoque
>   perire
> ocius et citius dissolvi <in> corpora prima,
> cum semel ex hominis membris ablata
>   recessit. (3.436-39)

quid dubitas tandem quin extra prodita
  corpus
imbecilla foras in aperto, tegmine dempto,
non modo non omnem possit durare per
  aevum
sed minimum quodvis nequeat consistere
  tempus? (3.603-6)

(and since cloud and smoke part asunder
into air, you must believe that the soul too
is scattered and passes away far more swiftly,
and is dissolved more quickly into its first-
bodies, when once it is withdrawn from a man's
limbs, and has departed.

Why do you doubt after all this that the
soul, if driven outside the body, frail as it
is, without in the open air, robbed of its
shelter, would not only be unable to last on
through all time, but could not hold together
even for a moment?)

The unending cycle of atomic dissolution and recombination—
the "endless way"—of *ASL* 32 is "the endless road" of *ASL* 60. "In
all the endless road you tread/There's nothing but the night." But
the perfect and desired cure for life is oblivion. There is no doubt
that Housman's intimate beliefs were rooted in such concepts as
those in the lines just quoted from Lucretius. We must not be
misled by his many allusions to Christian tenets since they eventually lapsed into little more than a manner of speaking. These
references and echoes correspond to the counterpart he elected
to act out in real life. "He conformed . . . in the outward observ-
ances of religion," Laurence Housman remarks in his memoir,
"approving of the Church of England as an institution, while
having no faith in its tenets."[13]

The clash of this prevalent biblical strain in Housman's poetry,
alternating as it does with his irreverent—not to say impious—
protests against the "iniquity on high," inevitably produces for
the average reader its embarrassing moments. These were not
unintentional. The three stanzas Housman composed under the
title "For my funeral" are, it has been pointed out, a masterpiece
of pseudo-piety. It seems strange indeed, at this distance, that

those who first read the poem and put it to its use failed to see, or could pretend not to see, that it is as pagan as Lucretius' invocation to Venus. There was just enough seeming-sanctity in such phrases as *thy mansion, thy children, tribes and nations* and in the archaic forms *dost, madest,* and *wilt* to lull both the ministrants and the laity into unthinking acceptance of the poem. It was his final sarcastic jest with God and man, and with supreme confidence he sharpened its point by a note warning that the printers would make an error in the Order of Service (they did) and by writing after his final stanza, "And then, unless forcibly restrained, the choir will sing"—concluding with the four lines of the Gloria.

In assembling *More Poems,* Laurence Housman placed "For my funeral" in the penultimate position and followed it with "Alta quies," which, like an echo, takes the reader to "Wake not for the world-heard thunder" (*LP* 29) and others of its kind. With them also is recalled Lucretius' solemn passage, 3.830 ff., beginning *Nil igitur mors est ad nos neque pertinet hilum . . .* (Death, then, is nought to us, nor does it concern us a whit). To Housman, as to other poets, time is nothing: he wrote the tremendous lines of this poem when he was twenty. Here there is no ambiguity. In contrast to the preceding lyric, the sincerity of "Good-night; ensured release . . ." rings clear, like a speaking voice. This is the authentic cry, the *verae voces . . . pectore ab imo* that may be heard in his most poignant lyrics addressed to dead or dying comrades against the thunder of breaking worlds. Here also are the familiar majestic images of the Latin poet: the earth's failing foundations, the mingling of sky, land, and ocean in the end of all.

V   *Other Sources*

The five sources just reviewed are by no means the only fountainheads that left their traces in Housman's poetry. There is strong evidence that he had a specific narrative poem in mind as he composed his longest piece in *Last Poems,* the gloomy fantasia, "Hell Gate." The central theme—comradely love will prevail against the gates of hell itself—is fitting enough; yet as a whole the poem is atypical. Beside its unexampled length (104 lines), there is its peculiar verse-structure used only here and in one other poem: octosyllabic couplets set to trochaic rhythm.

These outward and obvious particulars might declare themselves at once to the most casual reader. But that same reader
would probably feel in "Hell Gate" other qualities that make it
stand out as an odd number. Housman himself had deep misgivings about the poem. In a letter (already mentioned) asking
his former colleague of University College, J. W. Mackail, to
criticize the proofsheets of *Last Poems*, Housman remarked the
length of the poem might not be "its worst fault," and he added
that Mackail should be severely candid in his judgment of it—
"not afraid of stifling a masterpiece through a temporary aberration of judgment." Housman concluded by saying that he was
putting the suspect poem through the fire of the opinions of "one
or two other people."[14]

Part of the unlucky hang of the poem arises, I believe, from
the reader's sense that the poem is in some way incomplete, that
some important antecedents are missing. This feeling arises in
the very first line, where we are told of a road that led onward
again. The word *again* sets up an inquiry which holds like an
unresolved chord throughout the reading of the poem and recurs
as often as we think of the word. Where had the road begun?
Where had the travelers set foot on it? How had they met?
Reasons for the persistence of these queries, if not their answers,
might be found if we knew of a source or sources from which
Housman had derived some elements of his story.[15]

A few of these are easily identified: from *Paradise Lost* come
the grim warders, Sin and Death; the flaming sentinel and the
infernal firearms—not to mention the setting and description of
the city of Hell. I also suggest that Robert Browning's "Childe
Roland to the Dark Tower Came" might be responsible for the
heightening of some descriptive features of the blasted landscape, the lauding of soldierly fidelities, and the survival of the
undaunted traveler in a moment of supreme danger.

It was not only its length that made the poem so long in the
making; begun about 1905, it was not completed until the summer of 1922—just in time to be included in *Last Poems*. Housman
spread three labored drafts (of which only the first and third
survive) of this poem over eleven pages of his last notebook,
mingling in a way unusual for him both ink and pencil in successive couplets as tentative and final parts of the poem came
to him. These various peculiarities, internal and external, com-

bine to raise the question: Is there a model for "Hell Gate"? If
one could be found, an explanation of some of the oddities of the
piece might not be far to seek.

There is a definite source for "Hell Gate." It is the poem "Si
Descendero in Infernum Ades," written in octosyllabic couplets
and trochaic verse by an almost forgotten Victorian poet,
George Augustus Simcox, who published it in his *Poems and
Romances* (1869). Housman may have known Simcox was also
a Classical scholar, but it was by his poetry that he was introduced to the young collegian; for *Poems and Romances* went
with Alfred to Oxford, and from it he copied long passages into
his commonplace book.

Briefly, the substance of Simcox' 295-line romance is this: Part
I: Lady Rosalie lies dead in a church by the sea. A supernatural
element enters:

> And there waited through the night,
> Housed with silk, a steed of might,
> Half of gold and half of fire,
> Shod and bridled with desire.

A knight, the lady's paramour, comes to take her away. Victor
rouses her, rebukes her fears, and they ride off together. Part II:
On their journey they pass the place of their sinful love-tryst.
They are borne over the sea; and mention is made of a divine
presence that goes with them:

> . . . One with drooping head,
> Following ever as they fled,
> Bleeding as He too were slain,
> With one hand upon the rein.

They pass "the isle of evil graves" where Victor had lured
Rosalie's father to death. His spirit joins them as the steed
plunges with the two riders to the deeps of hell undersea. Part
III: It is in this part that the important situation is found. The
section opens:

> So they came unto the city
> Of the king who hath no pity;
> And that city needs for light
> Sun by day nor moon by night;
> It is lighted in such wise

By the king's devouring eyes,
Flashing through the dusky air,
For the eyes are everywhere.
And we call the city Hell,
But the people there who dwell
Name it by another name,
And no man may speak the same.
And the golden gates of it,
Where the purple shadows flit,
Where the mighty warders sit,
Are not shut by night or day.

The lovers, their supernatural companions still with them, are welcomed by the angel Azazel. Rosalie asks her father's spirit who the other is and is told it is the Christ. They stand before the throne of the King of Hell, but Rosalie is oblivious of all around her except

Only One who walked the night
Clad upon with tender light,
With a visage pale and sweet,
And with pierced hands and feet,
Saying, "Staunch My wounded side
With more kisses, O My bride!
For the shadows flee away
Into everlasting day."

Thus the poem ends with the veiled conclusion that divine love pardons the errors of human love and saves the faithful even in the very gate of Hell. So, *mutatis mutandis*, in "Hell Gate" Ned, who was also the silent comrade in "The West" (*LP* 1) and is now a taciturn guard of the desolate city, risks all for his friend, kills the Dark Conductor, and saves them both. This act of rescue is such as would become the idealized Moses Jackson, here and elsewhere in Housman's poetry his partner in fictive dangers.

Housman, knowing as he did the all-pervasive influence of Greek and Latin writers throughout modern literature, would have subscribed to Molière's comprehensive motto: "Je reprends mon bien où je le trouve." The extent of Housman's adaptations and borrowings probably will never be reckoned in full: one may expect to come upon the original site of another hidden bit of his "property" the next time he sits down to read, with Housman in mind, almost any respectable poet from Homer to Arnold. Taking "Hell Gate" once again, we observe that the Dark Conductor answers the shade's questions *before they are asked.* Where could this device come from if not from Dante's conversations with Virgil and Beatrice in the *Divine Comedy,* where it figures at least fifteen times? It should also be said that Dante's "Dead were the dead, and the living seemed living" (*Purg.* 12:67) contends with or supports Heine in affording Housman his two lines beginning the last stanza of "In midnights of November" (*LP* 19): "The living are the living/And dead the dead will stay."

"Loitering with a vacant eye" (*ASL* 51) may owe something to Wordsworth's "The Leech-Gatherer,"[16] which Housman admired and set among the best of the elder poet's lyrics. The two poems in their settings could hardly be more unlike, but they have important elements in common: beginning with a mood of depression, each describes the poet's meeting with a stranger whose harder lot, borne with dignity and courage, shames the more fortunate complainer to an acceptance of his own. The last line of Burns's spirited "Song of Death"—*O who would not die with the brave?*[17]—undoubtedly gave Housman his refrain line for "Lancer" (*LP* 6), and may also have added a dash of its derring-do to the poem as a whole.

Housman's adaptation from Southey in his humorous poem, "The Parallelogram or: Infant Optimism,"[18] is also worth citing to show how he could wear his borrowed plumage with a difference when he wanted a comical effect. The quotation is "My cheeks have often been bedewed/With tears of thoughtful gratitude." Southey in his "My days among the dead are passed" was giving sober thanks for the works of the "mighty minds of old." Housman's infant is overawed by Euclid's definition of the parallelogram.

CHAPTER 8

Retrospect and Summing-up

BOOKS, no less than their authors, have lives of their own; and *A Shropshire Lad* has had a history that is worthy of a brief review, which in itself may touch most of the salient points in its author's poetic career. Having been turned down by Macmillan on the advice of their reader John Morley,[1] Housman's first book was issued by Kegan Paul in an edition of only five hundred copies. It was not an "immediate success," as later claimed by some of Housman's overenthusiastic friends: two and one-half years passed before a second edition was forthcoming from the firm of Grant Richards.

Although not a first-rate businessman, Richards correctly surmised he had a valuable piece of property in *A Shropshire Lad*, which he nevertheless handled from the first with timidity. His first edition (1898) ran to only five hundred copies, and from that date to the beginning of World War I his press runs, occurring about every two years, were extremely unadventuresome, only one splurge of two thousand copies highlighting the year 1902. Over a longer span, in the first fifty years of its existence, from 1898 to 1948, *A Shropshire Lad* was reissued forty-eight times by the Richards firm.

It was a fortunate day for publisher and poet when in September, 1915, Sir Walter Raleigh asked Housman's permission to print some lyrics from his book in a collection of poetry intended for the men in the trenches. Housman agreed,[2] and a public who had never known him began reading and quoting his poems, and *A Shropshire Lad* shot up into something of a best-seller. The strong patriotic flavor in it, particularly in the opening poems—a feature Housman's first publisher, Kegan Paul, had wanted to make more of—now proved to be a great popularizer. In 1916 Housman whimsically told his publisher that he was expecting his book to perform one day the saving trick of diverting a bullet from the heart of one of his readers in uniform, and before the war ended he did hear of a copy of his book stained with a soldier's blood. Sales mounted, and an edition of *A Shropshire Lad* in 1918 ran to five thousand copies.[3]

Kegan Paul had sent one hundred and fifty copies of the first edition to John Lane of New York, where the book attracted the attention of a few influential readers, among them Richard Le Gallienne; Viola Roseboro', chief reader for *McClure's*; and Witter Bynner, also on the staff of that magazine. Bynner began running a series in *McClure's* of some of the poems from *A Shropshire Lad* that he liked best. Housman mentioned this early in his connections with Richards, little realizing that his American admirer would become not only an excellent overseas promoter of his book but a life-long correspondent. Housman had intentionally made no effort to obtain copyright restrictions in the United States, and by 1922 at least twelve different issues of his book had appeared in this country. At that date, however, when arrangements were being made for the sales abroad of his *Last Poems*, Housman informed Richards diffidently that he would be "prepared to receive royalty from America for the sale of *A Shropshire Lad*." So henceforth the editions of his first volume published by Henry Holt & Co., of New York, began to carry the line "Authorized Edition," although this designation had already been used by other publishers in America. In an appendix to his semicentennial edition of this book,[4] Carl Weber lists forty-five separate American editions of *A Shropshire Lad* from 1897 to 1946—not counting numerous reprintings, imports, and variants.

I *Illustrated Editions*

Needless to say, *A Shropshire Lad* has, over the years, given employment to an army of book-designers, illustrators, and printers, especially in the United States, where the book was a "free-for-all." Housman looked with disfavor upon "special" and decorated editions and killed them in the making when he could. But he never expressed regret that he had lost by default his copyright in America,[5] though his sacrifice did not increase his love for transatlantic printers and their countrymen. It is to be hoped that he never saw the Little Blue Book No. 306 of the Haldeman-Julius Publications, entitled *Hanging of Shropshire Lad*. It was listed in the firm's catalogue under "Murder and

Crime"! But publishers of far better reputation were guilty of gross neglect in printing and proofreading of *A Shropshire Lad*; and Carl Weber remarked in his Windsor Lecture (1952)[6] that, although a New York house contracted to observe scrupulously Housman's specific directions as to page-arrangement, punctuation, and spelling, "every one of his desires has been ignored."

It was not until 1906 that Grant Richards roused sufficient courage to show Housman a sample illustration by William Hyde, a well-known landscape artist, hoping to induce the poet to listen with approval to the suggestion of publishing an edition of his poems with Hyde's coöperation. Housman finally gave his grudging consent—"rather, I think, with the idea of humoring me than for any other reason," as Richards confessed;[7] and the illustrated *Shropshire Lad* was finally in the bookshops late in 1908. Its sale was not what its publisher expected; too often Hyde missed the point of the poems, and Housman objected that the illustrations on the end papers "seem to be letting the man do all the ploughing."[8] Housman had proved his point, but as late as 1919 he was twitting his publisher about the latter's "pet edition."

The failure of the 1908 experiment had put Richards in a poor bargaining position when in 1920 he again endeavored to tempt his canny author with some new illustrations, displaying this time a set of thirty designs by the painter Lovat Fraser. Housman did not conceal his dislike of this project and in a long letter,[9] in which he expressed moderate approval of six of the designs, he gave free vent to his feelings in general and in detail. He began dourly: "The trouble with book illustrators, as with composers who set poems to music, is not merely that they are completely wrapped up in their own art and their precious selves, and regard the author merely as a peg to hang things on, but that they seem to have less than the ordinary human allowance of sense and feeling." Some of his specific jibes at Fraser's drawings are worth quoting for the light they cast on Housman's temperament: "What a cherry-tree!"; "Lunatic at large"; "Satyr dressed up as John Bull: allegory, I suppose: quite inappropriate"; "No illustration: none possible"; "The poem is about black poplars growing by pools and whispering at night when there is no wind. The illustration displays Lombardy poplars in broad day and a furious gale. . . ."

Housman was better served by the artists after his death, in 1936. Four years later appeared a splendid illustrated edition of *A Shropshire Lad*, published by Harrap, of London. Its fifty-six engravings in black-and-white were the work of Agnes Miller Parker. Two of the most popular decorated editions of the book produced in the United States are those containing the designs of Elinore Blaisdell (1932) and Edward A. Wilson (1935).

Housman steadfastly refused to allow British anthologists to reprint selections from *A Shropshire Lad*,[10] but was more liberal in granting these liberties with *Last Poems*. He also deplored putting his two books of poetry within a single cover: "I think it a silly notion." Although the poems from these two volumes stand often side by side in his notebooks, they occupied entirely different areas of his affections. Percy Withers remarks that Housman's feeling for *A Shropshire Lad* was like that of a mother for her first-born. "Over and over again he showed a special, a tender, affection for it."[11] Nothing else of his was worthy of a place beside it, and we today understand the reason for Housman's affection: his book commemorates the great crisis of his life, Moses Jackson, the Oxford failure, and the saving relief that poetry bestowed upon him. When Poet Laureate Robert Bridges in 1926 broke into the sanctum and took three poems from Housman's first book for an anthology, Housman refrained from violence, but he commented firmly to his publisher: ". . . he does not pretend that I gave him permission to do so."

II *Musical Settings*

Housman was plagued, to use his word, by numerous requests from composers and publishers asking to be allowed to set his lyrics to music. Though he frequently gave permission, it was not without misgivings that his poems would be abridged or otherwise tampered with. Arther Somervell's *Song Cycle from A Shropshire Lad* (1904) acknowledges the "kind permission of the author" and carries at the foot of the title-page the monitory note: "These songs may be sung in public without fee or license. The public performances of any parodied version, however, is strictly prohibited." (For *parodied* read "with any changes whatsoever.") Housman pretended, justly perhaps, that he had no appreciation for music; and this lack may have made him less protective of his lyrics than he otherwise might have been. He was, however, not one to suppress his feelings at accompaniments he did not like; and, at a hearing of some of his lyrics set to music by Vaughan Williams, he fell into an attitude of extreme pain and seemed about to run headlong from the room—so Percy Withers reports.[12]

Though the common reader would probably have a more tolerant feeling, even a liking, for the poems in Dr. Williams' settings—provided he could be introduced to better vocalization than that of Mr. Peter Pears in the London Gramophone recordings—he has found enough in the poetry itself to be enjoyed without a bush. It belongs, of course, to the Georgian reaction against the indoor stuffiness of the Victorian age; and it fitted in with the use that a few of Housman's contemporaries were making of the simpler, homespun vocabulary to present alive everyday scenes and situations.

But it needs to be emphasized that Housman belonged to no school and founded none. He felt, and correctly, that he had no vital liens with other poets of his time. He wrote to Richards, who had forwarded to him a plea from A. J. A. Symons for permission to include some *Shropshire Lad* selections in an anthology: "to include me in an anthology of the Nineties would be just as technically correct, and just as essentially inappropriate, as to include Lot in a book on Sodomites. . . ."[13] What would have been his feelings, therefore, could he have known that a quarter-century or so after his death two of his poems would find their way into a widely circulated anthology of conventional religious verse?

It happened that the generation into which Housman was born took his poetry to its heart because it was melodious, alive, and had something important to say. He got the audience he needed and desired even though he pretended to be unaware of it and even stood it off when it pressed him too closely. While he never displayed any deep satisfaction in his enlarging reputation, there is little doubt that he felt it. Two years before his death he wrote to Mr. John Coghlan, of Dublin: "*A Shropshire Lad* has never been out of print since its publication in 1896, and for the last thirty years or more it has been procurable for eighteenpence." And he closed his letter with the name and address of his publisher.

[174]

Housman kept a businessman's eye on the sale of his books at home and in America, although he professed a strong distaste for nearly all transatlantic admirers—a feeling which probably was not mitigated upon learning that the famous American defense lawyer, Clarence Darrow, was using poems from *A Shropshire Lad* to move jurymen to look with pity upon young malefactors accused of capital offenses. In the United States Housman had few imitators, but some traces of his style and points of view may be seen in Witter Bynner, Edna St. Vincent Millay, Richard Le Gallienne, and George Santayana—to name only the outstanding few. Santayana on one occasion confessed, "I read *A Shropshire Lad*, always with tears. There is not much else than tears in them, but they are perfect of their kind."[14] Carl Van Doren once declared the first book he knew by heart was *Mother Goose*; the second, *A Shropshire Lad*.[15]

III *Critical Reaction*

A strong reaction against Housman's style and subject-matter broke out immediately after his death—as if his detractors, remembering the pilloried victims of his wrath, prudently waited for advantage before they dared to launch their attack. "There is," Lord Vansittart remarked, "usually a pause between death and belittlement, but Housman did not get it."[16] The leader of the reaction was Cyril Connolly, who only three weeks after Housman's funeral discharged in the *New Statesman* for May 23 a volley of missiles that was, and probably was intended to be, the signal for a running battle on a wide front. At least, such a battle threatened, for at the head of the "Correspondence" column in the next number the editor announced he was printing below only "a small selection of a large and learned correspondence excited by Mr. Connolly's article," and expressed his hope to publish more protests the following week.

Below this announcement were printed letters from four of the more vigorous objectors: F. L. Lucas, Martin Cooper, L. P. Wilkinson, and John Sparrow. Sparrow's reply—which began, "Late for the funeral, Mr. Connolly at least had the satisfaction of arriving in time to spit upon the grave . . . ."—was fired with a vituperative bitterness not exceeded by anything he later emitted in his long controversial campaign in defense of his critical sponsorship of Housman, over whom, from his earliest interest in the poet, he had assumed a kind of proprietary claim. The moderation and good sense of the letters of Lucas and Cooper whetted the appetites of the readers of the *New Statesman* for a continuation of the debate, but some behind-the-scenes influence prevented them and others from having their day in court against Mr. Connolly in the next issue of the *New Statesman*. Strangely enough, no one other than the arch-rebel himself was there in the correspondents' column to fire another, and the last, shot in the quarrel; he made a few concessions to the formidable quartet who had replied so effectively the preceding week but, in the main, stood his ground.[17]

Meanwhile Housman's poetry is being read and occasionally studied by the older and younger members of the generation that succeeded his.[18] He has been, and is being, copiously anthologized and written about; his bibliography is already mountainous. George Benjamin Woods included all the poems of *A Shropshire Lad* in his *Poetry of the Victorian Period*, and the paperback revolution is repeating what Sir Walter Raleigh did for the book fifty years ago. Dr. William White, of Wayne State University, who has since 1937 been aggregating a bibliography of Housman (now containing more than 2500 items), despairs of ever bringing it up to date. Poets of our recent past cannot be more than provisionally ranked in the long beadroll of their kind, but it is possible even this early to identify some of the strong survivors of the transition from the nineteenth to the twentieth century. Housman is one of these.

IV   *Housman's Enduring Fame*

One index of a poet's worth lies in his ability to escape the tenure of academic professionals and to serve the needs of the market place. Housman had a healthy distrust of the cloistered critic: he named bibliophiles "an idiotic class"; and he rejected his colleagues' high praise of him because they offended his judgment in their praises of one another. On the other hand, he never catered to the public, but he did want his poetry to become popular and he did not demur when it sometimes served decidedly unliterary ends, as for example when two lines of his "Merry Guide" were selling toilet water in the *New Yorker* of

November 7, 1931.[19] Twenty-four years later Housman headed the March of Dimes in that same magazine and in other journals throughout the nation. More recently, he has given a *frisson nouveau* to the readers of *Playboy Magazine*[20] and, to balance one extreme of grotesquery with another, twice answers roll call in the already referred to *Penguin Book of Religious Verse* (1963). His two poems are "Be still, my soul . . ." (*ASL* 48) and "On Wenlock Edge . . ." (*ASL* 31). In neither is the religious feeling significant.

Many of Housman's picturesque turns of language are returning, touched with a new aptness, to the mainstream of popular speech—one of the chief fountainheads of his own poetic diction. Somewhat as his scholarly reputation has for a half-century and more made his name a byword for accuracy and thoroughness,[21] so many of his pithy, keen-edged phrases have been picked up by Everyman and made to serve many and various causes. This is the way of poetry that lives. Such expressions as "proud and angry dust," "a world I never made," "shoulder the sky," "with rue my heart is laden," "to see the cherry hung with snow," and "land of lost content" are now firmly established commonplaces of everyday use wherever English is written. "And long 'tis like to be."

Books are perpetuated by books, and it is instructive to observe Housman's influence on authors who follow the amiable habit of naming their own productions from the writings of others. Any extensive list of new book-titles in, say, one non-special number of *Publishers' Weekly*, will include many titles chosen from literature. Over the years, the two sources one most frequently meets are the Bible and Shakespeare. A. E. Housman, albeit a long distance from second place, is in third. This is striking and incontestible evidence of his unfailing popularity in the English-reading world today. Since 1920, when Storm Jameson's *The Happy Highways* appeared, about eighty books —poetry, novels, collections of short stories, plays, autobiographies, and anthologies of different kinds—have been published under titles chosen from Housman's poetry. Among the best-known borrowers are James T. Farrell, *A World I Never Made*; Susan Ertz, *Anger in the Sky*; Dorothy Stockbridge, *Angry Dust*; Helen MacInnes Highet, *Neither Five nor Three*; Jocelyn Brooke, *The Flower in Season*; Drew Middleton, *The*

Sky Suspended; Patrick White, *The Tree of Man*; E. L. Wood-ward, *Twelve-Winded Sky*; Elliott Nugent, *Of Cheat and Charmer*.

Thus about every six months, over a period of forty-seven years, a new Housman book-title, whether immediately recognized or not, has been showing up in the bookshops of London and New York. Eventually phrases from the couplet "I, a stranger and afraid/In a world I never made" (*Last Poems* 12) may be appearing on book jackets as often as segments from Macbeth's farewell: "Tomorrow, and tomorrow, and tomorrow. . . ." Late in 1965 Helen Hudson's *Tell The Time To None* carried on the tradition; and one section of Barbara W. Tuchman's *The Proud Tower* (1966) displays a Housman title: "The Steady Drummer." I have a list of seven other book-titles awaiting confirmation of their origin.[22] It is abundantly evident that writers of books in English are joined in a kind of free conspiracy not to let A. E. Housman out of their sight or others'. This is fame.

Appendix

Themselves they could not save. *ASL* 1:16

himself he cannot save. Matt. 27:42; Mark 15:31

my threescore years and ten. *ASL* 2:5

The days of our years are three score years and ten. Ps. 90:10

trump of doomsday. *ASL* 3:21

the last trump. I Cor. 15:52
the trump of God. I Thess. 4:16

A careless shepherd. *ASL* 9:5

ye careless ones. Is. 32:11

the careless people. *ASL* 14:1

the careless Ethiopians. Ezek. 30:9

the heart's desire. *ASL* 10:18

his heart's desire. Ps. 10:3; 21:2; Rom. 10:1

the desire of his heart. *LP* 4:9

the desires of thy heart. Ps. 37:4

The far dwelling [= "the grave"]. *ASL* 11:9

their beauty shall consume in the grave from their dwelling. Ps. 49:14

. . . lust

the lust of the flesh. Gal. 5:16

In the house of flesh. *ASL* 12:5-6

the lusts of the flesh. II Pet. 2:18

house of flesh. *ASL* 12:6

our earthly house. II Cor. 5:1

house of dust. *ASL* 12:7

death . . . the house appointed for all living. Job 30:23

ye that dwell in the dust. Is. 26:19

clay's the house he keeps. *ASL* 25:14

them that dwell in houses of clay. Job 4:19

heart and soul. *ASL* 14:7, 20; *ASL* 27:14

heart and . . . soul. Deut. 11:13; Josh. 22:9; Matt. 22:37

World without end. *ASL* 14:8

world without end. Is. 45:17

son of grief. *ASL* 17:7

son of my sorrow. Gen. 35:18

son of sorrow. *ASL* 44:15

the world's ends. *ASL* 22:7

the ends of the world. Ps. 22:27; Rom. 10:18

watch them depart on the way that they will not return. *ASL* 23:12

I shall go the way whence I shall not return. Job 16:22

Ye shall henceforth return no more that way. Deut. 7:16

plain for her to understand. *ASL* 26:17

plain to him that understandeth. Prov. 8:9

a time at hand [= "time of death"]. *ASL* 26:18

My time is at hand. Matt. 26:18

the time is at hand. Rev. 1:3; 22:10

the time of my departure is at hand. II Tim. 4:6

builded of old. *AP* 21:36

wept of old. *ASL* 28:20

established of old. Ps. 93:2

fixt of old. *ASL* 48:2

appeared of old. Jer. 31:3; *et passim.*

winterfalls of old. *LP* 20:3

told lies of old. *LP* 25:4

the truceless armies yet/Trample, rolled in blood and sweat. *ASL* 28:25-26

every battle of the warrior is with . . . garments rolled in blood. Is. 9:5

None will part us. *ASL* 28:29

there was none to part them. II Sam. 14:6

makes one flesh of two. *ASL* 28:30

they twain shall be one flesh. Matt. 19:5; Mark 10:8

two shall be one flesh. I Cor. 6:16; Eph. 5:31

The stuff of life to knit me Blew hither. *ASL* 32:3-4

God . . . breathed into his nostrils the breath of life. Gen. 2:7

hearts that perish. *ASL* 33:1

the heart of the king shall perish. Jer. 4:9

powers on high. *ASL* 33:2

power from on high. Luke 24:49

[180]

The world might end tomorrow. ASL 33:7	the end of the world. Matt. 13:39; 24:3
You should not see the grave. ASL 33:8	he should . . . not see corruption. Ps. 49:9
	he . . . shall not see death. Ps. 89:48
	neither did his flesh see corruption. Acts 2:31
you should live forever. ASL 33:11	he should still live for ever. Ps. 49:9
	he shall live for ever. John 6:51
the enemies of England they shall see me and be sick. ASL 34:16	The wicked shall see it, and be grieved. Ps. 112:10
None that go return again. ASL 35:12	None that go . . . return again. Prov. 2:19
Hand, . . . Be clean. ASL 37:14-15	make my hands . . . clean. Job 9:30
	he that hath clean hands. Job 17:9; Ps. 24:4
From yon far country. ASL 40:2	from a far country. Prov. 25:25; Is. 13:5; Jer. 4:16
my bones within me say. ASL 43:3, 36	All my bones shall say. Ps. 35:10
proud in power. ASL 43:13	the pride of your power. Lev. 26:19
	the pride of her power. Ezek. 30:6
morn is all the same as night. ASL 43:28	the darkness and the light are both alike to thee. Ps. 139:12
Empty vessel. ASL 43:33	made me an empty vessel. Jer. 51:34
brave in season [= "opportunely"] ASL 44:7	spoken in due season. Prov. 15:23

in season. *LP* 13:21; *MP* 22:7, 11

The soul that should not have been born. *ASL* 44:12

Turn safe to rest. *ASL* 44:25

If it chance your eye offend you,
Pluck it out, lad, and be sound.
ASL 45: 1-2

And if your hand or foot offend
    you,
Cut it off, lad, and be whole.
ASL 45:5-6

play the man. *ASL* 45:7

stand up. *ASL* 45:7

"The Carpenter's Son" [Title]
ASL 47

And the people passing by/Stop
to shake their fists and curse.
ASL 47:13-14

                    right and left
Two poor fellows hang for theft.
ASL 47:17-18

stand and gaze. *ASL* 47:21; *AP*
7:2

Walk . . . in other ways. *ASL*
47:22

fulfilled in their season. Luke
1:20; in season, *passim*

it had been good for that man if
he had not been born. Matt.
26:24; Mark 14:21

thou shalt take thy rest in safety.
Job 11:18

if thy right eye offend thee,
pluck it out. Matt. 5:29; Mark
9:47

And if thy right hand offend
thee, cut it off. Matt. 5:30

And if thy hand offend thee, cut
it off. Mark 9:43

And if thy foot, etc. Mark 9:45

play the man. II Sam. 10:12

stand up against the Prince.
Dan. 8:25

the carpenter's son. Matt. 13:55;
Mark 6:3

And they that passed by reviled
him. Matt. 27:39

And they that passed by railed
on him. Mark 15:29

two thieves crucified with him:
one on the right hand, and another on the left. Matt. 27:38.

And with him they crucify, etc.
Mark 15:27

stand ye gazing. Acts 1:11

walk in the ways. Eccl. 11:9

walked not in his ways. I Sam.
8:3; *et passim*

Earth and high heaven. *ASL* 48:2

heaven is high above the earth. Ps. 103:11

fixt of old and founded strong *ASL* 48:2

Of old hast thou laid the foundation of the earth. Ps. 102:25

the heavens were of old. II Pet. 3:5

strong foundations of the earth. Micah 6:2

Then it was well with me. *ASL* 48:8

then it was well with him. Jer. 22:16

it is but for a season. *ASL* 48:11

it were but for a season. II Cor. 7:8

high heaven and earth ail from the prime foundation. *ASL* 48:13

from the foundation of the world. Matt. 13:35; *et passim*

the foundation of the earth. Heb. 1:10

the whole creation groaneth, and travaileth in pain. Rom. 8:22

doomsday may thunder and lighten. *ASL* 50:25

It thundered and lightened. II Esdras 6:2

out of the throne proceeded lightnings and thunders. Rev. 4:5

We both were fashioned far away. *ASL* 51:8

unto him that fashioned it long ago. Is. 22:11

men whose thoughts are not as mine. *ASL* 51:16

my thoughts are not your thoughts. Is. 55:8

quit you like stone, be strong. *ASL* 51:22

quit you like men, be strong. I Cor. 16:13

Be strong, and quit yourselves like men. I Sam. 4:9

no more remembered. *ASL* 52:9

no more remembered. Jer. 11:19; Zech. 13:2; Job 24:20

Where for me the world began. *ASL* 55:2

Since the world began. Luke 1:70; John 9:32; Rom. 16:25

"The Day of Battle" [Title] *ASL* 55; also *LP* 13:19	the day of battle. I Sam. 13:22; Job 38:23; *et passim*
while the sun and moon endure. *ASL* 62:45	as long as the sun and moon endure. Ps. 72:5
for ill and not for good. *ASL* 62:48	for evil, and not for good. Amos 9:4
In a weary land. *ASL* 62:52	in a weary land. Is. 32:2
	in a . . . weary land. Ps. 63:1
When your soul is in my soul's stead. *ASL* 62:56	if your soul were in my soul's stead. Job 16:4
In the dark and cloudy day. *ASL* 62:58	in the cloudy and dark day. Ezek. 34:12
A dead man out of mind. *ASL* 63:8	A dead man out of mind. Ps. 31:12
Some seeds the birds devour. *ASL* 63:9	Some seeds . . . the fowls . . . devoured. Matt. 13:3; Mark 4:4; Luke 8:5
As I gird on for fighting My sword upon my thigh. *LP* 2:1-2	Gird thy sword upon thy thigh. Ps. 45:3
My sword that will not save. *LP* 2:16	neither shall my sword save me. Ps. 44:6
Queen of air and darkness. *LP* 3:5	Prince of the power of the air. Eph. 2:2
	the power of darkness. Luke 22:53
Far from his friends and his lovers. *LP* 4:15	Lover and friend hast thou put far from me. Ps. 88:18
my friend and lover. *MP* 46:9	
in the grave, they say, Is neither knowledge nor device. *LP* 5:18-19	there is no . . . device, nor knowledge . . . in the grave. Eccl. 9:10
for a certainty. *LP* 9:9	for a certainty. Josh. 23:13

the estate of man. *LP* 9:19

the estate of the sons of men. Eccl. 3:18

The flesh will grieve on other bones than ours
Soon, and the soul will mourn in other breasts. *LP* 9:23-24

his flesh upon him shall have pain, and his soul within him shall mourn. Job 14:22

from eternity. *LP* 9:26

from everlasting. Prov. 8:23; Ps. 93:2; Micah 5:2

Bear them [troubles] we can, and if we can we must. *LP* 9:27

Truly this is a grief, and I must bear it. Jer. 10:19

The laws of God. *LP* 12:1

The laws of . . . God. Ezra 7:25

if my ways are not as theirs. *LP* 12:5

neither are your ways my ways. Is. 55:8

　　　　a stranger and afraid
In a world I never made. *LP* 12:18

they were strangers and pilgrims on the earth. Heb. 11:13

the hope of man. *LP* 16:3

the hope of man. Job 14:19

the house [body] is fallen. *LP* 18:21

if our earthly house . . . were dissolved. II Cor. 5:1

the keepers of the house shall tremble. Eccl. 12:3

That was the lover's hour,
The hour for lies. *LP* 22:3-4

this is your hour and the power of darkness. Luke 22:53

she and I should surely die. *LP* 25:8

thou shalt surely die. Gen. 2:17; 20:7; (surely die, *passim*)

never live again. *LP* 25:8

If a man die, shall he live again? Job 14:14

Sleep on now, and take your rest. *LP* 29:16

Sleep on now, and take your rest. Matt. 26:45; Mark 14:41

Clasp your cloak of earth. *LP* 29:19

Prepare raiment as the clay. Job 27:16

gate of hell. *LP* 31:12

gates of hell. Matt. 16:18

the slimepit and the mire. *LP* 31:31

the vale of Siddim was full of slime-pits. Gen. 14:10

everlasting fire. *LP* 31:32, 100

everlasting fire. Matt. 18:8; 25:41

Death and Sin
Rose to render key . . . *LP* 31:56

the keys of hell and death. Rev. 1:18

the heart of man. *LP* 35:11; *AP* 3:7; 15:20

the heart of man. Prov. 12:25; I Cor. 2:9; *et passim*

when heaven was falling, . . . when earth's foundations fled. *LP* 37:1-2

the earth and the heaven fled away. Rev. 20:11

earth's foundations. *LP* 37:2, 6; *MP* 26:7; 48:5, 7; *AP* 14:3

the foundations of the earth. Ps. 82:5; Job 38:4; Is. 24:18; *et passim*

the sum of things. *LP* 37:8

of the things . . . this is the sum. Heb. 8:1

And darkness hard at hand. *LP* 39:19

for it is nigh at hand; a day of darkness. Joel 2:1-2

And I knew all her ways. *LP* 40:6

and art acquainted with all my ways. Ps. 139:3

in that Syrian garden. *MP* 1:1

Now in the place where he was crucified there was a garden. John 19:41

ages slain,
You sleep. *MP* 1:1, 2

the Son of Man must . . . be slain. Luke 9:22

desired they Pilate that he should be slain. Acts 13:28

you [Christ] are dead in vain. *MP* 1:2

Christ is dead in vain. Gal. 2:21

Ascends in smoke and fire by day and night
The hate you died to quench. 1:4-5

It shall not be quenched night nor day; the smoke thereof shall go up for ever. Is. 34:10

son of man. *MP* 1:6

Son of man. Matt. 8:20; 9:6; *et passim*

the stone rolled by. *MP* 1:7

the angel . . . rolled back the stone. Matt. 28:2

the stone was rolled away. Mark 16:4; Luke 24:2; John 20:1

At the right hand of majesty on high You sit. *MP* 1:7-8	sat down on the right hand of the Majesty on high. Heb. 1:3
	set on the right hand . . . of the Majesty in the heavens. Heb. 8:1
Your tears, your agony and bloody sweat. *MP* 1:10	And being in an agony, he prayed more earnestly: and his sweat was as it were great drops of blood. Luke 22:44
Bow hither out of heaven and see and save. *MP* 1:12	Bow thy heavens, O Lord, and come down. Ps. 144:5
	he shall send from heaven and save. Ps. 57:3
When Israel out of Egypt came. *MP* 2:1	When Israel went out of Egypt. Ps. 114:1
	Israel when they came up out of Egypt. I Sam. 15:6 (Similar refs., *passim*)
Safe in the sea they trod. *MP* 2:2	the children of Israel walked upon dry land in the midst of the sea. Ex. 14:29. (Similar refs., *passim*)
By day in cloud, by night in flame. *MP* 2:3	the cloud of the Lord was upon the tabernacle by day, and fire was on it by night. Ex. 40:38
	in the day by a cloudy pillar, and in the night by a pillar of fire. Neh. 9:12
Went on before them God. *MP* 2:4	the angel of God which went before the camp. Ex. 14:19
He brought them with a stretched-out hand. *MP* 2:5	And brought Israel . . . with a strong hand, and with a stretched-out arm. Ps. 136:11-12
	I will bring you out . . . with a mighty hand, and with a stretched-out arm. Ezek. 20:34
Dry-footed through the foam. *MP* 2:6	the children of Israel went into the midst of the sea upon the dry ground. Ex. 14:22

over Horeb heard The blast of advent blow. *MP* 2:9-10	a great and strong wind rent the mountains [of Horeb]. I Kings 19:11
fire-faced prophet. *MP* 2:11	Moses . . . came to Horeb, and the Angel of the Lord appeared unto him in a flame of fire. Ex. 3:1-2
the cloudy flame. *MP* 2:13	a cloud covered the mount. Ex. 24:15
	the glory of the Lord was like devouring-fire on the top of the mount. Ex. 24:17
the mount of thunder. *MP* 2:14	there were thunders and lightnings . . . upon the mount. Ex. 19:16
The tokens that to Israel came. *MP* 2:15	this shall be a token unto thee, that I [God] have sent thee. Ex. 3:12
I see the country far away Where I shall never stand. *MP* 2:17-18	This is the land . . .: I have caused thee [Moses] to see it with thine eyes, but thou shalt not go over thither. Deut. 34:4
Our eyes were in the places Where we should never be. *MP* 33:7-8	
Content thee if thine eyes Behold it in thy day. *MP* 4:27-28	behold it with thine eyes. Deut. 3:27
	Only with thine eyes shalt thou behold. Ps. 91:8
the promised land. *MP* 2:20	the land which he [God] promised. Deut. 19:8
	a land . . . promised thee. Deut. 27:3
like Sinai staggered The . . . world. *MP* 3:7-8	the whole mount [Sinai] quaked greatly. Ex. 19:18
	the mountains melted . . . even that Sinai. Judg. 5:5

kingdom swept and garnished. *MP* 3:11

findeth it swept and garnished. Matt. 12:44; Luke 11:25

the perished nation. *MP* 3:19; *MP* 20:7

the whole nation perish. John 11:50

That never see the sun. *MP* 3:20

they may not see the sun. Ps. 58:8

They never see the morn. *MP* 4:24

they shall never see light. Ps. 49:19

heart is right. *MP* 4:1

Is thy heart right? II Kings 10:15

thy heart is not right. Acts 8:21

loins are girt. *MP* 4:2

having your loins girt. Eph. 6:14

they girded their loins. I Kings 20:32

be strong. *MP* 4:10

be strong, yea, be strong. Dan. 10:19

But think not . . .
To save thy soul alive. *MP* 4:19-20

he shall save his soul alive. Ezek. 18:27

none can keep alive his own soul. Ps. 22:29

will ye save the souls alive? Ezek. 13:18

altered is the fashion of the earth. *MP* 5:4

the fashion of this world passeth away. I Cor. 7:31

the fashion of his countenance was altered. Luke 9:29

Mine were trouble
And Mine were steady,
So I was ready
When trouble came. *MP* 6:13-16

I was not in safety, neither had I rest, neither was I quiet; yet trouble came. Job 3:26

It rains into the sea,
And still the sea is salt. *MP* 7:7-8

All the rivers run into the sea; yet the sea is not full. Eccl. 1:7

The rainy Pleiads wester,
Orion plunges prone. *MP* 11:1-2

which maketh . . . Orion and Pleiades. Job 9:9

Pleiades or . . . Orion. Job 38:31

singleness of heart. *MP* 12:3

the single-hearted. *ASL* 61:19

      so deep has cast
Its sure foundation. *MP* 12:7-8

perished people. *MP* 14:11

the heart would counsel ill. *MP* 17:8

hold its peace. *MP* 19:2

to earth and darkness. *MP* 21:7

To darkness and silence and slumber. *MP* 40:3

      to peace and darkness
And earth. *MP* 47:9-10

Ho, everyone that thirsteth
And hath the price to give,
Come to the stolen waters. *MP* 22:1-3

Come to the stolen waters. *MP* 22:3

Drink and your soul shall live. *MP* 22:4

desire shall fail. *MP* 22:8

free land of the grave. *MP* 23:8

singleness of heart. Acts 2:46; Eph. 6:5; Col. 3:22

digged deep and laid the foundation on a rock. Luke 6:48

the people perish. Prov. 29:18

out of the heart proceed evil thoughts. Matt. 15:19; Mark 7:21

the imagination of man's heart is evil. Gen. 8:21

hold your peace. Ex. 14:14 (hold . . . peace, *passim*)

darkness and the shadow of death. Job 10:21; Ps. 107:10

go down into silence. Ps. 115:17

the dust return to the earth. Eccl. 12:7

Ho! everyone that thirsteth, come ye to the waters . . . without money and without price. Is. 55:1

let him that is athirst, come: and whosoever will, let him take the water of life freely. Rev. 22:17

If any man thirst, let him come unto me and drink. John 7:37

stolen waters are sweet. Prov. 9:17

hear, and your soul shall live. Is. 55:3

thy soul shall live. Jer. 38:17, 20

desire shall fail. Eccl. 12:5

free among the dead. Ps. 88:5

earth's foundations will depart. *MP* 26:7	the mountains shall depart. Is. 54:10
he cleansed his heart And washed his hands in innocence in vain. *MP* 28:3-4	Pilate . . . took water and washed his hands. Matt. 27:24
	I have cleansed my heart in vain and washed my hands in innocency. Ps. 73:13
	I will wash my hands in innocency. Ps. 26:6
sons of Adam. *MP* 34:18	sons of Adam. Deut. 32:8
seed of Adam. *MP* 45:4	(Seed = "descendants," *passim*)
near at hand. *MP* 45:21	nigh at hand. Joel 2:1; Luke 21:30; John 19:42
send abroad thy children. *MP* 47:3	let us send abroad. I Chron. 13:2
all thy hand hath made. *MP* 47:6	all those things hath my hand made. Is. 66:2
	Hath not my hand made all these things? Acts 7:50
[God] wilt cast forth no more. *MP* 47:12	I [God] will cast thee forth. Ezek. 32:4
While sea abides, and land, And earth's foundations stand. *MP* 48:4-5	while the world standeth. I Cor. 8:13
braver than the heavens are high. *AP* 6:6	higher than the heavens. Heb. 7:26
sons she brings to birth. *AP* 8:30	Shall I bring to the birth? Is. 66:9
I shall not die today, no fear; I shall live. *AP* 15:5-6	I shall not die, but live. Ps. 118:17
the heavens stand fast. *AP* 15:13	By the word of the Lord were the heavens made . . . he commanded and it stood fast. Ps. 33:6-9

Bears up . . . that world-seen span. *AP* 15:19

I bear up the pillars of it [the earth]. Ps. 75:3

a taste for death. *AP* 16:4

should taste death. Heb. 2:9

shall never taste of death. John 8:52

the innocent trod
The grapes of the anger of God. *AP* 19:16

he treadeth the wine-press of the . . . wrath of Almighty God. Rev. 19:15

the great wine-press of the wrath of God. And the wine-press was trodden. Rev. 14:19-20

glory
Filling the house of the Lord. *AP* 21:7-8

I will fill this house with glory, saith the Lord. Haggi 2:7

There stood in the holy places
A multitude none could name. *AP* 21:13-14

[see] the abomination of desolation . . . stand in the holy place. Matt. 24:15

Who shall stand in his holy place? Ps. 24:3

stand in the holy place. II Chron. 35:5

made . . . lamentation. *AP* 21:27

made . . . lamentation. Acts 8:2; Ps. 78:64

make . . . lamentation. Jer. 6:26

Down ruins the ancient order
And empire builded of old. *AP* 21:35-36

I will raise up his ruins, and I will build it as in the days of old. Amos 9:11

We are come to the end appointed. *AP* 21:41

the end shall be at the time appointed. Dan. 11:27

All kindreds under the sky. *AP* 21:46

all kindreds. Rev. 13:7

all kindreds of the earth. Rev. 1:7
all the kindreds of the earth. Acts 3:25

We have seen his star in the west. *AP* 21:52

We have seen his star in the east. Matt. 2:2

had seen your star. *AP* 19:10

All flesh lies taken at his will. *AP* 22:7	taken captive . . . at his will. II Tim. 2:26
	(all flesh, *passim*)
every fowl of air. *AP* 22:8	every fowl of the air. Gen. 1:30; 9:2

The complete poems—about seventeen in all—and the fragments collected in *The Manuscript Poems of A. E. Housman* also contain their proportion of borrowings from the Bible:

have the grave to wife. Page 32	this damsel to wife. Gen. 3:34
The weapons of the war. Page 33	the weapons of war. II Sam. 1:27
underfoot to tread. Page 33	mountains tread him underfoot. Is. 14:25
the Lord hath lifted up therefor The darkness of his countenance upon her/And given her war. Page 35	Jehovah lift up his countenance upon thee and give thee peace. Num. 6:26
they waged aforetime. Page 38	As he did aforetime. Dan. 6:10
though the solid earth be shaken. Page 40	the earth shall be shaken. Is. 13:13
remove/the landmark. Page 52	Remove not the ancient landmark. Prov. 22:28
The shards of Dagon strew the temple floor. Page 84	Dagon was fallen upon his face to the ground. I Sam. 5:3
take and break your bow. Page 91	He breaketh the bow. Ps. 46:9

Notes and References

Preface

1. Cambridge, 1961.
2. New York, 1936.
3. See his "A. E. Housman" in *Eight Essays* (Garden City, 1954), p. 127. Wilson's suggestion was echoed by Professor Otto Skutsch in an address given at the University of London, September 3, 1959, during the observance of Housman's Centenary.
4. *Housman 1897-1936* (New York, 1942).
5. Laurence Housman, *My Brother, A. E. Housman: Personal Recollections together with Thirty Hitherto Unpublished Poems* (New York, 1938). (Throughout the text this volume will be referred to as Laurence Housman's memoir.)
6. *Thirty Housman Letters to Witter Bynner* (New York, 1957).
7. Among these are letters to Professor F. W. Oliver, a colleague at University College, London; to Grant Richards and T. S. Eliot; also the holographs of the letters to Witter Bynner; a rare reprint of "R.L.S.," etc.
8. Printed in Richards' *Housman 1897-1936* with Housman's reply, pp. 267-71.
9. A thirty-seven-page booklet describing the Collamore bequest contained an article by Fraser Bragg Drew that included seventeen of Housman's humorous poems written in the guest books.
10. In the section "Light Verse and Parodies," pp. 230-47.
11. This book was published the following year by Henry Holt & Co. of New York. The juvenile verses, humorous and serious, are on pp. 15-28. (This book will be referred to as the Holt memorial volume.)
12. In *Études Anglaises* (November, 1953), pp. 346-49. "The Death of Socrates" appeared in the *Publications of the Modern Language Association of America*, (September, 1953), pp. 913-16.
13. Pp. 797-808.
14. See memoir, pp. 256-72.
15. Published by the University of Minnesota Press, 1955. See pp. 120-37.

16. Published by Jonathan Cape, London.
17. *A. E. Housman: A Divided Life* (London, 1957).
18. *A. E. Housman: Man Behind a Mask* (Chicago, 1958).
19. Richards comments negatively on several of these in Chapter 34 of his memoir.
20. These documents could exist only in papers taken over by Housman's literary executor, his brother Laurence, who deposited with the British Museum in 1942 a manuscript (now designated Add. MS 45861) consisting of "extracts from A. E. Housman's diary, with a statement by Laurence Housman." The Keeper of Manuscripts at the Museum further informed me that the documents are "reserved for a period of twenty-five years from that date [1942]." The diary would seem to be the one mentioned by Mrs. Hawkins in her biography, pp. 116-17.
21. Now *Additional Poems* 12. Line three of this poem (*I never sigh, nor flush, nor knit the brow*) recalls his sister's comment: "Many things he did with an inner intensity that was obvious. You could see his feelings in his face." (From Mrs. Katharine E. Symons' chapter "Boyhood" in the Holt memorial volume, p. 29.)
22. Richards, *Housman*, p. 270.

Chapter One

1. The horoscope and its interpretation are reproduced in Laurence Housman's memoir, pp. 278-86.
2. Excellent photographs of the boyhood homes are given in the Holt memorial volume, pp. 6-10.
3. Mrs. Symons self-effacingly says of her only sister, Clemence, that "her abilities probably equalled Alfred's. . . . I was small and a dunce through my inveterate hatred of lessons. Basil, who came next, followed Alfred in orderly studiousness." Holt memorial volume, p. 16.
4. See Laurence Housman's memoir, pp. 22-23.
5. Alfred's early pedagogic habit of handing down judgments and assigning grades and rank seemingly passed into his magisterial tendency to put textual critics in their proper places: "Among the critics who have emended Ovid's *Heroides* since the time of Heinsius the first place belongs to Bentley, the second to Palmer, and the third to Madvig: van Lennep and Merkel may dispute for the fourth. . . . Palmer was a man more singularly and eminently gifted by nature than any English scholar since Badham and than any English Latinist since Markland. . . . Now the class which includes Heinsius includes also Gilbert Wakefield; and Palmer's rank is nearer to Wakefield than to Heinsius." From Carter's *A. E. Housman: Selected Prose*, pp. 90-91. See also pp. 121-23.

6. Since the punctuation of the text is sparse and irregular, a few signs have been added.

7. See Laurence Housman's "A Poet in the Making," *The Atlantic Monthly* (July, 1946), p. 120.

8. One of his earliest specific allusions in his poetry notebooks to his loss of faith occurs on A 67, only ten pages after the beginning of the serious poetry. An isolated couplet (about 1887) near the bottom of the page reads "Never, or ever, shine or snow,/That son of God I used to know." This means that his personal Saviour, once so unreservedly trusted, now having deserted him, can never in good circumstances or bad be called upon again.

9. Dr. White has corrected some errors in the *Messenger* printing, and his text also varies in a few slight details from a printing of the poem that appeared in the *London Magazine* for June, 1959. The editor was unaware of Dr. White's publication (1953) of the elegy and announced in his introduction to his reprint that the poem "was printed in the local press but has never appeared since." The *London Magazine* text, which the editor had from Laurence Housman, presents the better of the two readings, slight though the variations are.

10. In his memoir, p. 34.

11. The few later exceptions were among friends of his family and his early youth, notably three women living in Woodchester, his mother's old home. They were two sisters of the Wise family—their guest books were mentioned in the Preface (p. 9)—and a governess, Sophie Becker. The latter was fifteen years his senior. Grant Richards remarks in his memoir (p. 309) that Housman put her among his three greatest friends.

Chapter Two

1. See Laurence Housman's memoir, pp. 40-41.

2. The others, beside Poley, Housman, and Pollard were G. S. Edwards, F. Marr, and T. Anstey Guthrie, who became the author of the runaway best-seller *Vice Versa* (1882).

3. The Yale copy of this valuable set at one time belonged to Falconer Madan, the esteemed librarian of the Bodleian, who jotted down on the front fly of the volume the names and pseudonyms of the six editors, together with the names of their colleges, subjoining this certification: "Pollard supplied me with the above notes Jan. 6, 1893."

4. Pp. 22-23. The lines she quotes are, " 'Pigs on the front lawn again!' said the King, 'give me a cannon somebody!' No one gave him a cannon, so, seizing a teaspoon from the breakfast table, he . . .''

5. At this time Basil, five years younger than his eldest brother

(and present tutor), was in his senior year at Bromsgrove School and a member of the editorial staff of the *Bromsgrovian*. Mrs. Symons hints (23) that he was the one who "nefariously passed on" Alfred's short story to the school magazine. This betrayal caused the author much annoyance at the time for, in his state of mind during the winter of 1881-1882, he had no relish for public appearances. But he forgave and, in the last years of his life, wrote for Basil a short sequel to the story. Laurence gave Mrs. Hawkins permission to print in full the first of the eleven chapters of the narrative. See pp. 67-68 of her *A. E. Housman: Man Behind a Mask*.

6. Gow records in his *Sketch*, p. 6, that when he once asked Housman how his Oxford examiners could have used him so harshly, he replied that they had no option: he deserved to fail. Gow remarks further that he does not think Housman "bore them any grudge, and with two of them, Ingram Bywater and Herbert Richards [an uncle of Grant Richards] he was afterwards on friendly terms."

7. In reply to a formal questionnaire sent him January 30, 1933, by a French student, Maurice Pollet. See Richards' memoir, pp. 267-74. An article based on Housman's answers was published by M. Pollet in *Études Anglaises*, I, 5 (Sept., 1937).

8. Housman blamed only himself for his misfortunes and steadfastly referred to Moses Jackson as "my greatest friend." As Housman treasured every scrap of his mother's writing, he also preserved all of the forty-year correspondence from Jackson. Laurence recalls (memoir, p. 62) how, after his brother's death, he found among his papers a worn envelope marked "Mo's last letter." It had been written early in 1923 from Jackson's hospital bed in Vancouver, and Housman had traced in ink every word of the feeble hand.

9. It may have been a part of Housman's self-imposed penance that, although many scenes in his poetry as we now read it are sensuous, his notebook drafts, from first to final version, often show a retreat from personal or explicit statement and suggestion. For example, the last line of "Spring Morning" (*LP* 16) *Rouses from another's side* read in its first draft (C 30) *Sleeps against another's side*. The sixth line of "When I watch the living meet" (*ASL* 12), now reading *In the house of flesh*, was written in the sole notebook draft *In my house of flesh*. Again, the last line of "March" (*ASL* 10) *For lovers should be loved again*, as we now know it, was in the unique draft, on A 170, a continuation of the preceding line (*Ah, let not only mine be vain*) and a much more emotional appeal: *Who ask but to be loved again*. Line four of the final stanza of "O see how thick the goldcup flowers" (*ASL* 5) reads decorously *We might as well sit down*, but an intermediate draft on B 25 had it *We might as well lie down*.

Chapter Three

1. Laurence says (memoir, p. 62) that Alfred asked that he and Clemence not come to visit him when he was rooming with the Jackson brothers. Meeting Laurence at the home of a man they both knew, Moses Jackson was surprised to learn that Alfred had a brother and sister living near him.

2. Of Housman's first paper, "Horatiana," published in the *Classical Review* (1882), Gow says (*Sketch*, p. 11) that "it was an astonishing performance for a young man of twenty-three—astonishing both in its comparative maturity and in the extent to which it foreshadows what was to come."

3. The list included his old headmaster at Bromsgrove School, Herbert Millington; Housman's Oxford friend and co-editor, A. W. Pollard; and two Oxford professors, Robinson Ellis and Henry Nettleship, whom Housman had ridiculed in his *Rounde Table* lampoon, "The Eleventh Eclogue," fifteen years earlier. The former, one of Housman's teachers at Oxford, laid aside whatever personal rancor he may have had to remark in his testimonial letter that he had "always found Mr. Housman an amiable and modest man." Alfred retained a strong sense of detachment in his personal dealings with Ellis, and, according to Laurence (memoir, p. 88), left in his notebooks the acid comment, "Mr. Ellis' reluctance to accept the emendations of others is only equalled by the reluctance of others to accept the emendations of Mr. Ellis." Housman's other supporters in his candidacy were J. E. B. Mayor, R. Y. Tyrrell, Arthur Palmer, Lewis Campbell, T. Herbert Warren, T. C. Snow, Henry Jackson, Joseph B. Mayor, A. W. Verrall, J. S. Reid, G. M. Edwards, B. L. Gildersleeve, and N. Wecklein.

4. Alfred's departure may have had something to do with Jackson's decision to press his engagement the following year with Mrs. Rosa Chambers, whom he married in 1889. For Housman's part, it is unquestionable that the first news of his friend's plans came as a crushing blow.

5. This is very much in the spirit of "Because I liked you better" (*MP* 31), a poem of abnegation and farewell.

6. In his reply to the Pollet questionnaire. See Richards' memoir, pp. 270-71.

7. Another elegiac source was in the death of his youngest brother, George Herbert, "killed in action at Baakenlaagte, S. Africa, 30 October, 1901; buried on battlefield"—to quote from a family chart Housman made in 1908. Mrs. Symons in the Holt memorial volume (35-36), identifies other poems written to their brother's memory.

8. When, in the early autumn of 1939, Laurence and his two sisters were preparing the table of contents for the *Collected Poems* of their brother, the poem to Wilde was rejected during one session of the family council—probably on the suggestion of Mrs. Symons. Laurence's influence may be seen in the restoration of *AP* 18, a decision which aroused far less disturbance than the omission of the poem would have occasioned; for Laurence *had* published it in his memoir in 1937. Housman's regard for Wilde was very high. In his review of the eleventh volume of the *Cambridge History of English Literature* (*Cambridge Review*, XXXVI, 896 [January 27, 1915], 160-61) he declared, "from a European point of view the three great English poets are Shakespeare, Byron, and the late Mr. Wilde."

9. Housman gave his inaugural lecture on May 9, 1911. He had performed a similar duty in October, 1892, before beginning his Latin professorship at University College. This address was privately printed by the College—an honor not previously bestowed upon an introductory lecture—but Housman took very little pride in his, calling it "rhetorical and not wholly sincere." His Cambridge inaugural was never printed, not because he wished to have it forgotten, according to Gow (*Sketch*, p. 33, note), but because he was unable to verify an allusion made in it to a poem by Shelley.

10. Shortly after learning of his appointment, Housman expressed his feelings to his friends the William Rothensteins in a letter which, though humorous, squares with some of the conditions of his new duties as he foresaw them: "to have less work and more pay is always agreeable, and that will be the case with me. The drawback is that I shall be obliged to be less unsociable."

11. A former student, Professor Joshua Whatmough of Harvard University, has recorded his opinion: "Unfortunately he lived too long to command the kind of admiration with which he had first been greeted in Cambridge. By the twenties his lectures were not well attended, usually eighteen or twenty at the most, including a don or two." *Word Study*, XXVIII, 4 (April, 1953), 3.

12. Gow, *Sketch*, p. 46.   13. *Ibid.*, p. 50.

14. See Withers, *A Buried Life* (London, Cape, 1940), pp. 55-56.

15. The notebook draft of this famous poem, written on pp. 92-93 of Notebook C, is not with the other *reliquiae* in the Washington collection. Mr. Carter included it in an inventory he made of the manuscript pieces he received from Laurence Housman, but the authoritative Library of Congress checklist notes of this poem "no manuscript found." Evidently, between the purchase of the collection from Scribners of New York by a dealer in 1940, when every item was checked as present, and the compilation of the official list by the Manuscript Division of the Library of Congress in 1944, this precious item must have been detached. Others are not in the Wash-

ington papers, which are still in the order in which Laurence passed them on to Mr. Carter. Part of "The Recruit" (*ASL* 3) is absent from its mounting-sheet, No. 38, and one looks in vain for "I shall not die for you" (*AP* 2), which Mr. Carter listed in his final consignment from Laurence. Three humorous pieces in his list are also missing: "The Amphisbaena" and two others that have never been identified, "The Ballad of a Widower" and "The Illustrated Bible."

16. Housman's letter of refusal, together with six others of the same import, is now in the Lilly Library of Indiana University. The proffering institutions include the University of St. Andrews, the University of Oxford, the University of Liverpool, and the University of Wales.

17. Housman's declination of the Laureateship, offered to him in the last year of his life, Lord Robert Vansittart describes in his *The Mist Procession* (London, 1958), p. 535: how he sought out the poet in Cambridge and told him of the offer. (The Prime Minister had wanted Housman to succeed Bridges after his death in 1930.) "But the professor remained locked in his Latinity, and I was sorry."

18. Apparently no more than six *Last Poems* lyrics originated in Notebook D: nos. 8 ("Soldier from the wars returning"), 20 ("The night is freezing fast"), 22 ("The sloe was lost in flower"), 26 ("The halfmoon westers low, my love"), 32 ("When I would muse in boyhood"), and 40 ("Tell me not here, it needs not saying.")

19. Withers, *op. cit.*, p. 76.

20. *Ibid.*, p. 45.

21. *Mark Twain Quarterly* (Winter, 1936), p. 9.

22. A pathetically scrawled letter, probably his last, written eleven days before his death, testifies to his grim resolve to perform his professional duties as long as he could lift a hand. The letter was written to an Indian student asking comment on an enclosed article dealing with Housman's poetry. After an incoherent opening sentence he set down, "I take no interest in the matter," and inadvertently ended with a double signature.

23. Housman's bad luck in his life-long war against typographical mishaps literally dogged him to the grave, for the Order of Service, in place of the word *Ecclesiastes*, had *Ecclesiasticus*—a fault, by the way, which probably cannot be laid on the printer.

24. Possibly Laurence was not among these; for, as he listened to the choir intone his brother's hymn, he may have remembered a passage from his own *Englishwoman's Love-Letters* in which the writer protests against the scandal at the funeral of the village rector where Chopin's Funeral March was played, "a thing utterly unChristian in its meaning." See p. 103 of the *Letters* (New York, 1900).

Chapter Four

1. There was a strong counterbalance here in Housman's pride, which set some limits to the self-depreciatory tendencies he expressed in his poetry intended for publication. Take for example the deserter's confession in "My dreams are of a field afar" (*MP* 39). As a whole, the poem condemns the writer's cowardice, but the third stanza as it was first written was much more extreme than the stanza we now read. Hardly legible, on B 230, it runs:

> There nine shrewd fellows stand their ground,
>   The only fool was I,
> Who keep my carcass safe and sound
>   And left my soul to die.

Another example of his softening the tone of self-rebuke is seen in his handling of line 4 of "As I gird on for fighting" (*LP* 2), *Of better men than I.* Over *better,* in his unique draft of the lyric (B 7), Housman wrote *other;* however, his original reading went into printer's copy. Again, the unique draft of "Westward on the high-hilled plains" (*ASL* 55) shows line 13 thus: *There to clearer eyes than mine* (B 20-21). But, in a poem of places loved in his boyhood, Housman would not say that now any eyes could be *clearer* than his had been; so over the word he set *later,* and eventually the whole line was radically altered to *There, on thoughts that once were mine.*

2. Part of the latter section of Chapter 7 sums up the influence of Lucretius on Housman's poetry.

3. Two of the most easily accessible cis-Atlantic printings are those in the *Yale Review* (January, 1928) and the *Atlantic Monthly,* (July, 1946). The texts show numerous variations, as might be expected of the numerous unauthorized printings of Housman's poetry that appeared in the United States. A note accompanying the announcement of the *Fragment* in the New York *Herald Tribune* for June 14, 1936, says that the manuscript "finally came into the hands of Housman himself and is quite definitely known to have been destroyed by him personally."

4. Housman explained his meaning in *cut* in a letter to Houston Martin, one of the last he wrote, dated March 22, 1936. See the *Yale Review* (December, 1936), p. 284.

5. See Laurence's memoir, p. 157.

6. Pp. 45-46.

7. See my *Thirty Housman Letters to Witter Bynner* (New York, 1957), pp. 34-35.

8. Housman's debt to the English ballads is discussed at length in Chapter 6.

9. Memoir, p. 212.

10. Housman's first three notebooks show several instances of his working with set patterns of accent and rhythm, sometimes in uncompleted lines, again with patterns consisting only of signs indicating strong and weak syllables. On A 125, for example, he wrote line one of the poem that was to become *ASL* 39 thus: *'Tis time, I think, by* — ˘ *town.* He made a similar notation in a fragment jotted down on B 139: ˘ — *My love, that I shall not be true to.* An abandoned line in his dedicatory poem (B 146) to Moses Jackson opened thus: — ˘ ˘ — ˘ *suo diuisos orbe Brittanos . . .* On C 31 he began line 11 of "The Bay of Biscay" *Leave* ˘ — ˘ ˘ ˘ — ˘ *and the. . . .* In the upper left corner of A 140 he drew up this design for a stanza: a,a, b,b, c,b,c, d,d. This intricate eight-line stanza pattern was drawn up on A 157:

$$\smile \; - \; \smile \; - \; \smile \; - \; \smile$$
$$\smile \; - \; \smile \; -$$
$$\smile \; - \; \smile \; - \; \smile \; - \; \smile$$
$$\smile \; - \; \smile \; - \; \smile \; -$$
$$\smile \; - \; \smile \; - \; \smile \; - \; \smile$$
$$\smile \; - \; \smile \; - \; \smile \; -$$
$$\smile \; - \; \smile \; - \; \smile \; - \; \smile$$
$$\smile \; - \; \smile \; -$$

After the symbols in line 7 he wrote *But in my heart I carry;* the words for the next line are now illegible.

On B 137, where he began *LP* 1, Housman scribbled near the right margin the rhyming words *still, hill* and *resign, line;* and B 176 opens with this *esquisse:*

fighter, nitre
$$\smile \; - \; \smile \; - \; \smile \; -$$
$$\smile \; - \; \smile \; - \; \smile \; - \; \smile$$
$$\smile \; - \; \smile \; - \; \smile \; -$$
$$\smile \; - \; \smile \; - \; \smile$$

Laurence remarks in his Analysis of the notebooks (memoir, p. 267) that the last sixteen pages (now destroyed) of B were devoted to "tabulated rhymes, and vowel sounds, under various headings." Here may be the germ of Housman's remarkable footnote on page 4 of his "Name and Nature of Poetry," in which he raises a number of inquiries pertaining to English versification, some of which still await study.

11. Pp. 14-17.

12. To read H. B. Walters' *Church Bells of Shropshire* (Oswestry, 1915) is to relive a vital part of Housman's boyhood.

[202]

13. See p. 185 of Laurence's memoir, where it is quoted in a letter from Alfred.

14. Alexander Eliot, *Earth, Air, Fire and Water* (New York, 1962), p. 33.

15. Here Housman was describing what he had reported to J. W. Mackail in a letter (now in the Fitzwilliam Museum, Cambridge) dated July 25, 1922, about one of his lyrics under consideration for *Last Poems*: "25 dissatisfies me too. . . . The first and last stanzas came into my head; the middle ones are composed." In the same letter he comments on the diction in parts of "Hell Gate" that he "had to compose. . . . It is not what it should be, and I rather despair of mending it."

16. Some of Mr. John Crowe Ransom's remarks at the National Book Awards meeting, March 10, 1964, illuminate Housman's description: "The best the poet can do is to introduce words and phrases partly related to the argument, but partly going off tangentially and rather spectacularly as if heading for other structures. Students are taught to regard the act of composing a poem under the image of the rational mind furiously worrying and whipping the imagination to perform superhuman or at least irrational feats of language which the understanding cannot by itself discover. So the poet has hit awkwardly but truly upon the mystery of multiple creation." Quoted in *Publishers' Weekly* (March 23, 1964), p. 23. So much for the sovereignty of the creative imagination at its undirected and productive best.

17. George L. Watson, *A. E. Housman: A Divided Life* (London, 1957), p. 211.

18. A 237 is dated in Housman's hand "March 1895," and 240 is on the next to last page in the first notebook. B 3 is dated "April 1895"; so it is possible that only a few days elapsed between the two drafts of *ASL* 19.

19. See Nesca A. Robb, *Four in Exile* (London, 1948), pp. 12-13. The author has difficulty in showing the appropriateness of several of the poems, *e.g.* "The New Mistress" (*ASL* 34), not knowing that it was sent in after Housman's manuscript had gone to the printer, to take the place of "Yonder see the morning blink" (later *LP* 11). Her lack of acquaintance with the notebooks leads her to repeat the common error that the major part of *A Shropshire Lad* was written in the spring of 1895.

20. See Ian Scott-Kilvert, *A. E. Housman* (London, Longmans [c.1955]), p. 24. The quotations in this otherwise valuable brochure are unhappily disfigured by numerous misprints. A new amended edition is in the making.

21. Housman's own description of his ordering of the poems in his

first two books tends to refute the arguments of Nesca Robb and Scott-Kilvert. In the letter to J. W. Mackail (referred to in note 15 of this chapter), he said of the twentieth poem of *A Shropshire Lad* that he "only put it in for variety"—as he did another, once Number 15 of *Last Poems*. He went on to say of another lyric (on p. 20 of the proofsheets, of which he was writing) that he "stuck it in to keep apart two poems which should not come together."

22. In Vol. III, p. 95.

23. See Richards' memoir, p. 289.

24. The Library of Congress copy of the *Odes* is no. 18 of fifty large-paper copies intended for presentation only and signed by the editor. Housman's three pieces are on pp. 15; 85, 87; and 109, 111 facing the Greek texts.

25. The celebrated misprint of the hyphen in line two of the third translation occurred in the Stott printing: *Far-seeking and deep debate*. The correct printing (*Far seeking . . .*) was shown in the *Classical Journal*, XXIX, 2 (November, 1933), p. 119. Though Professor Harry J. Runyan early in 1940 passed on to American publishers Housman's request that his meaning be restored to the line by the dropping of the hyphen, this correction was not made in the London edition until the fourteenth impression of the *Collected Poems* in 1953. Professor Runyan publicized the error in an article published in *Modern Language Notes*, LVI, 6 (June, 1941), p. 458.

26. In the Trinity College Library there is a collection of Housman's books, among them *Greek Lyric Poets*, selected and translated by Francis Brooks (London, 1896). Housman had drawn a vertical line on page 48 opposite this translation from Sappho: "The moon has set, and the Pleiads, and it is midnight, and the hour goes by, but I lie down alone."

27. Proof that he had considered and rejected it is evident in the long wavy downstroke topped with an X, in the right margin of the page.

Chapter Five

1. These five eventually appeared in *More Poems*: "I did not lose my heart in summer's even" (37); "The world goes none the lamer" (21); "I to my perils" (6); "Young is the blood that yonder" (34); "Crossing alone the nighted ferry" (23).

2. On D 116. This is the only prose entry in the four notebooks: "I dreamt I was reading a passage of George Eliot, in which was quoted, printed in italics as prose, the verse 'The bogle of the [hairy weid]'*'". Three more lines complete the stanza. Below Housman added this note: "*understood as a heath or moor." (The brackets and asterisks are Housman's.)

3. The Handbook for the Housman Centenary Exhibition at University College, London, carried this revealing note (by Mr. John Carter) touching about a dozen posthumously printed poems for which we have no manuscript source: ". . . the drafts from which Laurence Housman drew them having been afterwards judged by him too fragmentary to be legitimately preserved." Knowing Laurence's blunders with sound copy, we may ask: What reliance can be placed in the texts of these unsupported poems?

4. On page 73, in a list of poems found carrying dates in the notebooks. (Three were overlooked: on B 36, B 95, and B 109.)

5. See "A. E. Housman, an Annotated Check-List, Additions and Corrections," by William White, John Carter, [and] R. C. Bald (London, 1942), p. 36.

The persistence of known errors in the texts of Housman's poems is equalled only by the longevity of the confusion of paragraphs in the opening of Chapter 49 of *Vanity Fair*, where paragraph 4 should be followed by 16 and 17—an error that has been faithfully carried into all editions of the novel since 1848, although Thackeray himself recognized it. In the first printing of *More Poems* the stanza in lyric 34 that should have been number 2—plainly so indicated in a near fair copy Housman wrote on D 121—was shuffled into number-five position and stayed there until 1955, through thirteen impressions of the comprehensive London edition.

6. Collected in *Essays and Studies of the English Association,* XXV (1939), The Clarendon Press, Oxford, 1940. See p. 7.

7. See his memoir, p. 212.

8. One of the most extreme and amusing protests was that of Mr. Stephen Spender, who in the correspondents' column of the *Observer*, December 8, 1957, lashed out at "the American professor who, *with the help of acids,* uncovered and published all of A. E. Housman's deletions in his notebooks."

9. See Richards' memoir, p. 22.

10. There were thirty-three changes in punctuation, six in spelling, and four errors resulting probably from broken type.

11. Richards *op. cit.*, p. 48.

12. Front page New York *Times Book Review*, by Ivor Brown, Mar. 29; same day front page New York *Herald Tribune Book Review*, by De Lancey Ferguson.

Chapter Six

1. Housman had a keen interest in tracing the literary antecedents of the poets he read. Percy Withers (*op. cit.*, p. 59) recalls how Housman, after praising Ralph Hodgson's "Song of Honour," threw in "Yes, but what a debt it owes to Smart's 'Song to David.'"

2. "Nature meant me for a geographer, but I had to abandon the study on rising above the lowest form at school."—Richards' memoir, p. 331. Why did Housman have to abandon this study? Was he at twelve feeling the scholar's need to narrow his reading? Or was he, when he made the statement Richards records, reading back into the motives of the Bromsgrove student the declaration of the scholar of many years later who felt he had to drop his pursuit of Greek because he could not attain to eminence in both Greek and Latin?

3. One of his most enthusiastic tributes went to "Wordsworth's Grave," by William Watson, a poem that Housman called "one of the glories of English literature, and a few more poems [by Watson] of about the same date had the same quality."—In a letter to F. C. Owlett, October 8, 1930.

4. See Laurence Housman, *The Unexpected Years* (London, 1937), p. 203. Alfred published "The Oracles" (later *LP* 25) in the first number of *The Venture* (1903), p. 39.

5. See Percy Withers, *op. cit.*, pp. 66-67.

6. *Ibid.*, p. 66.

7. See Laurence's memoir, p. 163.

8. Richards quotes Housman's rather elaborate explanation on page 192 of his memoir. Housman's subjunctive forms are frequent but often unnoticed by the reader. The last stanza of "The Immortal Part" (*ASL* 43) has perhaps the largest accumulation:

> Before this fire of sense decay,
> This smoke of thought blow clean away,
> And leave with ancient night alone
> The stedfast and enduring bone.

9. Originally published in five volumes by Houghton Mifflin Co., 1882-1898; reprinted in three volumes for The Folklore Press, New York, in association with the Pageant Book Company, London. (Oxford University Press, 1957.)

10. He answered an inquiry of J. W. Mackail, who, while reading the proofsheets of *Last Poems*, called his attention to an archaism in the last line of *LP* 26: "you do lie," thinking Housman wanted the form for a metrical purpose. Housman replied that the archaic expression "is not really for metre's sake, but an imitation, false I daresay, of the ballads, which I do imitate."

11. Housman's macabre absorption in the gallows, reflected in some of his most vivid poems—"On moonlit heath and lonesome bank" (*ASL* 9); "The Culprit" (*LP* 14); and "Eight O'Clock" (*LP* 15)—may date from near-at-hand experiences of his childhood since public executions were not outlawed in England until 1868, when he was nine. John Masefield, born in 1878, has this to say of his early

fears of the gallows: "The fear . . . was real, and the memory of the gibbet still clear. I well remember the stump of the upright of a gibbet, under which people hardier than myself used to grub for bits of old highwayman."—*So Long to Learn* (New York, 1952), p. 39. Mrs. Hardy in her *Early Life of Thomas Hardy* (New York, 1928), p. 37, tells how young Thomas in his late or middle 'teens (the date about 1860) watched through a telescope a hanging three miles distant: "At the moment of his placing the glass to his eye the white figure dropped downwards, and the faint note of the town clock struck eight."

12. Richards' memoir, p. 270.

13. The poem may actually have been started on p. 235, for Housman sometimes wrote his first draft on the recto of two open pages and used the one on the left as a testing-field for stanzas he had to "compose"; or he might continue his draft on it after filling the recto page.

14. See "Some Unpublished Housman Letters," by Cyril Clemens in *Poet Lore*, LIII, 3 (Autumn, 1947), p. 259.

15. There can be no doubt about the sincerity of Housman's patriotism, which was one of his earliest, as well as one of his longest-lasting, sentiments. Frank Harris relates how at a luncheon of four he quoted to Housman the last stanza of *ASL* 1, "1887":

> Oh, God will save her, fear you not:
> Be you the men you've been,
> Get you the sons your fathers got,
> And God will save the Queen.

Harris went on to praise the "splendid mockery" of the poem and its denigration of the patriotic idea. This—as it probably was intended to do—roused the lion in Housman, who retorted bitingly: "I never intended to poke fun, as you call it, at patriotism, and I can find nothing in the sentiment to make mockery of: I meant it sincerely; if Englishmen breed as good men as their fathers, then God will save their Queen. . . . I can only reject and resent your truculent praise."—*Latest Contemporary Portraits* (New York, 1927), pp. 279-80.

Chapter Seven

1. "The Name and Nature of Poetry," pp. 39-40.

2. In a very similar way, the word *tokens* in "The lads in their hundreds . . . (*ASL* 23) links Housman's poem with a line in Juvenal (Sat. 10:196) which he had translated in an article, employing the

word *tokens.* Both contexts describe a concourse of young men: thus it was natural that the word came and fell neatly into its place when it was needed in *ASL* 23: "I wish one could know them, I wish there were tokens to tell."

3. See Don Cameron Allen's *The Moment of Poetry* (Baltimore, 1962), pp. 82-83. Mr. Wilbur points out that his interpretation of the line makes the poem at war with Housman's general view; he then goes on to speculate on "the sort of person whose view it might be." This wasted effort would have been spared if Shakespeare's *wages* had been seen in Housman's line.

4. See "The Application of Thought to Textual Criticism" in John Carter's *A. E Housman: Selected Prose* (Cambridge, 1961), p. 136.

5. In A. L. Rowse's, *William Shakespeare* (New York, 1963), p. 199.

6. See Laurence Housman's memoir, pp. 103-5.

7. The story is told and the passage quoted in Gow's *Sketch*, pp. 53-54.

8. *Ibid.*, pp. 12-13.

9. John Carter and John Sparrow, *A. E. Housman: An Annotated Hand-List* (London, 1952), p. 27.

10. Translations follow those in Cyril Bailey's edition: *Titi Lucreti Cari, De Rerum Natura, Libri Sex* (Oxford, 1950).

11. In "Some Reminiscences" in the Holt memorial volume, pp. 39-40.

12. Quoted from my *Manuscript Poems of A. E. Housman*, p. 77.

13. Laurence's memoir, p. 111.

14. From a letter dated July 18, 1922, thanking Mackail for agreeing to read the proofs of *Last Poems.* In a second letter dated one week later, Housman returned to his misgiving about "Hell Gate": "the whole thing is on the edge of the absurd."

15. The experiences of a soul being escorted by Hermes to the afterworld Housman had developed in his long poem "The Merry Guide" (*ASL* 42), written perhaps fifteen years before the earliest draft of "Hell Gate."

16. Renamed by the poet "Resolution and Independence" and found under that title in most of the modern editions. Laurence included the poem in his small *Wordsworth Anthology* (New York, 1947).

17. The rhythm of the refrain *O who would not sleep with the brave?* is typical of the whole poem, which has the pace and spirit of Burns's:

   Scene—A Field of Battle—Time of the day, evening—The

wounded and dying of the victorious army are supposed to join in the following song.

> Farewell, thou fair day, thou green earth and ye skies,
>   Now gay with the broad setting sun;
> Farewell, loves and friendships, ye dear tender ties,
>   Our race of existence is run!
> Thou grim King of Terrors; thou Life's gloomy foe!
>   Go, frighten the coward and slave;
> Go, teach them to tremble, fell tyrant! but know
>   No terrors hast thou to the brave!
>
> Thou strik'st the dull peasant—he sinks in the dark,
>   Nor saves e'en the wreck of a name;
> Thou strik'st the young hero—a glorious mark;
>   He falls in the blaze of his fame!
> In the field of proud honour—our swords in our hands,
>   Our King and our country to save;
> While victory shines on Life's last ebbing sands,—
>   O who would not die with the brave?

18. First published in the *Union Magazine* (University College), I, 1 (1904).

Chapter Eight

1. See Richards' memoir, p. 12 and notes 1 and 2.

2. Housman gave his consent partly because of his high regard for Raleigh's judgment in literary criticism—something he said was "quite beyond" him. See Gow's *Sketch*, pp. 20-21.

3. Early in World War II *The Selected Poems of A. E. Housman* (New York, [n.d.]) was printed for the Armed Services, Inc., an organization established by the Council on Books in Wartime. All of the *Collected Poems* were included, except five with the sourest smack: "On the idle hill of summer" (*ASL* 35); "The Day of Battle" (*ASL* 56); "The chestnut casts his flambeaux" (*LP* 9); "Oh stay at home, my lad" (*ASL* 38); and "Farewell to a name and a number" (*MP* 40).

4. Published by the Colby College Library, of Waterville, Maine, 1946.

5. In his note to the semicentennial edition, Carl Weber (p. 92) quotes Richards' comment on a notable American "pirate": "Mosher

did as much as any man to make *A Shropshire Lad* known to his compatriots and, in doing so, in no way vexed its author, who never hid from his American correspondents that his book enjoyed no copyright in the United States."

6. Printed in *Nineteenth-Century English Books* (Urbana, 1952). See pp. 45-47.

7. Richards' memoir, p. 75.

8. *Ibid.*, p. 85.

9. *Ibid.*, pp. 181-83. The letter is now in the Lockwood Memorial Library of the University of Buffalo.

10. Anthologies printed in the United States, like new editions of *A Shropshire Lad* in this country, were not under Housman's ban. In reply to an inqury of Professor C. Ralph Bennett, of the University of Cincinnati, Housman wrote March 6, 1927: "I cannot be expected to give my express approval to the inclusion [of my poems] in anthologies published in the United States; but I have neither the power nor the wish to prevent it."

11. Withers, *op. cit.*, p. 69.

12. *Ibid.*, p. 82.

13. Richards' memoir, p. 245.

14. Quoted in Weber's semicentennial edition, p. 125.

15. Quoted in the *Mark Twain Quarterly*, I, 2 (Winter, 1936), p. 17.

16. See his *Mist Procession* (London, 1958), p. 535.

17. These sallies are reprinted in Mr. Connolly's *Condemned Playground* (London, 1946), pp. 47-62.

18. Frank Halliday's testimonial in his *Indifferent Honest* (London, 1960), p. 82, expresses a typical point of view: "I read his verse not only for its poetry, but also because he gave my own thoughts articulate form. And what form! His poetry has the classical perfection of Landor's, but whereas Landor's is cold, marmoreal, mere statuary, Housman's is pulsating with life, and almost every poem has the grace and precision of a trained athlete; no wonder he disliked the puffy, out-of-condition flatulence of so much eighteenth-century verse."

19. This amusing relic, together with a prim note from Housman, may be seen in the Washington collection.

20. See the number for November, 1963, p. 179.

21. One of the most recent appeals to his authority in the abstract was in the following, from the editorial column of the *Times Literary Supplement* for April 9, 1963, p. 21: " 'mental discipline' can in fact be obtained from other training than that of Latin grammar, good

classical scholars can, *iudice* Housman, write execrable English . . ." Mr. Peter Alexander in the *Supplement* for April 23, 1964, p. 327, comments at some length on some of Housman's allusions to Shakespeare.

22. *The Hands of Innocence* by Jeffrey Ashford; *Doomsday Morning* by Wynwode Reid; *The Everlasting Fire* by Jonreed Lauritzen; *Fancy's Knell* by Babs H. Deal; *No More to the Woods* by Laurence Moody; *Angry Dust* by Clement R. Hoopes; *In a World I Never Made* by Barbara Wootten.

Selected Bibliography

Housman's bibliography is mountainous both in its mass and its variety. Gow's List of Writings in his *Sketch* fills fifteen pages and his Indexes to the Classical Papers take up forty-six more. *The Annotated Hand-List* of Carter and Sparrow (London, 1952) comprises forty-two pieces, of which the following are the most important:

"The Death of Socrates" (*The Bromsgrove Messenger*, 1874).
Three Translations in *Odes from the Greek Dramatists* (London, 1890).
"Introductory Lecture" (Cambridge, 1892).
A Shropshire Lad (London, 1896).
Manilii Astronomica (London, 1903-1930).
Iuvenalis Saturae (London, 1905).
"The Application of Thought to Textual Criticism" (London, 1922).
Last Poems (London, 1922).
Lucani Bellum Civile (Oxford, 1926).
Biographical Preface to *Nine Essays* by Arthur Platt (Cambridge, 1927).
The Name and Nature of Poetry (Cambridge, 1933).
More Poems (London, 1936).
The Collected Poems (London, 1939).

*   *   *

Complete Poems: The Centennial Edition (New York 1959).

SECONDARY SOURCES

This list of books about A. E. Housman is intended as a supplement to the source materials described in the Preface. The Notes and References also cite location of articles from collections and from the scholarly journals.

CARTER, JOHN and SPARROW, JOHN. *A. E. Housman: An Annotated Hand-List*. London: Hart-Davis, 1952. Provides bibliographical descriptions in chronological order, 1874-1936.

Selected Bibliography

CONNOLLY, CYRIL. *The Condemned Playground.* London: Routledge, 1945. "A. E. Housman: A Controversy" (1936), 47-52, is famous for sparking, so soon after Housman's death, the debate over his reputation. The essay is followed by four spirited protests, to which Connolly replies unrepentant.

HABER, TOM BURNS. *The Manuscript Poems of A. E. Housman.* Minneapolis: University of Minnesota Press, 1955.

HAWKINS, MAUDE M. *A. E. Housman: Man Behind a Mask.* Chicago: Regnery, 1958. Supports George L. Watson's belief that Housman's personal tragedy lay in his unorthodox affection for Moses Jackson. The author drew largely on letters and counsel from Laurence Housman.

HOUSMAN, LAURENCE. *My Brother, A. E. Housman.* New York: Scribner's, 1938. A random biography valuable for several letters, thirty new poems, and an analysis of the poet's four notebooks.

————. *The Unexpected Years.* London: Cape, 1937. Mainly of value for its details of early home life; ends with recollections of the brothers' last exchanges.

MARLOW, NORMAN. *A. E. Housman: Scholar and Poet.* London: Routledge & Kegan Paul, 1958. Says regrettably little of Housman's scholarship; provides a survey of the main literary influences in his poetry.

RICHARDS, GRANT. *Author Hunting.* London: Unicorn Press, 1960. First published in 1934; Chapter Ten, "A Shropshire Lad," describes first contacts with Housman; also frequent later mention. Places *Last Poems* above *A.S.L.*

————. *Housman 1897-1936.* New York: Oxford, 1942. Chatty and uncritical but provides a wealth of firsthand author-publisher information; excellent index. The Appendix offers a miscellany of ten pieces by various hands: a former student of Housman, university colleagues, and others.

ROBB, NESCA A. *Four In Exile.* London: Hutchinson, 1948. The essay "A. E. Housman" explores the poet's twofold world, "a mingling of the intensest beauty and delight with appalling pain and evil"; elaborates a sequence theory of the poems of *A Shropshire Lad* not borne out by the evidence of the manuscripts.

ROBINSON, OLIVER. *Angry Dust.* Boston: Bruce Humphries, 1950. A competent sketch of the poet's life and the forms and content of his poetry. Useful fourteen-page bibliography.

SCOTT-KILVERT, IAN. *A. E. Housman.* London: Longmans, Green, 1955. Brief (thirty-seven pages), but one of the best straight biographies, barring its misquotations.

WALLACE-HADRILL, F., Editor. *Alfred Edward Housman.* New York:

Holt, 1937. Reminiscences, (some twice-told) of the family, school friends, and others.

WATSON, GEORGE L. *A. E. Housman: A Divided Life.* London: Hart-Davis, 1957. A discreet but thorough appraisal of Housman's involvement with his Oxford roommate, Moses Jackson, and its evidence in the poetry.

WILSON, EDMUND. *Eight Essays.* Garden City, New York: Doubleday, 1954. The third, "A. E. Housman," originally published in *The Triple Thinkers* (1938), sums up Housman's scholarly output, comments on the immature lament of his poems.

WITHERS, PERCY. *A Buried Life.* London: Cape, 1940. Invaluable for its recollections of a close personal attachment over the last nineteen years of the poet's life.

Index

Index

Index

Index

Index